KV-031-397

The Indispensable
DRINKS BOOK

The Indispensable
DRINKS BOOK

JOHN DOXAT
MICHAEL JACKSON · JANCIS ROBINSON
RICHARD CLARK · LEONARD KIRSCHEN

MACDONALD & CO
LONDON & SYDNEY

First published in Great Britain in 1982 by
Macdonald & Co (Publishers) Ltd
London & Sydney

Maxwell House
Worship Street, London EC2A 2EN

ISBN 0 356 07545 1

Conceived, edited and designed by
Harrow House Editions Limited
7a Langley Street, Covent Garden, London WC2H 9JA

Editors
Hazel Songhurst
Liz Wilhide
Gill Rowley

Designers
Nigel Partridge
David Fordham

Picture Researchers
Maggie Colbeck
Elizabeth Rudoff
Georgina Steeds

Production Manager
Kenneth Cowan

Production Editor
Fred Gill

Filmset in Century Schoolbook by
Pierson LeVesley Limited, Oxshott, Surrey, England
Illustrations originated by
Reprocolor Llovet S.A., Barcelona, Spain
Printed and bound by Dai Nippon, Hong Kong

16 15 14 13 12 11 10 9 8 7 6 5 4 3 2 1

CONTENTS

INTRODUCTION

"What would you like to drink?" is a deceptively simple question. Today the variety of wines, beers and spirits, not to mention soft drinks, available to the ordinary consumer in local shops, restaurants, cafés and pubs can seem confusing, even daunting. The dangers are only too obvious. Ordering an inappropriate wine is bad enough, spending a fortune on it is even worse. Trying out a new cocktail whose name gives no clue as to its ingredients can leave you reaching for the sodium bicarbonate. Few people order steak and chips every time they go out to eat; it is just as unadventurous to sample only one type of drink when such an interesting selection is available. Unfortunately experts can be remarkably unhelpful, often insisting on a standard of connoisseurship that most people don't have the time or money to develop. The quantity of publications on specialized aspects of various beverages would be quite an investment in themselves.

The purpose of this book is as described in its title – to be indispensable. Collected together here is a wealth of information on every conceivable type of drink – from champagne to cognac, from Harvey Wallbangers to mineral water, from stout to jasmine tea – providing the general reader with the first comprehensive guide to the world's beverages. Each section begins with a lively and entertaining account of the subject in question and continues with a detailed breakdown according to country, region or type, as applicable. The result is informative, up to date and fully international. It may seem ambitious, or even arrogant, to describe a book as indispensable. But this guide is as useful for planning cocktail parties as it is for deciding what to order in a restaurant; it is full of suggestions for wine and beer drinkers at home and abroad, and unique in its treatment of non-alcoholic beverages: it certainly merits its description on the grounds of usefulness alone.

Cheap travel and mass marketing have brought the exotic produce of other lands to the attention and appreciation of a wider range of people than ever before. In many cases, what could only be obtained on holiday in some distant spot can now be bought at the local shop. This book aims to fill the gap that inevitably arises when information has not caught up with the enterprise of retailers. In other words, it will help all would-be *bon vivants* to choose and enjoy new drinks and to understand more about their favourites. Drinking is a pleasure: it reminds us of foreign delights, homely comforts, the company of friends. Reading about drinking can only make the pleasure more assured.

WINE

Red, white or *rosé*; sparkling or still; dry, medium or sweet – there are wines to suit most palates, and most pockets. Although half the world's wine comes from only two countries – France and Italy – the vine has been cultivated all over the globe, wherever conditions allow it to flourish. Port, sherry and other fortified wines add to the variety of style, taste and region – a variety which creates much of the fascination and excitement of wine.

WINE

It is extraordinary that one unremarkable plant, the vine, can give rise to so much pleasure, passion, enthusiasm and controversy all over the world. A library of books about potatoes or an international association of potato-tasting societies, for instance, would seem absurd, but the comparison is apt – wine is above all an agricultural product.

Only in the last few centuries have winemaking techniques become sufficiently sophisticated for the emergence of wine connoisseurship, but the potential was always there, for the vine is a complex and varied *genus* (botanical name *Vitis*). There are many different vine species, of which *Vitis vinifera*, the "wine-bearing vine", is the one most commonly responsible for wine.

The exact date when our ancestors realized that wild vines could produce a delicious drink is not known. Noah's activities on Mount Ararat in Armenia are sometimes cited as the first example of intentional winemaking. Claims are made for ancient winemakers in the Far East, and there is certainly evidence that the Egyptians were making wine more than a thousand years BC. (It is strange that none of these supposed birthplaces of wine is a major wine region now.)

As early as 1000 BC wine was taken to the two countries that now account for nearly half the world's total wine production: France and Italy. As the Greeks enlarged their empire, they took both the vine and the traditions of their god Dionysus with them, and Dionysus was adopted with relish by the Romans under the name of Bacchus. It is likely that the wine produced at this time was fairly crude and needed the addition of some preservative or flavouring to keep it drinkable until the next vintage. It may well have been at this time that the process of resinating wine began, still seen today in Greek retsina.

While the Greeks kept their wine in open amphoras, the Romans managed to develop wine containers not unlike the barrels and bottles of today and so made great strides towards the development of wines that were built to last and mature. Vineyards were developed north and west of Marseilles. By AD 400 there were vines being cultivated to

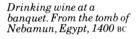
Drinking wine at a banquet. From the tomb of Nebamun, Egypt, 1400 BC

produce wine throughout the south of France, around Bordeaux, along the valleys of the Rhône and the Loire, in Burgundy and Champagne and even along the two great German wine rivers, the Rhine and Moselle. The fact that wine was easily transported by river doubtless played a part in the siting of these ancient vineyards.

By about AD 1000 wine was being made all over Europe, largely by the Church, which had a monopoly on vine-growing and winemaking skills, not to mention land. In the Middle Ages there were even vineyards all over southern England, but the dissolution of monasteries under Henry VIII brought a four-hundred-year pause in the cultivation of the vine in Britain.

The British did not stop drinking wine, however, and continued to play an important part in shaping the world's wine industry. In the twelfth century, when Bordeaux and Aquitaine were ruled by Henry II, the important trade in wine between western France and Britain began. The word "claret" is a corruption of the light, red *clairet* wines produced by the French and sent to Britain. More recently "clarets" have been made all over the world. *Clarete* is still an established style of wine in Spain, for example. The one country in which the word claret is hardly ever used is, ironically enough, France.

"Sherry" is another term used the world over, with the exception of its birthplace, Jerez in southern Spain. Again it was trading links with northern Europe that established sherry's worldwide reputation. The "sack" of Shakespeare's time is thought to have been dry or *seco* wine from Jerez.

The Methuen Treaty of 1703 between England and Portugal played a major part in the development of the port wine industry. Preference was granted under this treaty to wines from Portugal and this provided great stimulus to the wine producers in the hinterland of Oporto. This original port is emulated today from Berkeley to Barossa.

Over the last three centuries *Vitis vinifera* was taken from Europe to almost all the corners of the globe in which it could possibly flourish. Monks in the retinue of Spanish and Portuguese *conquistadores* brought their winemaking traditions to Central and South America and up the west coast to North America. Dutch settlers took the vine to their new territory on the Cape, just as the British developed a wine industry in Australia.

King Ashurbanipal feasting and drinking with his Queen in the Royal Garden, Assyria, 668 BC

Lady at a champagne bar. "Rotkappchen" by Hans Rudi Erdt

This 1926 cartoon by Aubrey Hammond portrays the fashionable attractions of a London night club during the Jazz Age

The prospects were good for the world's wine drinkers when disaster suddenly struck in the second half of the last century. In the 1860s *vignerons* in the Avignon area in southern France were alarmed to witness what seemed to be a serious epidemic that was rapidly destroying their vines. The destruction was the work of the *Phylloxera vastatrix*, a plant louse native to the east coast of America, where only wild vines grew. The louse must have made its transatlantic journey on a botanical specimen and it took some time for the full impact of its importation to be realized. It became apparent that *Phylloxera* had a particular passion for the roots of the cultivated *Vitis vinifera*, which it would munch avidly, finally leaving the plant to wither and die.

The epidemic was disastrous, not just for the winemakers of France, where the *Phylloxera* spread first, but for those in almost every other wine-producing area in the world. By the end of the last century, there were few vineyards that had not been affected by this tiny aphid. Desperate *vignerons* tried spraying, flooding, replanting, all without success. The only successful solution they found was to graft European *Vitis vinifera* on to rootstock of those American wild vine types that were known to be resistant to *Phylloxera*, and this practice continues today as an insurance measure against the disaster that hit the wine industry a century ago.

Although some wine is made directly from the "wild" vine species, chiefly in New York state, *Vitis vinifera* can take the credit for all the world's greatest wines. It comes in many varieties and it is this variation that creates much of the excitement and fascination of wine. There are many hundreds of different grape varieties from which wine can be made. A few are particularly successful.

King of red wine grapes, and a wonderfully hardy traveller, is the Cabernet Sauvignon, a concentrated, long-living grape which produces the great world-famous clarets and also some excellent wines in California and Australia. Pinot Noir, the perfumed grape of the world's great red burgundy, is much less likely to produce great wine outside the tiny Côte d'Or region that is its Burgundian home. Australia's best-known red wine grape, Shiraz, is related to the noble Syrah of Hermitage in the Rhône, while California's Zinfandel is not known elsewhere.

To the Germans, Riesling is the king of white wine grapes. With many lesser varieties sharing the same

name, true "Rhine Riesling" is capable of making racy,
aristocratic, honeyed wines with great potential for ageing.
This last quality is also true of the Chardonnay, which
Burgundians would doubtless nominate as the leading
white wine grape. Great Chardonnay such as Le Montrachet is a powerful dry wine that is capable of developing
great layers of flavour as it matures. Sémillon is the classic
Sauternes grape and in good years, treated carefully, can
produce luscious dessert wines of the quality of Yquem.
Sauvignon is the other white bordeaux grape, grown extensively outside Bordeaux but designed for wines drunk
young and fresh. Muscat of various sorts is grown in almost
every wine area and is, curiously, the only variety that
makes wine actually smelling of grapes.

If choice of grape variety plays a vital part in the final
flavour of the wine, this is equally true of where the grapes
are grown. Cabernet Sauvignon in the temperate climate
and poor gravel of Médoc in Bordeaux makes a lighter,
more complex wine than that made from Cabernet planted
in rich soil in one of the hotter wine areas of Australia.

Vines need a reasonably temperate climate: enough sun
to ripen the grapes, enough rain to swell them, a cold
enough winter to allow the vines to rest but not so cool as to
make frosts too much of a problem. This is why wine is
produced in areas that, broadly speaking, fall into two
bands half-way into the Northern and Southern Hemi-
spheres, with the greatest concentration of vineyards lying
around and just to the north of the Mediterranean.

Climate can affect grapes by as little as a matter of
yards. There are vineyards in Bordeaux and Burgundy
separated only by the width of a road, but, because of
differences in, say, susceptibility to frosts or winds, are
capable of producing wines of quite different qualities.
Each small area has its own "micro-climate" and study of
this is vital when deciding where to site a new vineyard.

Soil also has a great effect on the resultant wine. In the
past it has been thought that the general rule is "the
poorer the soil, the better the wine" and it is certainly true
that the world's great clarets come from mean-looking
gravel, moselles from precipitous slate, port from almost
impermeable schist and Châteauneuf from land littered
with unaccommodatingly large stones. Some very good
wines are being made in North America, however, from
vines planted in relatively fertile soil, and, though much
research is still to be done, it seems that the most important

(top) 1922 advertisement for Italian sparkling wine. (bottom) Advertisement for marsala, a type of rich Italian fortified wine

factor is that the soil be well drained. This means that the vine has to send its roots down deep in search of moisture, and the deeper the roots go, the more interesting trace elements they will take up from the soil. These trace elements play an eventual part in determining the nuances of flavour in the wine.

The aim of any serious vine grower is to be able to present the winemaker with fruit in the best possible condition at vintage time. Just after the vintage, the grower's annual cycle of work begins with a general tidying of the vineyard. During the winter months the vines are severely pruned so that all that is left to show that the land is a vineyard are the rows of little black stumps.

By early spring the sap is beginning to rise and a few young shoots start to appear which, in some areas, may be at risk from the spring frosts. Some years vine growers go to great lengths, using wind, flame or water, to try to prevent frost damage.

The flowering of the vine usually takes place in June in the Northern Hemisphere. Continuously warm weather is important during flowering for the crop to be of good, even quality. The grapes form, ripen and swell during the summer, according to the amount of sun and rain. The vines may be pruned again in the summer to prevent foliage shading the grapes from the sun, or to concentrate the vines' energies on developing ripe grapes rather than luxuriant leaves. The vines are also sprayed several times against the alarming variety of pests and diseases to which they are prone, and then all the grower has to do is to make his most critical decision of the year: when to pick. The grower wants to wait until the grapes are as ripe as possible, but he doesn't want to risk their being shattered by hail, diluted by rain during picking, or even frozen in below-zero temperatures.

In the Northern Hemisphere, the vintage can take place as early as August in the hotter wine regions, where grapes may have to be picked before they are fully ripe in order to keep them tart enough. In cooler regions the grapes can be picked much later, sometimes well into November if the grower is trying to produce wines that are very high in sugar. In the great dessert wine vineyards in Germany and Sauternes, pickers may go through the vineyard several times picking out individual bunches according to how ripe they are. In this case, they will be delighted if the grapes succumb to a certain type of rot, "noble rot" (*pourriture noble* in French, *Edelfäule* in German, *Botrytis cinerea* in Latin). This process shrivels the berries, covers them with a peculiarly unsavoury-looking grey dust and concentrates their sugar content so as to make the grapes capable of producing truly great sweet wines. Sémillon is planted in Sauternes, for instance, because it is particularly susceptible to *pourriture noble*.

Whatever sort of wine winemakers intend to make, even the driest of dry, they like to receive grapes that are as high as possible in sugar, because sugar is their essential raw material. The principle of fermentation is that sugar reacts together with yeast to form alcohol. The more sugar the grapes contain, therefore, the higher the potential alcoholic strength of the wine.

The grape is a remarkable example of a do-it-yourself winemaking kit. It not only contains sugar inside the pulp, it also has thousands of yeasts on the skin which accumulate there from the natural atmosphere in the vineyard. Whenever a grape is crushed some form of alcoholic fermentation can begin, and this is presumably exactly

how the first wine was "discovered" by our ancestors.

Modern winemakers like to leave as little as possible to chance, so they may well decide to kill off all the yeasts present on the skin and to apply their own specially cultivated yeasts, which have been proved to be particularly successful for the sort of wine they want to make. They will certainly make sure the grapes are chemically "clean" before winemaking starts, usually by killing off bacteria with sulphur dioxide.

If the winemaker wants fermentation to take place in contact with grapeskins, an essential requirement for red and *rosé* wine as there is no colouring matter in the pulp of most red grapes, the grapes will be lightly crushed. Most grapes will also be separated from their stalks as these can make the wine too hard to taste. The mushy mixture known as "must" is moved to scrupulously clean fermentation vats, usually made of stainless steel, and the yeasts get to work on the sugar. In really well-equipped wineries there are means of controlling the temperature of this fermentation to make sure that the wines will get maximum flavour from the grapes. If the grapes are particularly low in sugar, sugar may be added before fermentation to ensure that the resultant wine will be sufficiently high in alcohol. This does not necessarily make the wine sweeter, just stronger. This very common process is known as "chaptalisation" after a French Minister of Agriculture called Chaptal. The winemaker has to decide whether to stop fermentation before all the sugar, whether naturally present or added, is used up, or whether to ferment the wine out to dryness.

Most wines still have some sugar left in them. Above a certain strength, the alcohol overcomes the yeast and fermentation ceases naturally. After fermentation the juice that is now new wine is run off and the remaining mixture of skins, pips and juice will then be pressed to get the rest of the wine out before the pomace is either distilled to produce *marc* or used as fertilizer. For white wines not fermented on their skins, the grapes are carefully pressed before fermentation, which generally takes place at a lower tem-

A Paris café is not just a place to drink wine but also can be a rendezvous for friends or even somewhere to sit quietly and write letters

Label from a bottle of Swanbridge wine, produced in Wales

perature than red wine fermentation in order to maximize the wines' fruitiness and freshness.

The next decisions concern the type of material in which the wine will be stored before bottling and how long it will be stored. A period of many months in small oak casks is an integral part of making most great red wines, the sort of wines that are built to last, but the proportion of wine made today that has never come into contact with wood is surprisingly high. All whites, except the finest Chardonnays and Sauternes, and most everyday reds, will go straight into large tanks to be bottled within a year of the vintage for consumption as soon as possible. It is important that the wine should come into contact with air as little as possible to prevent the wine becoming "oxidized" – flat, stale and prematurely aged. To this end, some wines are kept beneath a "blanket" of inert gas such as nitrogen.

Scientists believe that wine undergoes a very slow and slight process of oxidation in wooden casks and this can have a great effect on the final taste of the wine. The size of the casks is important: larger ones, such as those used traditionally for Barolo, allow a much smaller proportion of the wine to come into contact with air than smaller ones. The exact sort of wood used also has a great effect on the taste of the wine and warrants a book in itself.

In any case it is vital that wine maturing in cask is kept topped up regularly as there is an inevitable amount of evaporation which could cause undue oxidation if small quantities of wine were not added at regular intervals. During this process of maturation there is also the essential business of "racking", pumping the wine off the dead yeast cells and other solids that form a deposit at the bottom of the wine. Most wine drinkers nowadays are unduly suspicious if their wine is not completely clear, so winemakers go to great lengths to ensure that their wines are "star bright". This process may start with centrifuging the must, in addition to filtering the wine before bottling. Most wines are also refrigerated before bottling so that the tartrates, the harmless solids that can look like white crystals in white wine, dark specks in red, are precipitated. Such is the importance of the customer's every whim in the winery!

The wine is now ready for bottling, usually on a highly automated bottling line. Some winemakers have a policy of giving their wines some bottle age in addition to ageing in cask. Really long livers such as first-growth clarets, vintage ports, the *crème de la crème* of what Germany has to offer, deserve, indeed demand, a certain amount of time to mature in bottle. A young vintage port, for instance, is no fun at all to drink. The process of ageing in wine is not fully understood, but it is thought that it involves a very slow process of oxidation. The wine mixes with the small amount of air in the wine, or allowed in by the cork.

Experiments have shown that for everyday wines which will be consumed within a year or so of being bottled, it does not matter whether they are stoppered with a cork, a crown cork, or even something as unromantic as a plastic plug. For great wine, however, no expert has come up with a viable substitute for the porous, malleable, robust cork. Without such a suitable stopper as cork, and without the benefits of such an inert, cheap material as glass, blown into the easily stacked bottle shape, the fine-wine drinker would be lost.

But this book is not designed exclusively for fine-wine drinkers. It is meant for everyone whose palate is sufficiently titillated, whose intellect is sufficiently intrigued, to want to learn about one of Nature's generous gifts, wine.

Label from a bottle of Castell Coch, another Welsh wine

FRANCE

To wine drinkers and winemakers all over the world, France is the cradle of truly great wine, providing models to which all may aspire but will rarely match.

Although the "New World" producers in California and Australia are catching up fast, they have yet to reach that state of maturity in their winemaking traditions that gives them wines of the greatness and complexity of first growth clarets, the finest white burgundies, classic sauternes and those under-appreciated treasures, the best wines of the Rhône and the Loire. France is fortunate in containing regions ideally suited to the production of fine wine within her frontiers, but this is not the whole story. There are many other parts of the world at least as capable of making truly great wine because of their geographical and meteorological situation. The reason that they are not yet doing so is that their wine industries are either very young or, in the case of China for instance, simply non-existent. The French, however, have been making wine since colonization by the Greeks and Phoenicians. Their development of winemaking skills later received a great boost when Aquitaine in the west came under the sway of the English in the twelfth century. The thirsty English and, in particular, Scottish, encouraged trade in wine between themselves and Bordeaux and La Rochelle, just as a trade was built up in exporting the wines made further east to other parts of Britain and elsewhere. The French have a tradition of making and drinking wine that goes back so very much longer than most of their wine-making rivals, it is small wonder that they are capable of making such sublime wines.

Until recently there has been a tendency for *all* French winemakers to bask in the reflected glory of the finest of her wines, the top one per cent perhaps. It has been all too easy for the French to trade on their name and their wines have accordingly become increasingly expensive. There are now signs that they are becoming aware of the fact that there are winemakers in other countries, and relatively successful ones at that. At the top end of the wine market there have been some embarrassing comparisons between, say, classed growth clarets and Californian Cabernet Sauvignons, just as Burgundy has had to see some of her finest wines rivalled by the best of Australian Pinot Noirs and California Chardonnays.

At the other end of the scale, the French are at last starting to realize that the quality of their *vin ordinaire* must be improved if it is to satisfy consumers, and warrant all those thousands of acres planted with grapes in the south of the country where the bulk of the grape harvest is produced. France vies with Italy each year to be the world's biggest wine producer, but well over half, and often as much as three-quarters, of what she produces is ordinary table wine, *vin de table*, the majority of it red and of pretty mediocre quality.

The French government is trying to encourage the planting of better-quality grape varieties in the place of the very high-yielding sorts that have been popular in the past. And they are trying to elevate more wines from the straight *vin de table* category to the next quality level up, *vin de pays*. To qualify as a *vin de pays*, a wine must come from a certain specified region, be made from certain specified grape varieties in not so great a quantity that the

Wine is the accompaniment to a fashionable yet decorous dinner party. By Cardona from Lè Rire

Champagne seems to have added to the riotous atmosphere of a night on the town. By Cardona from Lè Rire

(left) Pouring out the wine. Detail from "Les Vendanges", Burgundian tapestry, circa 1500 (right) The gentleman complains that the wine is "corked", only to be told by the waiter that his nose has deceived him! Paris Brilliant, *March, 1890*

grape juice is "stretched", and must be subjected to official tasting tests. The development of this *vin de pays* category has brought about a rise in quality of the wines that are made in these southern "workhorse" regions of France.

The French have always been pioneers in wine legislation and these *vin de pays* laws were modelled, albeit further down the scale in quality, on her famous *Appellation d'Origine Contrôlée* (AC) laws, which have been developed throughout this century and on which so many other systems of designating "quality wines" have been based throughout the world. The French system uses as its basic tenet that the quality of a wine is determined most importantly by the exact spot where it was produced. For a wine to qualify as *Appellation "X" Contrôlée* it must have been made from very carefully controlled quantities of prescribed grape varieties grown in a vineyard in the exactly delimited area of "X" and made to certain specifications. This is the highest official national quality designation in France and about fifteen per cent of all wine produced in France each year is AC. The AC system operates in a series of ever more specific delimited areas, rather like a set of Russian dolls, so that the less general "X" is, in terms of the geographical area it describes, the better any wine described as *Appellation "X" Contrôlée* is likely to be. For example, Pauillac being a village, or *commune*, in the Médoc region in Bordeaux, means, AC Pauillac is likely to be better than AC Médoc (which could come from anywhere in the Médoc), which in turn is likely to be better than AC Bordeaux, which could have come from any of the fringe, lesser areas of Bordeaux which have not earned themselves their own specific reputation.

There is a small fourth category of wines in France which fits in above *vin de table* and its superior *vin de pays*, but below AC wines, and that is VDQS, *vins délimités de qualité supérieure* (better quality wines coming from a delimited area). Here the rules are not quite so strict as for AC in some respects and the category has in effect become a sort of staging post for regions *en route* for full AC status.

In line with the French mania for categorizing everything, every wine made in France must fall into one of these four categories. But that is not to say that all *vins de table* are worse than all *vins de pays*, which in turn are worse than all VDQSs, themselves worse than all ACs.

Much depends on the skill of individual producers and shippers (*négociants*). In addition to this there are all sorts of quirks in the details of legislation which, for instance, make a perfectly respectable wine, Sauvignon de St Bris, a VDQS only because it is made inside the limits of the Burgundy region while Sauvignon is not one of the grape varieties prescribed by law as being permissible for an AC Burgundy. Or there is VDQS Minervois, from which some high-class grape varieties are excluded which may perfectly well be used in a *cuvée* (blend) for a local *vin de pays*.

At the Café Tortoni, Paris, 1889

The French, in wine as much as in sport, newspapers and customs, are nothing if not regionalized. Most Bordelais know nothing of the wines of Burgundy; the inhabitants of the Muscadet region see no reason to look as far east as Alsace to provide white wine drinking variety. While this is a shame from the point of view of those living in France, it is up to the rest of us to realize our good fortune in being able to draw on the variety France has to offer the wine drinker. Over the years she has managed to find out exactly which sort of wine each region can produce best. The sharp, firm wines of Champagne have been adapted to produce uniquely classy sparkling wines. Winemakers in Alsace, near the German border, have combined the best of French winemaking techniques with the best of German wine grapes to produce another unique style of wines. For centuries in Burgundy, Pinot Noir and Chardonnay grapes have been producing consistently high-quality wines in conditions that seem tailor-made for them. Along the Loire each sub-region has discovered what it is best at: dry whites at the mouth of the river, moving up through honeyed dessert and medium dry whites of Vouvray and Anjou to the much more austere whites of the Central Vineyards around Sancerre and the Pouilly Fumé region. The vineyards that follow the course of France's other "wine river", the Rhône, have for years produced some of her finest, richest reds as well as pockets of dry whites the like of which are not seen anywhere else in the world. In the southwest of the country, wine buyers from abroad are rapidly finding out what goodies the locals have been keeping to themselves all these years, while Bordeaux continues to arrest the attention of serious wine lovers the world over with the sheer class of what it is capable of producing. *Vive la France!*

BORDEAUX

For a wine lover to say he didn't like bordeaux would be about as likely as for a musician to say he didn't like Mozart. Bordeaux must produce the most interesting wines, and more of them, than anywhere else in the world. Their fascination lies in their ability to last, to develop such nuances of flavour at each different stage of their maturity, their capacity to differ so captivatingly according to the exact spot or precise year the grapes were grown. Claret and port are the two wines that are capable of provoking endless discussion.

Red bordeaux has been called claret ever since the very much lighter reds shipped from Aquitaine to the England of Henry II were known as *clairet*. The British and Dutch have always been particularly fond of it, though it is now shipped to wine connoisseurs all over the world. The characteristics of red bordeaux are that it is a dry, fruity wine when young, one that is not as high in alcohol as some produced in less temperate climates. Although there is an increasing tendency to make wines for earlier consumption, particularly the cheaper wines, the best wines are built to last. They are vinified so as to extract maximum fruit, colour and tannin from the grapes and it is the tannin that keeps the wines lively over the decades while they mature into wonderfully complex liquids with different "layers" of flavour that can be relished as the wine develops in the bottle, and even in the glass. Bottles of claret made in the last century are still delighting those who can afford them.

The other great classic of the Bordeaux region is sauternes, wonderfully rich, golden wines that taste as good as they look, though without the cloying aftertaste of cheaper sweet whites. Château Yquem is the most famous and most expensive of these unfashionably sweet wines.

Bordeaux also produces huge quantities of lesser white wine; about one-third of all produced each vintage is white. Some of this is still fairly mediocre quality, but there is increasing skill there in producing dependably crisp and inexpensive dry whites for early consumption. Care should be taken when choosing bottles of white bordeaux as it is not always made crystal clear which are dry and which are medium dry or sweet. There is a trend towards putting the dry wines in green bottles and the sweeter ones in clear glass. A small proportion of the dry white bordeaux produced is worth maturing to produce wines of the classic greatness of a Château Laville-Haut Brion and other good white Graves properties. Very little *rosé* is produced in the Bordeaux region.

The most basic sort of wine that can be recognized as bordeaux is straight *Appellation Bordeaux Contrôlée*. This may be a blend of wines from more than one *appellation* within the Bordeaux region, or it may come from a part of the region not entitled to its own AC, or the bottler may decide to sell it as AC Bordeaux rather than the more complicated or less fashionable AC to which it is also in fact entitled.

Many of these AC Bordeaux, both red and white, carry the name of a "château" on the label. This does not necessarily serve as evidence that there is indeed a sumptuous building of that name, which is surrounded by the vineyard from which the wine came. There is an official register of all these so-called *petits châteaux*, and so long as the

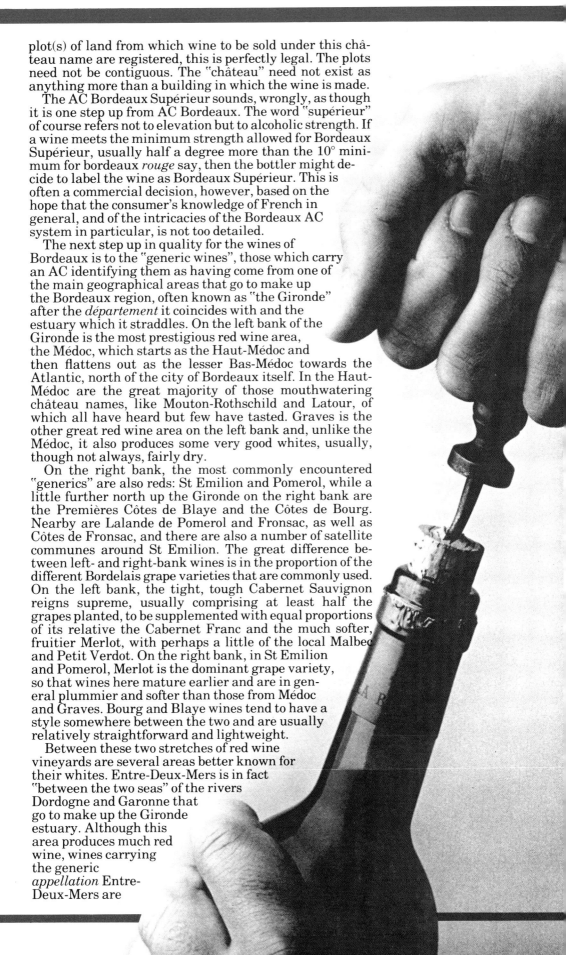

plot(s) of land from which wine to be sold under this château name are registered, this is perfectly legal. The plots
need not be contiguous. The "château" need not exist as
anything more than a building in which the wine is made.

The AC Bordeaux Supérieur sounds, wrongly, as though
it is one step up from AC Bordeaux. The word "supérieur"
of course refers not to elevation but to alcoholic strength. If
a wine meets the minimum strength allowed for Bordeaux
Supérieur, usually half a degree more than the 10° minimum for bordeaux *rouge* say, then the bottler might decide to label the wine as Bordeaux Supérieur. This is
often a commercial decision, however, based on the
hope that the consumer's knowledge of French in
general, and of the intricacies of the Bordeaux AC
system in particular, is not too detailed.

The next step up in quality for the wines of
Bordeaux is to the "generic wines", those which carry
an AC identifying them as having come from one of
the main geographical areas that go to make up
the Bordeaux region, often known as "the Gironde"
after the *département* it coincides with and the
estuary which it straddles. On the left bank of the
Gironde is the most prestigious red wine area,
the Médoc, which starts as the Haut-Médoc and
then flattens out as the lesser Bas-Médoc towards the
Atlantic, north of the city of Bordeaux itself. In the Haut-
Médoc are the great majority of those mouthwatering
château names, like Mouton-Rothschild and Latour, of
which all have heard but few have tasted. Graves is the
other great red wine area on the left bank and, unlike the
Médoc, it also produces some very good whites, usually,
though not always, fairly dry.

On the right bank, the most commonly encountered
"generics" are also reds: St Emilion and Pomerol, while a
little further north up the Gironde on the right bank are
the Premières Côtes de Blaye and the Côtes de Bourg.
Nearby are Lalande de Pomerol and Fronsac, as well as
Côtes de Fronsac, and there are also a number of satellite
communes around St Emilion. The great difference between left- and right-bank wines is in the proportion of the
different Bordelais grape varieties that are commonly used.
On the left bank, the tight, tough Cabernet Sauvignon
reigns supreme, usually comprising at least half the
grapes planted, to be supplemented with equal proportions
of its relative the Cabernet Franc and the much softer,
fruitier Merlot, with perhaps a little of the local Malbec
and Petit Verdot. On the right bank, in St Emilion
and Pomerol, Merlot is the dominant grape variety,
so that wines here mature earlier and are in general plummier and softer than those from Médoc
and Graves. Bourg and Blaye wines tend to have a
style somewhere between the two and are usually
relatively straightforward and lightweight.

Between these two stretches of red wine
vineyards are several areas better known for
their whites. Entre-Deux-Mers is in fact
"between the two seas" of the rivers
Dordogne and Garonne that
go to make up the Gironde
estuary. Although this
area produces much red
wine, wines carrying
the generic
appellation Entre-
Deux-Mers are

usually whites, dry whites. Up in its northwest corner is another, much smaller generic *appellation*, Graves de Vayres (nothing to do with Graves which is much further south), which again is a dry white bordeaux *appellation*.

To the south and west of Entre-Deux-Mers are the sweet white bordeaux *appellations*, of which the best known are Premières Côtes de Bordeaux, Loupiac, Ste-Croix-du-Mont, Cérons, Barsac and, giving its name to wines all over the world, Sauternes. Barsac and Sauternes are both capable of producing superb wines (which will probably not be sold as simple generics), while the other generic *appellations* can often produce sound, clean dessert wines.

Above all of these generic wines in terms of quality are those entitled to the *appellation* of a single *commune*, and this group includes the *crème de la crème*, individual "classed growths", those properties that have been included in the official classifications of the best wines of the Bordeaux region. The most famous of these is the 1855 Classification of the Médoc and Graves. This is often referred to as a "first growth claret".

In the Médoc the "best classified" *commune* is Pauillac, which includes three of today's five first growths within its parish boundaries. Other prestigious *communes* include Margaux and St Julien, with St Estèphe housing classed growths too. Five of the sixty-two châteaux included in the 1855 Classification have to make do with the *appellation* Haut-Médoc, since they do not fall within the boundaries of *communes* with their own AC. Added to the Médoc Châteaux Lafite, Latour, Margaux and (added later) Mouton-Rothschild, in the lofty ranks of 1855 first growths, is Château Haut-Brion which, together with its neighbour and rival Château La Mission-Haut-Brion, ranks as one of the best properties in the Graves, whose wines have a curious "stoney" texture to them. Top properties across the river in St Emilion are Châteaux Ausone and Cheval Blanc, which manage to fetch even higher prices than Médoc first growths, as does the supreme wine of Pomerol, Château Pétrus.

In Sauternes, where the Sémillon grape so obligingly ripens and then succumbs to *pourriture noble* (see page 14) to produce rich, luscious dessert wines in good years, the most prestigious property is Château d'Yquem, not just a *premier cru* but the only *premier grand cru* in Bordeaux. Here the Marquis de Lur Saluces painstakingly makes the world's most famous sweet white wine, with several of his neighbours providing treats for discriminating wine lovers.

BURGUNDY

The Burgundian may question the Bordelais' claim to make the finest red wines in the world, but in the sphere of dry whites, he is confident of having no serious rival. While it is fair to say that Burgundy owes much to supple, fulsome reds for its reputation, it could be argued that this is being maintained largely on the basis of the powerful whites, which are made nowhere else in the world.

Burgundy is a region fraught with difficulty for the wine drinker. One of the chief drawbacks is its size, or rather lack of it. This means that the topflight wines are produced only in very limited quantities and only at very high prices. A further difficulty is that quality is so much more variable, and so much more difficult to assess from the label or wine list. Because the individual vineyards tend to be split in several small plots, sometimes hundreds of small plots, there is no consistency between different bottles carrying the same vineyard name. *Négociants*, or shippers, rather than individual vineyard owners, are all-important in Burgundy. They will buy in many different parcels of wine, each entitled to the same name, and blend them together to sell their own style of, say, Gevrey-Chambertin or Chambolle-Musigny Les Amoureuses. It is important, therefore, to find out which *négociant* produces consistent wines, in a style that you like.

As if all this were not complicated enough, there is the tricky naming within the region. Gevrey-Chambertin is a village as is Chambolle-Musigny, whereas Les Amoureuses is a vineyard in Chambolle-Musigny. One would expect, therefore, Chambolle-Musigny Les Amoureuses to be a finer wine than straight Chambolle-Musigny, or Gevrey-Chambertin. These two villages were originally called simply Chambolle and Gevrey, having later added the name of their most famous vineyards, Le Musigny and Le Chambertin respectively. So a fair rule when buying Burgundy is "the longer the name the smarter the wine" – unless it's "Le something" (Le Musigny, for example).

Burgundy is not one homogeneous region, but the name is used to include Chablis in the north, the prestigious heartland of the Côte d'Or, the Côte Chalonnaise and the Mâconnais in the south and even, sometimes, Beaujolais.

Chablis is sixty miles to the northwest of the start of "Burgundy proper" and produces, from the Chardonnay grape, very dry whites, sometimes with a tinge of green. The greatest of these, Grand Cru Chablis, are capable of maturing over many years into firm and fascinating wines.

The Côte d'Or (golden slope) is where Burgundy's greatest wines are made. In the northern half, known as the Côte de Nuits and centred on Nuits-St-Georges, are most of the finest red burgundies: Le Chambertin, Le Musigny and the wines of the prestigious and wildly expensive Domaine de la Romanée Conti. The classic red burgundy grape Pinot Noir has yet to find a home as accommodating as the vineyards around Gevrey-Chambertin, Morey-St-Denis, Chambolle-Musigny, Vosne Romanée and Nuits-St-Georges. The Côte de Beaune, the southern half of the Côte d'Or is centred on the town of Beaune, where the famous Hospices de Beaune charity wine auction is held every year. Great white burgundies such as Corton Charlemagne, Le Montrachet and Meursault are made on the Côte de Beaune, whose villages Aloxe-Corton, Savigny-lès-Beaune, Pommard, Volnay, Monthélie, Auxey-Duresses

and Santenay are capable of producing fine burgundy.

The classic white burgundy grape is Chardonnay and is more reliable from year to year than Pinot Noir. In most years white burgundy is dependable (if expensively so), but there have been disappointments with red burgundy. At its best it can be sublime, but many wine drinkers outside Burgundy itself are taking their time getting used to the lighter "French" style of red burgundy that is now more common than the fuller, heavier "English" style burgundies that some merchants exported when *Appellation Contrôlée* laws were not quite so strict.

The most basic "generic" burgundy is Bourgogne Grand Ordinaire, usually rather lighter than the next step up, AC Bourgogne. Bourgogne Passe-tout-grains is a mixture of Gamay and Pinot, with Pinot characteristics becoming stronger as the wine matures. The most basic white burgundy is Bourgogne Aligoté, Aligoté being a local grape producing tart, light wines. Côte de Beaune-Villages and Côte de Nuits-Villages come from special vineyards.

In the hinterland of the Côte d'Or are the Hautes Côtes, which are producing lighter wines made from Pinot and Chardonnay, and these grapes are also capable of producing sound, attractive wines when planted further south around Rully, Mercurey, Givry, Montagny and Buxy.

In the Mâconnais to the south of this, Mâcon Blanc and its popular neighbour, Pouilly Fuissé, are better bets than Mâcon Rouge; the latter is usually made from Gamay grape, which produces mediocre wine in northern Burgundy, while the former must be made from Chardonnay.

The Gamay comes into its own, however, in the Beaujolais region immediately to the south. Here the grape is solely responsible for those juicy reds, Beaujolais, Beaujolais-Villages and, at the top of the scale, the Beaujolais "crus": Moulin-à-Vent, Morgon, Juliénas, Côte de Brouilly, Brouilly, Fleurie, Chénas, Chiroubles, and St Amour in descending order (approximately) of firmness. Unlike burgundy from further north, these are wines to be drunk young. This principle has been taken to its logical conclusion in the appearance of beaujolais *nouveau*, or beaujolais *primeur*, every November 15. These wines, vinified fast and bottled only weeks after the harvest, should be drunk (and forgotten?) as soon as possible.

RHONE

The Rhône is now well past its heyday, when Hermitage was thought of as the king of wines and Châteauneuf-du-Pape was a prerequisite for any wine list. These two are the region's most famous wines, one from the north, the other from the south, the two zones into which the Valley is climatologically and viticulturally split. In the north the great, dark Hermitage is made from the Syrah grape along with other similar, though usually lesser, reds such as Côte Rôtie, Cornas, St Joseph and Crozes Hermitage. Also in the north are two white "curiosities", Condrieu and Château Grillet, both made from the Viognier grape and both deliciously dry, yet flowery.

To the north of Avignon, much of the wine qualifies only as AC Côtes-du-Rhône, slightly spicy, "warm" tasting wine. The wine on which these everyday wines are modelled is Châteauneuf-du-Pape, of which there are as many styles as there are grape varieties in the average blend. The best are broad, peppery and strong and will last for many years. Gigondas and Vacqueyras are made in the same mould around villages of the same names to the northeast towards Côtes de Ventoux, which has its own *appellation* for its Grenache-based reds and *rosés*.

Other similar wines of this region, the fringes of the southern Rhône valley, are Coteaux du Tricastin, Côtes du Vivarais and Côtes du Luberon.

As this region is so close to Provence, it is hardly surprising that a high proportion of *rosés* are made, the local grape Grenache being particularly suitable for pink wines. Lirac and Tavel are the best known, the latter being very strong indeed. This is not great white wine country.

ALSACE

After being fought over for hundreds of years, the inhabitants of this absurdly pretty region have stopped worrying about whether they are German or French and have got on with developing a uniquely Alsatian style. This goes as much for winemaking as anything else.

The wines of Alsace combine the flowery, fragrant grape varieties of Germany with the techniques of French winemakers. All wines are fermented out to dryness in such a way as to minimize the use of chemicals and maximize the amount of fruit, with the aim of encapsulating in the bottle the exact flavour of the grapes that went into it.

It is not surprising therefore that winemakers in Alsace (who incidentally have managed to stave off takeovers from mammoth outside concerns better than any of their counterparts elsewhere in France) have chosen to name their wines so simply, after the grape varieties from which they were made.

In Alsace the entire region there has just one AC, Alsace (currently being supplemented by the much disputed new AC Grand Cru), and to this is added on the label the name of the grape. In Alsace the Riesling is recognized as king, as it is on the other side of the Rhine in Germany, and this produces the noblest and longest-living wines of Alsace. Outside Alsace, however, the best known variety is often Gewürztraminer, literally "spicy Traminer", whose aroma is uniquely perfumed and exotic, only to be followed by that characteristically Alsatian surprise, a dry finish on the palate. Another noble grape variety in Alsace is Pinot Gris or Tokay d'Alsace. This has no connection with the famous Hungarian Tokay and here makes heady, rich yet dry wines. Muscat, which is planted all over the world, from Asti to Setubal, retains its typically grapy smell in Muscat d'Alsace, and yet its lack of sweetness in the mouth makes it particularly popular as an aperitif.

Rather lesser grape varieties, though they are still often named on the label, are Sylvaner and Pinot Blanc. There has been an increasing tendency to plant the latter rather than the former as it gives "rounder" wines that are not quite so sharp. Neither of these varieties makes wines that are meant to be aged. Other, slightly cheaper Alsace wines will be sold as Edelzwicker, or sometimes under a brand name such as Chevalier or Flambeau d'Alsace. These will usually be mixture of grape varieties, usually Sylvaner and Pinot Blanc in the main. They have the characteristic fragrant "nose" with a dry taste, unlike the much sweeter wines made from similar grapes in Germany.

Almost all Alsace wine is bottled in Alsace itself, a policy which usually achieves its desired effect of keeping a certain quality and freshness in the wines. They can be spotted by their tall, elegant green *flûte* bottles, and by the fact that most labels seem to carry an unusual mixture of German and French words on them. Careful scrutiny of Alsace wine labels pays off as makers call their best wines "Réserve Personnelle" or perhaps "Sélection Exceptionelle", but these terms, which can make all the difference between a straightforward wine and a great one, are usually printed unduly modestly.

Vendange Tardive is the Alsatian equivalent of Late Harvest Spätlese and these wines are keepers.

A small amount of Pinot Noir is grown to make light, red wines for local consumption.

LOIRE

You can find any wine you like along the banks of the beautifully languid Loire: red, white or pink; still or sparkling; bone dry to lusciously sweet.

There are several distinct winemaking areas as one travels up the river. Around Nantes at the mouth are the Muscadet vineyards, where the Muscadet grape is planted to produce light, dry, sharp wines, the sort with so few distinguishing marks that they are the blind taster's *bête noire*. Among the Muscadet is planted another grape variety, Gros Plant, which is responsible for similar though tarter wines, Gros Plant Nantais.

Moving upriver there is Anjou, most famous for its *rosé*, which some may find rather more medium than dry. There is a classier version, Cabernet d'Anjou, which gets its perfume from the noble Cabernets Sauvignon and Franc and is usually a little drier too. Cabernet Franc is responsible for the Loire's best-known red wines, Chinon and Bourgeuil, light and dry with a curious scent to them.

A little downstream from the town of Angers is a quirk of nature, a tiny area that is capable of producing wonderfully rich dessert wines from the Chenin Blanc grape grown on the Coteaux du Layon. Bonnezeaux and Quarts de Chaume are the *appellations* here.

Chenin Blanc is the usual white wine grape of this middle Loire section around Angers and Vouvray and is put to work to produce honeyed, flowery wines of all degrees of sweetness, the best of which can last for decades. It is often forgotten that Vouvray can produce some of the world's most classic white wine, unyielding, long-lasting and very rewarding for those in search of a sweet or medium dry white which, if well made, can mature in bottle for years while never losing the honeyed delicacy of the Chenin grape. Savennières has its own *appellation*, though the most commonly seen are the medium dry Vouvrays made for early consumption.

Also made around Vouvray and, particularly, Saumur, are sparkling wines made by the *méthode champenoise* and often good value alternatives to champagne. There are also some reds produced here: Anjou Rouge, Rouge de Touraine, Saumur-Champigny and, to take the place of over-priced beaujolais, Gamay de Touraine.

Sauvignon de Touraine is its white wine equivalent and the blackcurrant-fresh dry wines made from this grape, widely planted in Bordeaux, are particularly popular in the Central Vineyards of the Loire. Best known are Sancerre and Pouilly Fumé (nothing to do with Burgundy's Pouilly Fuissé), which even experts find hard to distinguish. They are made very close to each other around the villages of Sancerre and Pouilly-sur-Loire on opposite sides of the river well south of Orléans. Other, similar wines come from Menetou-Salon, Quincy and Reuilly.

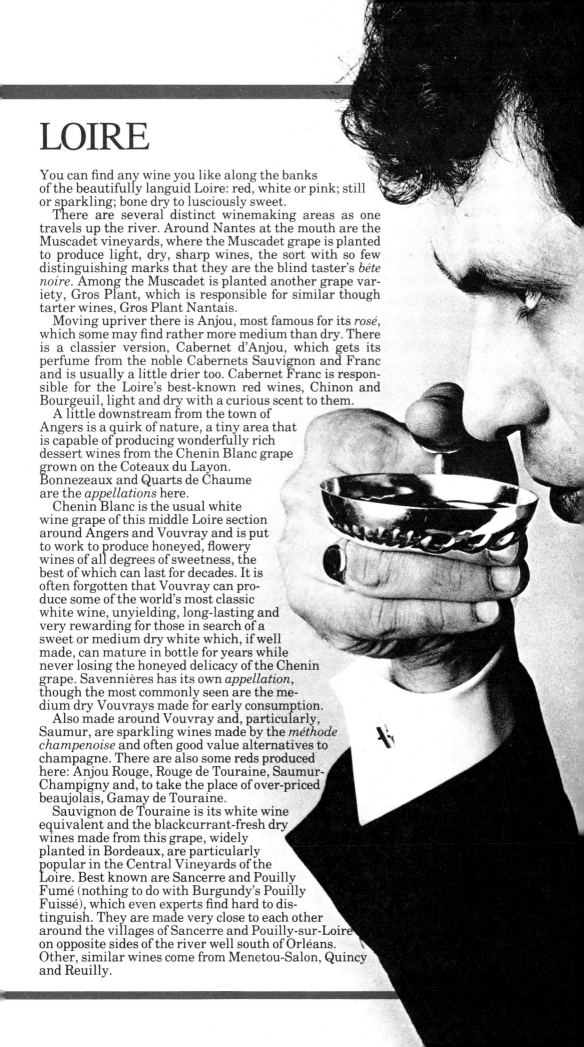

FRENCH SPARKLING WINES

There is nothing more excitingly special than a really good champagne. There are few drinks as nasty as a cheap sparkling wine. In Europe and most of the rest of the world (though not the USA) only the sparkling wine made in the Champagne region in northeastern France by the famous *méthode champenoise* may be called champagne. Everything else is just sparkling wine.

There are several ways of putting bubbles into wine to make it sparkling, each of which has a different effect on the resulting wine, which of course is a function of the initial quality of the still wine. There seem to be no still wines more suited to being turned into sparkling wines than the firm, dry wines of the Champagne region. Those in other parts of the world who aspire to making a really great sparkling wine always try to use a base wine as similar as possible to the still wines of Champagne.

Any method of making wine sparkle involves getting carbon dioxide into the wine in order to form bubbles, as small and as long-lasting as possible, when the wine is eventually opened. The *méthode champenoise* is the classic way of achieving this.

A careful blend of still base wines is made and, together with specially cultivated yeasts and a little bit of sugar, is put into champagne bottles and sealed with a crown cork. The bottles are left to rest in the cool, dark cellars of the Champagne region usually for up to three years. The sugar and the yeast react together to provoke a second fermentation, thereby increasing the alcoholic content of the wine, and giving off as a by-product carbon dioxide (see page 15).

The sediment that forms as a result of this alcoholic fermentation eventually falls to lie on the underside

of the bottle and the wine gains in complexity as it matures in contact with this mixture of dead yeast cells.

The liquid in these bottles is now good, dry champagne, but the sediment has to be removed if we are to persist in our liking for crystal clear wines. The development of a technique for removing this sediment, together with the advent of strong bottles and champagne corks, was the most important part of the evolution of champagne. The bottles are moved gently from their horizontal position and put into *pupitres*, racks with holes for bottle necks which are gradually tilted so as to take the bottles from nearly horizontal to nearly vertical upside-down. Each time this is done, by dextrously skilled workers called *remuers*, literally "shakers", they are also given a little twist, which encourages the passage of the sediment from the underside of the bottle to the cork. The bottles are then moved, still upside-down and vertical, to baths of a special solution which freezes the neck of the bottle and the sediment inside so that when the crown cork is popped off, this is ejected as a frozen pellet, a process called *dégorgement*. The bottles are then filled with wine mixed with a little bit of sugar, the *dosage,* according to how sweet the champagne is designed to be. The driest are usually called Brut, then comes Extra Dry, Sec, Demi Sec and Rich in ascending order of sweetness. There are very few champagnes indeed, even those called Brut, which do not have a little sweetness added to them at this stage. After a few months' rest to "marry" the *dosage* and the wine, the wine is ready for shipment and sale.

The transfer method of making sparkling wines relies on the same principle of inducing a second alcoholic fermentation in each bottle as the *méthode champenoise*. The difference is that bottles are not individually disgorged. The sediment is removed by emptying, filtering and refilling the bottles under pressure.

The tank method (*cuve close,* bulk fermentation or Charmat process) is one of the most common methods of making sparkling wine. Instead of inducing a second fermentation in individual bottles, so as to get the benefit of maturing the wine on the sediment in as small a container as possible, the yeast and sugar mixture is added to the still wine as it is stored in huge tanks. After fermentation the sediment is filtered out and the wine bottled under pressure straight from the tank. This is not allowed in France for any AC sparkling wine (*vin mousseux*).

The cheapest method of making sparkling wine is carbonation: simply injecting carbon dioxide into the tanks holding the wine. This usually produces wines that have very large bubbles that cause a great commotion when the bottle is opened, but don't last for very long in the glass. This method is used only for the cheapest wines.

CHAMPAGNE

Champagne is recognized, not just in France but throughout the world, as the ultimate in celebration drinks, "the king of wines and the wine of kings". It is the only AC wine in France that does not have to have *Appellation Contrôlée* spelt out on the label. "Champagne" is enough.

It is commonly thought that the reason for the Champenois supremacy in the field of sparkling wine-making lies many feet below the surface of the vineyards, in the unique chalky subsoil of the region, whose composition was determined by a series of prehistoric earthquakes. Certainly the wine made from the Pinot Noir, Pinot Meunier and Chardonnay grapes grown here seems ideally

suited to champenization. With this mix of grapes, the Champenois have to a certain extent made life difficult for themselves; the majority of grapes grown in the Champagne region are black rather than white, so the process of pressing is an extremely critical one. It is vital to press the grapes so gently that none of the pigment from the black skins colours the juice, and the winemakers in Champagne take only the juice from the first pressings. Vineyards in Champagne are carefully graded according to the quality of the wine they produce, so there are a number of factors which can govern the ultimate quality of the champagne: the initial quality of the grapes, the length of time the wine is allowed to mature, the exact blend of wines used as base still wines. Each champagne house tries to keep their own consistent style of champagne in their non-vintage blend, a blend of wines from different vintages. In particularly good years they will also make a vintage-dated wine which combines their own style with the characteristics of that particular year, and in recent years there have also appeared "de luxe" champagnes, vintage dated and made only from the best grapes. Dom Perignon was the first, but there are now many more.

A *blanc de blancs* champagne is one made only from white grapes, Chardonnay. A *blanc de noirs* is made only from Pinot, and will probably have more body and depth than the average champagne, which is made from a mixture of white and black grapes.

The two most important champagne towns are Rheims and Epernay, though the much smaller town of Ay also has a few champagne houses. The *grandes marques* are those houses which have developed an international reputation for their wines, but in addition to them, an increasing number of growers make their own champagne, particularly popular with Parisians, who can combine a weekend expedition with a champagne-buying trip.

OTHER FRENCH SPARKLING WINES

The French term for a sparkling wine is a *vin mousseux*, the best of which come from Saumur in the Loire, from chalky cellars remarkably like those in Champagne. These wines are usually made from the Chenin Blanc grape, however, which gives them a quite different flavour from the uncompromising Chardonnay and Pinot blend. Similar, though usually rather less distinguished sparkling wines are made in Vouvray, Touraine and Anjou.

Burgundy has long had a tradition of making sparkling wines, in all grades of sweetness and shades of colour. The increase in prices of burgundy, and in the policing of its cellars, is making this a declining trade now.

Two AC sparkling wines are made in and around the Rhône Valley. St Péray is a fairly full-bodied wine made from local grapes near Cornas in the northern half of the valley, while Clairette de Die comes from the Drôme tributary of the valley to the northeast of Montelimar of nougat fame. Brut is the dry version, while Tradition includes Muscat in the blend and is sweeter.

Blanquette de Limoux is an oddity, a clean, fairly dry sparkling wine made in the Languedoc-Roussillon region not otherwise associated with such elegance. In addition to these officially classified wines, there are many brands of French sparkling wine, some made around Bordeaux where there has traditionally been an ample supply of inexpensive dry white wine.

OTHER FRENCH WINES

A number of good French wines are made in areas not traditionally thought of as wine-producing regions. Others don't fit into any geographical category. Good varietal wines are made at the Haut Poitou just south of Tours in the Loire, for instance, while St Pourçain-sur-Sioule, also on the fringes of the Loire, is producing reds and whites. Good Gamays come from the Côtes du Forez near Lyons as well as from the Auvergne and near Roanne.

In the north of Burgundy is the dry white Sauvignon de St Bris as well as the light red Irancy, not unlike the still red wines of the Champagne region, all of which are called Coteaux Champenois. They can be either red or white, and one of the best known reds is Bouzy Rouge.

MIDI AND PROVENCE

More than one in every two bottles of wine produced in France comes from the grapes grown in the vast arc of vineyards that sweeps round the hinterland of the Mediterranean coast in the south and west of France. This is called the Midi or the Languedoc-Roussillon region of France and the regular wine lover may be puzzled by the fact that he reads and hears relatively little of what is surely a most important wine-producing area.

The explanation is simple: the majority of wine produced is not the stuff of which books or lectures are made. Most of the wine is red, much of it devoid of character, most of it produced by growers who have been encouraged to be more interested in quantity than quality. This is the territory of high-yielding grape varieties like the Aramon, which would be frowned upon by those winemakers who are trying to produce fine wine.

Thanks to a more far-sighted approach now being adopted by some producers there, the proportion of "nobler" varieties grown, such as the Syrah, Merlot, Cabernet and Grenache, is increasing and some wines of character are now coming out of the Languedoc-Roussillon. These include the *vins de pays*, often with the name of one of the Midi departments – Pyrenées Orientales, Aude, Hérault, Tarn, Gard and Var – specified. To qualify as a *vin de pays* a wine must come from a specified area, must usually reach 10° alcoholic strength (this depends on the latitude of the area) and must be made according to certain specifications which, among other things, restrict the yields allowed from the grapes, and must be approved by a tasting panel. This excellent step in the direction of quality in the Midi is complicated for the consumer only by the complexity of the names of the areas.

In addition to these *vin de pays*, a number of areas have earned their own reputation and, in an increasing number of instances, their own *appellation*. Coteaux du Langue-

doc, Côtes du Roussillon, Fitou, Corbières, Minervois and St Chinian are all names to look out for. These names are increasingly earning themselves the right to full *Appellation Contrôlée* status and, if they are made well, can be excellent value for money.

Further east are the light red wines of Costières du Gard, the expensive ones of Coteaux des Baux and the Provençal wines Coteaux d'Aix-en-Provence and Côtes de Provence, specializing in dry *rosés* from the Grenache grape. Other than these more general Provence *appellations* there are the rich reds and *rosés* of Bandol, as well as the wines of Palette, Cassis (no connection with *vin blanc cassis*) and Bellet, near Nice, where there are too many restaurants to allow much to escape the region itself.

Corsica falls within the scope of the French wine authorities and there are those who think they have been too liberal in their awards of ACs to the island. This may be true, but the *vins de Corse* are still good value for those in search of fiery reds and *rosés*.

JURA

The Jura is a strangely isolated region in the hills between Burgundy and the Swiss border. It is the homeland of the nineteenth-century scientist Louis Pasteur, who did so much work in the study of the ageing process in wine. Today it is the preserve of wine producer Henri Maire, who controls a high proportion of production there.

The main wine names are Château-Chalon (not the name of a castle, but the name of a town), Arbois and l'Etoile. A whole range of wines – red, white, *rosé*, still, sparkling – are made in the Jura, but its two specialities are *vin jaune* and *vin de paille*. *Vin jaune*, or "yellow wine", is the nearest France comes to producing sherry (though there is a village called Rasteau off the Rhône Valley that comes close to making a sweet version). Wine made from the Savignin grape is kept for many years in wood, where it gets stronger and darker and, it is thought, is subjected to the *flor* yeast that is also present in Jerez (see page 66). This is a speciality of Château-Chalon in particular. *Vin de paille* is made by drying out grapes on straw mats (hence the name) and is therefore similar to the *vino passito* made in Italy. To complete the list of the Jura's oddities, there is also *vin gris* (actually pale *rosé* rather than grey) and Vin Fou, Henri Maire's brand of fizzy wine.

SOUTHWEST FRANCE

One of the areas of France of most interest to those looking for well made though not necessarily expensive wines off the beaten track is that known commonly as the southwest of France. It is not a very satisfactory description, to punctilious geographers at least, but encompasses those wines made in the important vineyard areas to the east and south of the Bordeaux region. Many of the reds have much in common with the style of claret and there have been times when their wines have rivalled those of Bordeaux. Traditionally one of the best known was Cahors, whose "black wines" were renowned for their longevity. Today most of them are vinified so as to be ready rather earlier, but still taste like full-bodied, coarser versions of claret. Bergerac is another important area whose wines, both red and white, are very similar in style to their counterparts in Bordeaux. Côtes du Marmandais is close to Bergerac, both geographically and in the style of wine it produces, as is Côtes de Duras in Dordogne country. Pécharmant is another local red wine *appellation* and the wines of the Côtes de Buzet, most of them made at the local co-operative, are rapidly earning themselves a reputation abroad as having good staying power. Montravel white, made increasingly dry, is similar to white Bergerac, while Monbazillac produces sweet whites. These are sometimes referred to as "the poor man's sauternes".

In the southwest corner, towards the Pyrenées, Madiran, Jurançon and Irouléguy, are, respectively, red, white and *rosé*, made from local grape varieties. Jurançon as a full, sweetish wine was famous as a "keeper". The Brut version made now is much drier. Tursan is a similar VDQS *appellation* producing both red and white wines.

SAVOIE

The Savoy region lies to the south of Geneva and its best known names are Crépy, Seyssel and Apremont. Wines here are similar to those made over the border in Switzerland. The best wines of this region are light, dry whites, some of them sparkling.

VINS DOUX NATURELS

These are not, strictly speaking, "wines" in the fully fermented sense of the word. They are lovely golden grapy drinks, usually made from the Muscat grape, by adding grape spirit to only partially fermented grape juice so as to retain much of the sweetness. These are a speciality of the south of France, with the Muscats of Beaumes-de-Venise, Lunel, Frontignan and Rivesaltes being the varieties which are particularly well known.

"Nosing" or smelling a wine is considered the most important part of wine tasting; only the nose is sensitive enough to detect nuances of flavour. To nose a wine: half-fill a narrow glass with wine and hold it by the stem so as not to affect the temperature of the wine. Rotate the glass and breathe in deeply

GERMANY

Feasting in Bavaria in the Middle Ages. From a woodcut by Gunther Schmidt

Along with their counterparts in Bordeaux and the Douro in port country, German winemakers have traditionally been numbered among the world's great classic wine providers. Their wonderfully honeyed, concentrated dessert wines, usually made from the fragrant, racy Riesling grape, will always deserve a place in any collection of the world's great wines.

All of Germany's great wines are white – indeed only about ten per cent of her vineyards are planted with red wine varieties and these are made into wines that are usually consumed locally. Germany is too far north to be capable of producing really fine red wine; her triumph is in matching a cool climate with just the sort of grapes that will be capable of ripening into light, white wines of great delicacy and, in good years, richness. German wines are rarely more than ten per cent alcohol (while the average claret, for instance, is more than eleven per cent and some Italian reds as much as fifteen per cent), and her really special dessert wines are designed for the contemplative sipper rather than the alcohol enthusiast.

Unlike the French and Italian systems of describing better-quality wines, the German system is not based on geography but on ripeness. They have a very strict hierarchy of different grades of wine, but these are not governed by the exact spot where the grapes were grown. The criterion used instead is that of the sugar content of the grapes used. This means that in a very warm year, such as 1975 and 1976, a very high proportion of the wine was regarded as top quality, while in a lean year with less sunshine, the proportion is very much lower.

"Müller Extra" by Julius Klinger

The reason for this difference of approach is simple. The most difficult and therefore the most prized achievement for a German wine-grower is to harvest grapes that are high in sugar.

The most basic level of German wine is *Tafelwein* or table wine. This constitutes less than ten per cent of a typical German vintage, however, and the most commonly exported grade of wine is the next one up, *Qualitätswein bestimmter Anbaugebiete* or, rather more comfortably for non-German speakers, "QbA". This is wine coming from a particular specified wine region, of which Germany has eleven: Ahr, Mosel-Saar-Ruwer, Mittelrhein, Rheingau, Nahe, Rheinhessen, Rheinpfalz, Hessiche Bergstrasse, Württemberg, Baden and Franken. Wines in this category have to reach a certain minimum level of quality, but conditions are much more stringent for Germany's top-quality wines, *Qualitätswein mit Pradikat* (QmP), wines with one of the following "predicates", in ascending order of richness: *Kabinett, Spätlese, Auslese, Beerenauslese* and *Trockenbeerenauslese*. Each of these terms owes its origins to the literal meaning of the words, but nowadays the methodical Germans do not leave such things to the vagaries of interpretation. The exact "must" weight (sugar content of the grapes) is laid down for each level of quality, each grape variety and each wine region by the German Wine Law. The most expensive wines in Germany are those painstakingly produced *Trockenbeerenauslesen*, so preciously (and expensively) unctuous that they are often put only into half-bottles.

Eiswein is another rarity, wine that is made from grapes picked when the juice is frozen and concentrated. This term may be added to any of the "predicates" which are described above.

The naming of German wines on the label is easy for the producer, though not always so easy for the drinker. Most quality wines are described by the name of the village they come from (say Bernkastel), suffixed by "er" (e.g. Bernkasteler), followed by the name of the vineyard (e.g. Bernkasteler Doktor in the case of the famous top-quality Doktor vineyard). The confusion arises in that there are many much bigger collections of assorted vineyards that are grouped together under the name of the most famous vineyard in the collection. Bernkasteler Badstube, for instance, is a *Grosslage* (collection of sites) rather than an *Einzellage* (a contiguous plot such as the Doktor vineyard).

Added to this name will also be the "predicate" if the wine is entitled to one and sometimes the grape variety. Riesling is the most noble of all grape varieties planted in Germany, but it is losing ground to varieties that are easier to cultivate though perhaps have much less class. Müller-Thurgau is widely planted and produces wines with something of the fragrance of a Riesling, but without the staying power. Silvaner is another fairly well-established variety, but there are an increasing number of new varieties developed especially for Germany's northern climate by viticultural researchers.

German wine is easy to spot in its tall, tapered bottles, green for the wines of the Moselle or Mosel, brown for wines coming from the Rhine regions, the wine the British have called "hock" since the days of Queen Victoria. Perhaps the most common form of Rhine wine is Liebfraumilch, which may be any QbA wine with the characteristics of one made from Riesling, Müller-Thurgau or Silvaner. Rheinhessen is the chief supplier of this bland but very commercial wine.

Advertisement for champagne, showing the traditional tulip glasses

Art nouveau advertisement for champagne

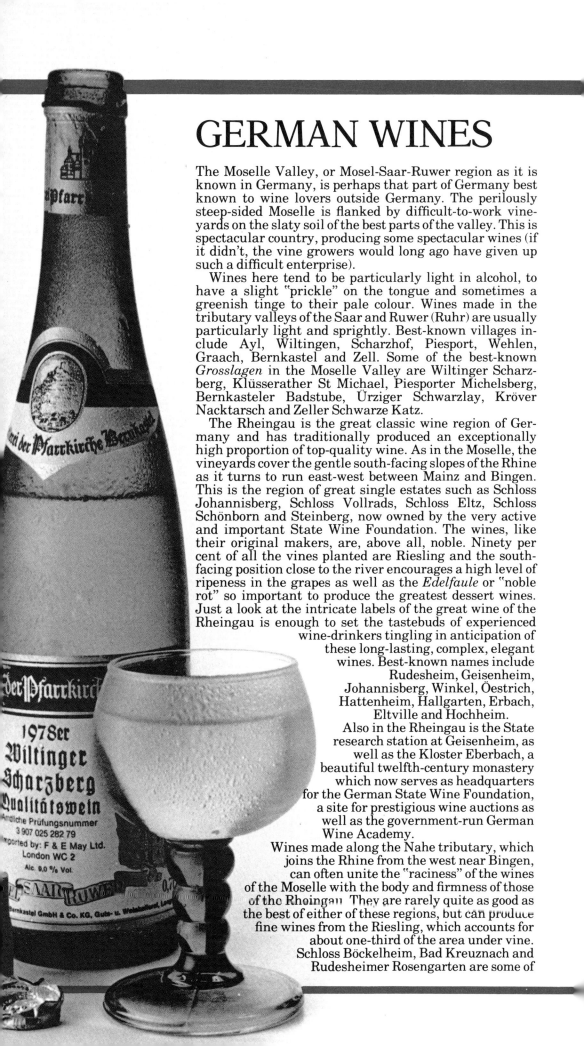

GERMAN WINES

The Moselle Valley, or Mosel-Saar-Ruwer region as it is known in Germany, is perhaps that part of Germany best known to wine lovers outside Germany. The perilously steep-sided Moselle is flanked by difficult-to-work vineyards on the slaty soil of the best parts of the valley. This is spectacular country, producing some spectacular wines (if it didn't, the vine growers would long ago have given up such a difficult enterprise).

Wines here tend to be particularly light in alcohol, to have a slight "prickle" on the tongue and sometimes a greenish tinge to their pale colour. Wines made in the tributary valleys of the Saar and Ruwer (Ruhr) are usually particularly light and sprightly. Best-known villages include Ayl, Wiltingen, Scharzhof, Piesport, Wehlen, Graach, Bernkastel and Zell. Some of the best-known *Grosslagen* in the Moselle Valley are Wiltinger Scharzberg, Klüsserather St Michael, Piesporter Michelsberg, Bernkasteler Badstube, Ürziger Schwarzlay, Kröver Nacktarsch and Zeller Schwarze Katz.

The Rheingau is the great classic wine region of Germany and has traditionally produced an exceptionally high proportion of top-quality wine. As in the Moselle, the vineyards cover the gentle south-facing slopes of the Rhine as it turns to run east-west between Mainz and Bingen. This is the region of great single estates such as Schloss Johannisberg, Schloss Vollrads, Schloss Eltz, Schloss Schönborn and Steinberg, now owned by the very active and important State Wine Foundation. The wines, like their original makers, are, above all, noble. Ninety per cent of all the vines planted are Riesling and the south-facing position close to the river encourages a high level of ripeness in the grapes as well as the *Edelfaule* or "noble rot" so important to produce the greatest dessert wines. Just a look at the intricate labels of the great wine of the Rheingau is enough to set the tastebuds of experienced wine-drinkers tingling in anticipation of these long-lasting, complex, elegant wines. Best-known names include Rudesheim, Geisenheim, Johannisberg, Winkel, Öestrich, Hattenheim, Hallgarten, Erbach, Eltville and Hochheim.

Also in the Rheingau is the State research station at Geisenheim, as well as the Kloster Eberbach, a beautiful twelfth-century monastery which now serves as headquarters for the German State Wine Foundation, a site for prestigious wine auctions as well as the government-run German Wine Academy.

Wines made along the Nahe tributary, which joins the Rhine from the west near Bingen, can often unite the "raciness" of the wines of the Moselle with the body and firmness of those of the Rheingau. They are rarely quite as good as the best of either of these regions, but can produce fine wines from the Riesling, which accounts for about one-third of the area under vine. Schloss Böckelheim, Bad Kreuznach and Rudesheimer Rosengarten are some of the best-known names among the wines of this area.

The Rheinhessen is a large region that rarely produces wines of great distinction but is a valuable source of medium dry, easy-to-drink wines of the Liebfraumilch genus. This is the flatter, less interesting country that lies to the south across the Rhine from the classic Rheingau. A wide variety of different grape varieties is planted here and one would not expect great longevity from many of them. Niersteiner Gutes Domtal and Oppenheimer Krötenbrunnen are the best-known *Grosslagen* here.

The Rheinpfalz or Palatinate region to the south is altogether more interesting, producing full, sometimes fat wines with plenty of aroma and character. Bürklin-Wolf is the best-known producer here and has done much to get these wines better known outside Germany. Others with larger estates include Bassermann-Jordan and von Buhl. Forster Jesuitengarten is one of Germany's better-known *Einzellagen*, while the corresponding *Grosslage* is Forster Mariengarten. Deidesheim and Bad Durkheim are also in the Rheinpfalz.

Even further to the south, just across the Rhine from Alsace, is the long strip of vineyards that constitute the Baden region. These vigorous wines, made chiefly by the co-operatives and from a wide range of grape varieties, are becoming increasingly better known outside Germany. The wines tend to be relatively low in acidity, but often appeal to those who find other German wines too sweet.

In the east around Würzburg, Franken (or Franconia) has built up such a following for its lively, slightly earthy wines, sometimes called Steinwein, that they are now relatively expensive and tend to be consumed locally. The green flask-shaped *Bocksbeutel* is used for Franken wines.

Other German wine regions whose wines are not often seen abroad are the red wine Ahr region to the north of the Moselle Valley; the fruity wine region of the Mittelrhein just across the Rhine from the Ahr; her smallest wine region, Hessische Bergstrasse; and Württemberg, on the Neckar tributary, where robust Riesling whites and Trollinger reds are made and consumed with relish by the locals.

Researchers, notably at the Geisenheim viticultural station, have been experimenting with grape types that can give the same sort of fragrance as the Riesling but that are easier to grow or give higher yields. They include Morio Muskat, producing an intensely grapy wine; Scheurebe, which is widely planted in the Rheinpfalz, where it makes full, fat wines; Bacchus with its concentrated but short-lived scent; the light flowery Kerner; and the showy Huxelrebe. But only the noble Riesling gives growers the wines they need if Germany is to continue its tradition of supplying the world with complex, elegant, aristocratic wines. Other more traditional varieties planted in Germany include the Ruländer (the Pinot Gris in Alsace), which produces fairly flabby wines, the undistinguished Gutedel (Chasselas in France) and the Spätburgunder (Pinot Noir) and Portugieser red wine grapes.

It is common in Germany to add a proportion of sweet unfermented grape juice, *Süssreserve*, to the wine after fermentation to make it sweeter. There is now a vogue for *Trocken* (dry) or *Halbtrocken* (half-dry) wines which have either no or less *Süssreserve* added to them.

Superior estate-bottled wines will be labelled *Erzeugerabfüllung*, while those produced by co-operatives have *Winzergenossenschaft* (co-operative) on the label.

The Germans are enthusiastic makers and drinkers of *Sekt*, sparkling wine.

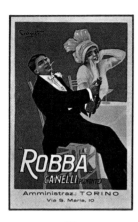

Italian sparkling wine advertisement by Codognato

ITALY

It is strange that Italy, a country that in many years produces more wine than any other, is still struggling to establish herself as an important force in the world of top-quality wine. As much commonplace or even disappointing wine is made each year in France as in Italy, but the French at least are confident in their supremacy at the top end of the quality scale. The Italians on the other hand are quite sure of their ability to impress the inhabitants of Turin with the best of their Barolos, the inhabitants of Florence with their Chianti Classico Riservas or the mightily priced Brunello di Montalcino, but none of these wines has yet won its place as of right on the top wine lists of the world beyond the Italian frontier.

Wine is as much a part of the Italian landscape as any other agricultural crop, perhaps rather more so as the vine can be cultivated right from the top to the tip of the boot that is drawn by her coastline and frontiers. Even Sicily, which can be fiercely hot in summer, is a prodigious producer of grapes for wine.

In terms of total quantities produced, Sicily and the hot southern tip of the country, Apulia, are major producers of wine in Italy and much of this is shipped north by tanker to add strength and colour either for the blenders of northern Italy, or those in southern France, or the makers of vermouth and sparkling wines. These wines are full bodied, ripened up to staggeringly high alcoholic strengths by the heat of the Mediterranean sun.

But the best wines of Italy, those which have won national, if not international, repute, come from the Alpine foothills of Piedmont in the northwest, Barolo, Barbaresco and Asti country, and from the less dramatic but more classical hills of Tuscany, the land of Chianti, Brunello di Montalcino and Vino Nobile di Montepulciano. The Veneto centred on Verona in the north has been responsible for putting Italy on the world wine map with its trio of Soave, Valpolicella and Bardolino, while the varietal wines of the far northeast, Fruili-Venezia-Guilia, are fast making a name for themselves.

Italy is popular with all major wine drinking countries as a source of good-value, dependable cheaper wines and a is major supplier of most northern European countries as well as the United States, where she is by far the most important source of imported wine.

Spumanti Beccaro – an Italian sparkling wine

A factor in this great commercial success has been the tightening up of her wine legislation, now based on *Denominazione di Origine Controllata* (DOC), itself modelled on the French *Appellation Contrôlée* system. If a wine is described as DOC it must come from the area specified and be made according to the laws for that particular DOC, usually arrived at on the basis of tradition in consultation with the local producers. This has not always meant that the very best possible wine in a given area has been encouraged, only that which has traditionally been the most popular with the locals.

Perhaps some official recognition that such a problem exists came with the proposal of "DOCGs", *Denominazione Controllata e Garantita*. This is designed to be a sort of "super-DOC", an order into which only the very best wines will be allowed to enter. Wines so far proposed for membership include Barolo, Barbareso, Brunello di Monatalcino, Vino Nobile di Montepulciano and Chianti Classico.

ITALIAN WINES

Barolo has traditionally occupied the throne as king of Italian wines. One would expect the crown to go to a red wine, for it is reds that are imbued with the most character in the cellars of Italian winemakers. Most whites tend to taste either too heavy or characterless in this hot climate. To the average Italian the deep, dark wines of the Barolo region to the south of Turin, with their usual ten-year sentence to cask ageing, seem all that they desire: manly, uncompromisingly chewy, fiercely strong. To non-Italian palates, many of them can seem too short on fruit, too long on wood, so it is important to be aware of this problem. The Barolo made by someone who puts his wines in wood for only a carefully judged period rather than until he receives an order for his Riserva can be a scented, mysterious, adult wine, but it is wise to check that the wine has had some bottle age.

There are many wines made from the Nebbiolo grape grown in the misty hills of Piedmont. Some wines may simply be called Nebbiolo, and these will in general be rather lighter than most Barolos, as is Barbaresco, which comes from a little further down the valley than Barolo. Gattinara and Spanna, Ghemme, Sizzano and Carema are all made from the Nebbiolo grape from which they get their intense mulberry colour. They are usually vinified so as to be ready sooner than classic Barolo. Further north, almost on the Swiss border, are the similarly made, though evilly named, Grumello and Inferno.

The other important red wine grape in Piedmont is the rather fruitier and tarter Barbera, more of a picnic wine than a grand dinner wine, though the complexity and diversity of its DOCs belie this, there being carefully delineated Barberas of Asti, Albi and Monferrato. Dolcetto is another red grape grown commonly in Piedmont, making wines of character but without the depth of flavour of Nebbiolo. There are Dolcettos d'Alba, d'Asti and d'Acqui.

Of the white wines of the region, the sweet fizzy Asti Spumante is by far the best known, though this is rapidly being replaced by the rather less expensive Moscato Spumante. These wines are refrigerated when only halfway

through fermentation so as to retain sweetness at the expense of alcohol. Otherwise, there are few well-known whites here, though Gavi is developing a certain following.

Further north and east is the Italian Tyrol, the Alto Adige, which, not surprisingly, has much in common in winemaking terms with the Austrian Tyrol just across the border. The wine industry there is centred on Bolzano or Bolzen. Best-known reds include Santa Maddalena and Kalterersee, but whites made of Riesling and Gewürztraminer are of particular interest to those who normally associate

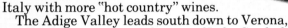

Italy with more "hot country" wines.

The Adige Valley leads south down to Verona, centre of the area just to the east of Lake Garda from which so much Soave, Valpolicella and Bardolino is shipped to thirsty wine drinkers the world over. The best dry white Soave is Soave Classico from the heartland of the original winemaking zone. Garganega and the ubiquitous Italian white wine grape Trebbiano are responsible for this wine, which can at best display some zesty almondy characteristics. The best of Valpolicellas can similarly give the taster a hint of bitter cherries. Bardolino is similar, but is usually a little lighter and tarter. One of the specialities of this Veneto region is Recioto, wine made from grapes that have been allowed to start to dry up before they are fermented. Recioto di Soave is a rich, sweet white wine, and Recioto della Valpolicella is its red counterpart. The most commonly exported Recioto is the dry version of the latter, Recioto Amarone della Valpolicella, a heady, slightly bitter red often called simply Amarone. Gambellara is very similar, and close, to Soave.

Made just south of Lake Garda, the sprightly Lugana is one of Italy's prettier white wines..

The Fruili-Venezia-Guilia region to the northeast of Venice is one that shows great promise and has already produced some fine varietally labelled wines from Merlot, Cabernet, (Italian) Riesling, Tocai, Pinot Grigio and Sauvignon. Some of the best of these "varietal" wines come from the Grave del Friuli region near Udine and the Colli Orientali del Friuli and Colli Goriziano around Gorizia on the Yugoslav border. Verduzzo is one of the better known whites from this area.

Between this region and the north of Tuscany are the plains, and the great Lambrusco vineyards around Modena. Lambrusco is usually a sweet fizzy red that can't be all bad as it accounts for more than half the total American imports of Italian wine. To the south and east are the rather more serious, but good value, wines of Emilia-Romagna, the reds made from Sangiovese, the whites from Trebbiano.

In the centre of Italy, on the cypress-clad Tuscan hills, is one of the oldest wine districts, Chianti country. Well might the more fastidious producers employ the warning: "Beware inferior imitations", for chianti can vary from

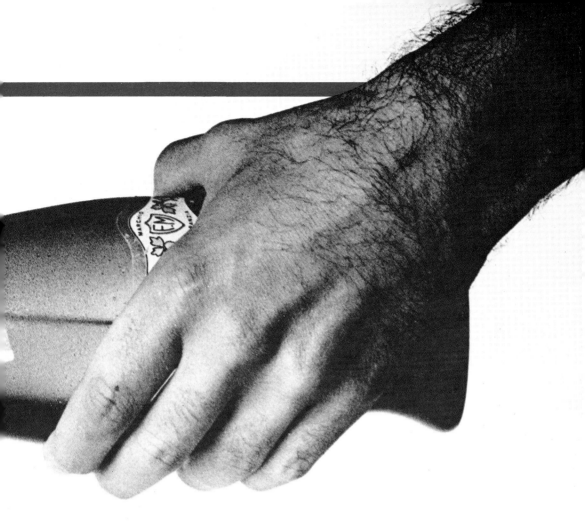

insipid fermented fruit juice to truly great, mature and above all balanced wine, usually with a characteristically "vegetable" smell. (This may well owe something to the fact that many vines are still planted in among rows of other crops in traditional Italian peasant farmer tradition.) The law specifies quite carefully what proportion of grapes may be used in Chianti: mainly Sangiovese with up to thirty per cent white grapes. There are many different styles of winemaking, however, some of which produce wines with a certain amount of "prickle" (this using the *governo* system) designed for early consumption. Chianti Classico again comes from the heart of the region and all wines so designated have to pass rigorous analysis and tasting tests. They can be spotted by their black cockerel seal. Chianti Putto has a cherub symbol.

Similar, though headier and often longer-lasting red wines made in Tuscany, are the two proposed for DOCG Brunello di Montalcino and Vino Nobile di Montepulciano as well as a Cabernet Sauvignon curiosity, Sassicaia. Whites are now relegated to the name Toscano Bianco and tend to be sold under a brand name. In the northwest of Chianti country, producers in the Chianti Montalbano area may add in a small proportion of Cabernet grapes to their standard Chianti mix to produce Carmignano, while even further out, the crisp white wine of Montecarlo is made near Lucca. Vernaccia, a heady white grape, is grown in Tuscany, notably at San Gimignano. Parrina, brand name for an unusual pair of red and white wines, is made near Orbetello on the Mediterranean coast, while Vinsanto, a white dessert wine, is a Tuscan speciality.

Dr Lungarotti's Rubesco Torgiano is one of Central Italy's best made reds and comes from Umbria.

Just to the south of Tuscany is a region known particularly for its whites, of all degrees of sweetness, Orvieto,

while over on the Adriatic coast by Ancona is the much crisper Verdicchio in its special amphora-shaped bottle. Est! Est!! Est!!! is made near Orvieto, but is seen less and less, other than in wine books.

Italy's other famous white wine, Frascati, is made in the hills to the south of Rome, traditionally by fermenting the wine on the skins, which accounts for its strangely grapy flavour. Marino is nearby and similar.

Way down south of Naples there are more wines whose names are better known their taste: Lacrima Christi, Capri and Gran Caruso di Ravello. This is the start of the country where enormous quantities of wine are produced, but there are very few internationally known names, usually quite rightly. The strong red Aglianico del Vulture must get points on the basis of its name alone, but otherwise there is little to capture the imagination until the mainland is left behind.

Sicily's best-known wine today is probably Corvo di Salaparuta, both red and white versions being daringly high in alcohol. Sardinia is the home of many a DOC, characteristically and traditionally fairly sweet. The producers and shippers Sella & Mosca, however, have pioneered a wine industry more in tune with the demands of today's wine drinker for crisp, dry whites and well-balanced, firm reds.

(top) Battersea enamel port label by Ravenet (1736); cruciform decanter (1710); sealed bottle (1703). (bottom) Enamelled port decanter and selection of decorated glasses

SPAIN

For years Spain was seen only as a useful source of cheap
wines for cheap brands, but her better-quality wines have
rapidly been earning themselves a reputation abroad, especially as rising French wine prices have set wine lovers
looking for bargains elsewhere.

Spain's major fine wine-producing region is Rioja, wild
hilly country in the north of Spain. It is significant that
when phylloxera hit the vineyards of Bordeaux, many
winemakers made their way south across the Pyrenees
to the Rioja region, where their influence can still
be seen from just a glance into any bodega, piled
high with Bordeaux-style *barriques*, oak casks.
These casks play a major role in determining rioja's
unique warm vanilla flavour, and it is wood that
imparts this. Few of the main wine producers, or
bodegas, own a large vineyard holding. Most of the
Rioja vines are tended by peasant farmers, who sell
their crop to bigger concerns that actually make the
wine. This means that a wide variety of different
grapes can go into each blend, whose final taste is
governed by the amount of time it spends in these
American oak casks. There was a time when too
much rioja spent too long in cask, but producers
are realizing the value of allowing the wine to
mature in bottle as well as in wood.

Rioja's best wines are the more
elegant reds, robust enough
to withstand being opened
hours, sometimes days,
before being drunk, yet
soft enough to appeal to
the most inexperienced
wine-drinker. Tradition-
ally, white rioja was
made just like red rioja,
which often meant it was
too old and tired by the
time it was eventually
bottled. Today there are
still a few very good wines
made in this way, Marques
de Murrieta white for instance
can taste not unlike a good
white burgundy – but an increasing
number of bodegas are experimenting
with modern white wine vinification
methods to produce fresh, crisp whites
for early consumption.

This pattern is being reflected elsewhere
in Spain, where reds still appeal more to
non-Spaniards than the often stale whites
and heavyweight *rosados* (*rosés*).

Just as there is variation in the style of
white riojas now being produced, there have
always been a number of different styles of
reds. Some bodegas make it easy for the
consumer by putting their richer,
"burgundy-style" wines into sloping-
shouldered bottles, while their lighter,
drier *claretes* go into claret bottles.

Another exciting area for

good-quality Spanish wine is Penedes, in Catalonia, to the west of Barcelona. Here there are a number of firms making wines for export, and this is also the centre of Spain's enormous sparkling wine industry, but Torres of Vilafranca del Penedes must be regarded as the pioneer. In a region where most grapes are local varieties destined for the large *méthode champenoise* sparkling winemakers such as Codorniu and Freixenet, Miguel Torres has experimented with most of Europe's classic grape varieties, often with excellent results. On his return from the oenological school at Montpellier he planted Pinot Noir, Cabernet Sauvignon, Gewürztraminer and many more. Vina Sol is the Torres standard white, while Coronas and Tres Torres are two of their reds. Other still wine producers of Penedes include Masia Bach, Freixedas, René Barbier and Marques de Monistrol. There is a host of sparkling wine producers, Vilafranca being Spain's Rheims and Epernay rolled into one, who use the same methods as in Champagne to make their wines. The main difference is that instead of the classic grape varieties, they use a mixture of local white Spanish grapes.

Just to the north of the rioja region is Navarre, whose wines can be very similar to rioja, though are usually a little coarser. Castillo de Tiebas is a name to remember for those who can take a lot of alcohol in their wine.

Another small region producing wines of almost indecent strength – though sometimes with enough character to warrant it – is Priorato in the hinterland of Tarragona, itself a well-known name for strong, rather sweet red wine in the past. To the south and west of this, most wine produced is very heavyweight red that may be a useful addition to blends for branded wine, but is often not fine enough to be savoured on its own merits. Jumilla, Yecla, Valdepenas, La Mancha, Mentrida, Utiel Requena, Manchuela, Cheste, Almansa and Alicante would all like to prove that they have sufficient attributes to make them worthy of note to wine drinkers the world over and some big companies are investing large sums in new wineries in the hot central plains of Spain. They will doubtless do their best to bring modern winemaking methods to these regions and may well be producing huge quantities of inexpensive, sound, full-bodied wine before long.

Another promising area is Leon in the northwest, where the climate is tempered by the Atlantic, a factor which also plays a part in the type of wine produced in Ribeiro and Valdeorras just to the north of the Portuguese border. This is an example of how little vines care for national frontiers, for the wines made here are like nothing more than wines of Vinho Verde country just across the border.

A curiosity from Spain also comes from the northwest. Vega Sicilia has developed such a following that its sales are rationed. This very concentrated red was kept for all of ten years in wood, and still manages to have enough fruit to stand up to this Barolo-like treatment. But inflation at last caught up with its maker, Don Jesus Anadon, and he has developed a five-year-old version too.

Drinking from a wineskin. Wineskins, sewn from the skins of whole goats, are now only commonly used in certain rural areas of southern Europe, and most often contain the roughest local wine

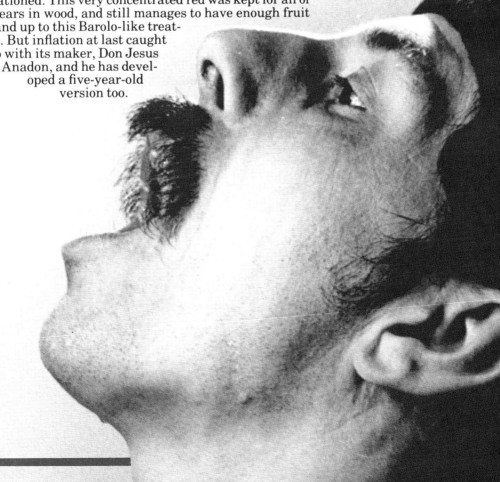

PORTUGAL

The extraordinary thing about Portugal is how underappreciated are her best wines. It is sad to think that most non-Portuguese know little of any Portuguese wine other than port and that well-known fizzy pink one.

As any visitor to Portugal knows, the country has much more to offer the world's wine drinkers than Mateus *rosé*, although the Portuguese themselves are some of the world's most enthusiastic wine drinkers. With the exception of the Vinho Verde wines of the north, which are spefifically designed to be drunk young, Portugal's *madura* or mature wines are remarkable for the concentration of their flavour. Like their Spanish counterparts, Portuguese winemakers are keen on leaving their wines in wood for some time, but the wines also seem to receive a fair time in bottle too and it is still possible to find old vintages at old prices.

Portugal is still working on her equivalent of an *Appellation Contrôlée* system and some of her best wines, such as Ferreirinha Barca Velha and Perequita, are sold simply under a brand name. Her best-established red wine region is Dão (pronounced, almost, "dow") to the south of the Douro valley of port fame. The wines are rich with lots of alcohol. They are usually given several years in wood and deserve a few more in bottle. As in Rioja, the whites can seem too heavy or flat. Local grapes are used here, with Touriga being the prominent red wine grape.

North of the Douro, in the Minho, Vinho Verde is made. Light and high in acidity, these wines often have a slight "prickle" of carbon dioxide. The "Verde" refers not to their colour but to the ripeness, or rather the lack of it, of the grapes when they are picked. More red Vinho Verde than white is made, but most of the red is consumed locally. The vines are trained high on trellises to keep acidity levels high and this tartness really does characterize a typical Vinho Verde. Some firms sweeten up their wines for export.

Mateus, the wine that is neither red nor white, still nor sparkling, dry nor sweet, is made in this northern region. Other wine regions which have earned themselves reputations in the past are Bucelas dry whites, Carcavelos sweet whites, and Colares reds made in the phylloxera-free sandy vineyards now swamped by Lisbon suburbs. Good table wines of the future are expected to come from the Douro, Estremadura on the coast north of Lisbon, Ribatego to the east, Bairrada and Lafoes.

YUGOSLAVIA

It would be absurd to expect a country such as Yugoslavia to present itself as a cohesive whole to the wine drinker any more than it does to the geographer, historian or sociologist. It has as many regions as frontiers.

Up in the northeast in Slovenia, the wines produced are obviously related to their counterparts across the border in Austria and Hungary: full-flavoured whites with a nice nip of acidity to keep them in balance. The wine consumed locally is often considerably drier than that exported, and most popular grape varieties, usually specified on the label of Yugoslav wines from any region, are Laski Riesling (a relative of Italian Riesling, not Riesling as in Germany and Alsace), Sauvignon and the full, "spicy" Traminer.

In vineyards in the northwest of the country are the same varieties as are grown so successfully in the northeast of Italy: Cabernet, Merlot, Pinot Bijeli (Bianco) and Tokaj (Tocai). Down the Dalmatian coast the grapes planted are usually local specialities and the wine not much exported, though the pungent white Zilavka from around Mostar has its followers abroad. The heady and almost unpronounceable red Vranac is Montenegro's chief contribution to Yugoslavia's wine repertoire, while further south in Macedonia the reds (and whites) are even more robust, reminding the visitor of his proximity to Greece. Here, and in the great wine-producing republic of Serbia to the north, are planted a wide variety of grapes, with Prokupac being a vigorous red. The vineyards of the Fruska Gora Hills, north of Belgrade, produce Sauvignon and Traminer.

HUNGARY

Hungary's reputation as a wine producer was made by one wine, the supposed "essence of life", Tokay. Tokay is still made today under the auspices of Hungary's State Wine system, but, rather like petrol, is now available in a number of different "grades". It is made from Furmint grapes grown around the town of Tokaj, in the far northeast of the country. "Noble rot" (see page 14) is encouraged and concentrates the sugar already present in the grapes to a state of great richness. The best grapes are kept separate, crushed and retained as a luscious paste. Tokay Aszu is the dessert wine, sold in strange half-litre flasks, made in various concentrations of this paste. Each measure of paste is called a *puttonyo* and the richest version sold is five *puttonyos*. The State is also rumoured to harbour small quantities of Tokaj Essencia, the "essence" of this unique, rich, spicy wine. Tokaji Szamorodni Dry has no sweetness added and tastes more like sherry than a table wine.

Hungary's best-known red wine is Bull's Blood – Egri Bikaver in its native land – a full, aggressive wine with lots of character. While the native Kadarka is her most common red grape, its white counterpart is Olasz Riesling, similar to the Laski Riesling of Yugoslavia and sometimes exported carrying the name of Pecs, a town in the south towards the Yugoslav border. Her most interesting whites come from the shores of the vast Lake Balaton, and are made from local grape varieties.

CZECHOSLOVAKIA

Czechoslovakia's reputation for beer so far outstrips its reputation for wine that one is tempted to forget that it produces twenty million gallons of wine a year.

So far very little has been exported, though it is clear that its geographical position, just north of wine-producing regions in Hungary and Austria, should qualify Czechoslovakia admirably as a maker of good white wine. Czechs seem to favour a full, dry, slightly pungent style.

RUMANIA AND BULGARIA

Rumania is another Eastern European wine producer with interesting potential, particularly for whites. Here the vineyards are still in private hands and a wide variety of grapes is grown, including Italian Riesling, Furmint, Muscat, Pinot Gris and Sauvignon as well as Kadarka and classic French red grape varieties. Cotnari is Rumania's answer to Hungary's Tokay, but the wines to look out for are the rapidly improving table wines.

Bulgaria has also been experimenting, with marked success, with classic European grape varieties in its vineyards, which are almost as extensive as those of Hungary, but only two-thirds those of Rumania.

Some remarkable Cabernets and Chardonnays have been produced by the state-run Vinprom organization. In addition to these are many Balkan grape varieties, such as Hungary's red Kadarka, its own rich red Mavrud, the more ordinary Pamid and the space-age-sounding Melnik. Misket is Bulgaria's version of Muscat, the sweet white grapiest of grapes, and Hemus is similar.

After years of Muslim rule, Bulgaria is a relative newcomer as a wine producer, but is already one of the world's biggest wine exporters, chiefly to Germany and Russia.

USSR

The Soviet authorities are not known for the generosity with which they dispense statistics and assessment of Russia's wine industry has to rely considerably on conjecture.

What is certain is that the authorities are keen to develop wine as a gentler alternative to vodka among the Russian people. This means that they import huge quantities of wine from all over the world, wherever the price is right, and they have no spare wine for export.

It is doubtful in any case whether many Russian wines would be that popular in the West. Perhaps because of their fierce winters, Russians seem to like their wines strong and sweet. They are avid consumers of sparkling wine, *shampanskoe*, and have a similar disregard for the proprietorial rights of the producers of sherry and port.

SWITZERLAND

From the Soviet Union to Switzerland – there could hardly be more of a contrast, except that both of them are enthusiastic importers of wine in bulk. Wine made from Switzerland's precipitous vineyards is necessarily expensive and there is much blending of imported cheaper wine.

Most Swiss wine is white, light and dry, particularly in the best-known regions around Lake Geneva (Vaud) and in the upper Rhône valley (Valais). Chasselas, a grape consigned to the fruit basket elsewhere, is popular here for Dorin in the Vaud and Fendant in the Valais. Johannisberg has slightly more flavour and is made from Sylvaner grown in the Valais.

The most popular red is Dôle, a light red not unlike Beaujolais, from the Valais, although the Swiss can also draw on the vineyards of the Ticino in the south, whose wines of course have Italian characteristics, with Merlot making round reds, the best of which are called Viti.

AUSTRIA

Austria's neutrality in European alignments has tended to keep the world's wine drinkers in ignorance of the remarkable value of its wines. The wines are anything but neutral, with lots of character and substance, like rather spicier versions of much German wine. Vinification techniques are advanced and most wines are well made.

The Austrians themselves are keen on the light, rather sweet reds of the Tyrol, but it is the better-quality whites that are of particular interest. Austria has developed a precise quality designation system based on the German one for its wines, with the same *Kabinett* to *Trockenbeerenauslese* range of "predicates". This is logical since its vineyards are in many ways similar to those on the Rhine, planted with grape varieties such as the Rheinriesling, the Riesling of Germany, and Müller-Thurgau. The lower latitude makes most Austrian wines stronger in alcohol and all quality wines have to be at least 10.5°.

The character of Austrian wine is exemplified by the native grape, the Grüner Veltliner, which combines a slight pungency with a good racy dash. Other local specialities include the heady wines of Gumpoldskirchen, made from the strangely named Rotgipfler and Zierfandler grapes and *Heurigen* that are so popular in special cafés of the same name in the suburbs of Vienna. *Heurigen* serve wine of the most recent vintage by the jug, and very good it is too. Lively dry whites are part of Viennese life.

Vienna is at the centre of Austria's wineland (though well distanced from the less interesting vineyards of the Tyrol). To the west is Wachau, where the firm of Lenz Moser is located, pioneers of the "high culture" system of planting vines far apart and training them high for mechanical harvesting. From this firm comes the branded wine Schluck. There are also extensive vineyards to the north of the city as well as Gumpoldskirchen to the south and Burgenland, particularly good for Austria's undervalued dessert wines, to the southeast towards the Hungarian border. Oggau and Rust are wine centres here.

GREECE

Greece gave us Dionysus, the later Bacchic god of wine, but has yet to match that gift in today's world of wine. The Greeks themselves like their reds tough and coarse, their whites resinated, though there are signs of increasing adaptation to the tastes of non-Greek wine drinkers.

Achaia Clauss are major producers and responsible for the strong red and white Demestica, lubricator of many a moussaka. D Courtaki is a leading producer of retsina, the speciality of Attica, which is resinated white, and sometimes pink, the wine tasting more as though it should be bought at a hardware shop than a wine merchant. They are also experimenting with Cabernet and Merlot and are producing a branded red wine called Apollo, which is not unlike a rioja. Château Carras is another attempt at importing winemaking techniques from Bordeaux.

Traditional specialities of Greece include the dark, sweetish red Mavrodaphne and the Muscat dessert wine of Samos. Naoussa is a strong dry red, Casteli Danielis rather lighter. Robola from the island of Cephalonia is one of the freshest dry whites made in Greece.

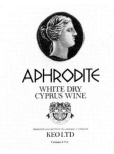

CYPRUS

Cyprus has been acutely sensitive to British influence and for some time concentrated on producing light Cyprus sherry for penny-conscious Britons. In recent years the price of "proper" sherry from Jerez has remained so stable as to allow the Cyprus sherry trade to decline. It is likely therefore that winemakers in Cyprus will be concentrating increasingly on providing good-value table wines.

Wine production is in the hands of three major firms who are anxious to woo foreign customers; Cypriots themselves are not over-keen wine drinkers. Bellapais, a semi-sweet slightly sparkling white, has clearly been developed to follow in the footsteps of Mateus rosé. Like most other Cyprus whites, it has a certain muskiness about it that some may find attractive. Aphrodite is a medium dry white, Arsinoe one of the best-known dry whites, while the far-from-delicate Othello is Cyprus's red answer to Demestica. Commanderia, the raisiny dessert wine, can be very good.

LUXEMBOURG

Luxembourg's small wine industry is centred on the town of Remich, just a few miles over the border from the Saar tributary of the Moselle, and indeed there is a similarity between the wines produced in these two wine areas.

Luxembourg wine is white, light and usually characterized by a high degree of acidity. Lack of body makes these wines ideal for slimmers and diabetics, and they should usually be drunk as young as possible. The sometimes eye-wateringly tart Elbing is cultivated widely, and Perlewein, slightly sparkling, is a local speciality.

ENGLAND

Like their counterparts in Luxembourg, aspiring wine-makers in England are pushing their luck, only more so, as they are even further north with even less sunshine to help them ripen their grapes.

It is surely no accident that interest in English wine increased so dramatically during and immediately after the two exceptionally hot summers of 1975 and 1976, when the sun shone long and hard to produce ripe grapes and a record vintage of half a million bottles in 1976. The vagaries of the British climate have brought wildly varying yields in subsequent years, but there seems to be an enormous amount of enthusiasm for reviving an art that lapsed in England with the Dissolution of the Monasteries when monastic vineyards were dismantled.

There are now well over two hundred vineyards in production in the British Isles, mainly in southern England, but also in southern Wales and Ireland. The average vineyard holding is only about three acres and vine cultivation tends to be a weekend activity, though some farmers in Kent and Sussex are producing wine on commercial lines.

Almost all vines planted are white, though some growers have managed to produce a fair red wine with Zweigelt grapes. One would expect English vineyard planters to look to Germany for inspiration when it comes to choosing grape varieties and Germany's convenient and most popular grape, Müller-Thurgau, is widely planted in Britain too. Some feel that the other newer German crosses such as Reichensteiner, Scheurebe and Schönberger are capable of producing more exciting wines in more reliable quantities. The American hybrid Seyval Blanc is grown successfully in England to produce fairly neutral wines that have no hint of the flavour usually associated with American vines.

The wines taste perhaps closest to German Trocken wines, having no apparent sweetness, though the latitude usually demands the addition of sugar to the must, or chaptalisation, to bring the alcoholic strength up.

English wines are necessarily expensive as they are all produced on a small scale and their makers, and buyers, are heavily taxed.

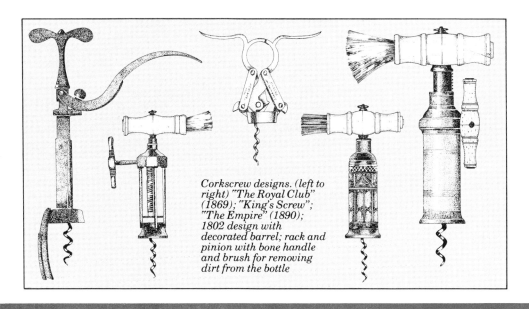

Corkscrew designs. (left to right) "The Royal Club" (1869); "King's Screw"; "The Empire" (1890); 1802 design with decorated barrel; rack and pinion with bone handle and brush for removing dirt from the bottle

SOUTH AFRICA

The South African wine industry has benefited enormously from considerable investment in recent years and is trying hard to gain itself the same sort of reputation for exciting progress as has been won by other "New World" wine producers, California and Australia.

Wine has been produced on the Cape ever since the first European settlers arrived there, and its Constantia dessert wine enjoyed great fame in the early part of the last century. More recently the South African wine industry is unique in that about half of every vintage, harvested of course in February/March in the Southern Hemisphere, is promptly despatched to the government-run distilling industry to be made into the brandy and other spirits that are so popular within South Africa.

The quality of the wine not disposed of in this way has been rising steadily, with the Cape's "estate" wines representing the best that South Africa has to offer wine lovers. Enthusiastic winemakers on these estates have been encouraged by South African wine companies' interest in exporting, and in the establishing of the annual Nederburg Wine Auction as an encouragement to high standards in the winery.

Modern vinification equipment has been installed in most establishments so that the whites are now fermented at low temperatures. The reds are also fermented in temperature-controlled conditions and most wines now avoid the fault of being too alcoholic or coarse. There is still work to be done in the vineyards to improve the matching of grape varieties, or cultivars as they are called on the Cape, to specific areas and to ensure that grapes are harvested in the healthiest condition possible.

The South Africans have devised a detailed but easy-to-understand quality designation system. Better-quality wines are known as "Wines of Origin", the best ones as "Wines of Origin Superior". A neckband designates each wine with a quality control number and also indicates how specific its guarantee of quality is by a series of different coloured bands. A blue band indicates that the wine is from one of South Africa's fourteen designated wine areas. A red band shows that the wine is from a single specified vintage. A green band shows that the wine is made from at least eighty per cent (one hundred per cent for a Superior wine) of a single cultivar. "Estate" wines are also specifically designated on the neck label, as well as having to conform to certain rules. It is just as well that it is easy to spot these estate wines as some of their individual estate names can be difficult for non-Afrikaans speakers. South Africa's more ordinary wines should not be overlooked, however, as many of them are considerably better than their counterparts in, say, France or Italy, and the South Africans are keen to keep export prices low.

Pinotage is the most common red wine grape, a Cape speciality, a cross between Pinot Noir and the Cinsaut of the Rhône, sometimes confusingly known as Hermitage – hence the name. The strength and body of most South African Pinotage wines suggest that the grape takes more of its character from the Rhône than Burgundy. Cinsaut is also grown fairly widely on its own and some estates put it to good use with Cabernet Sauvignon to make a blended claret-style of wine. (At this point it is appropriate to point out, pausing only to pat them on the back, that the South

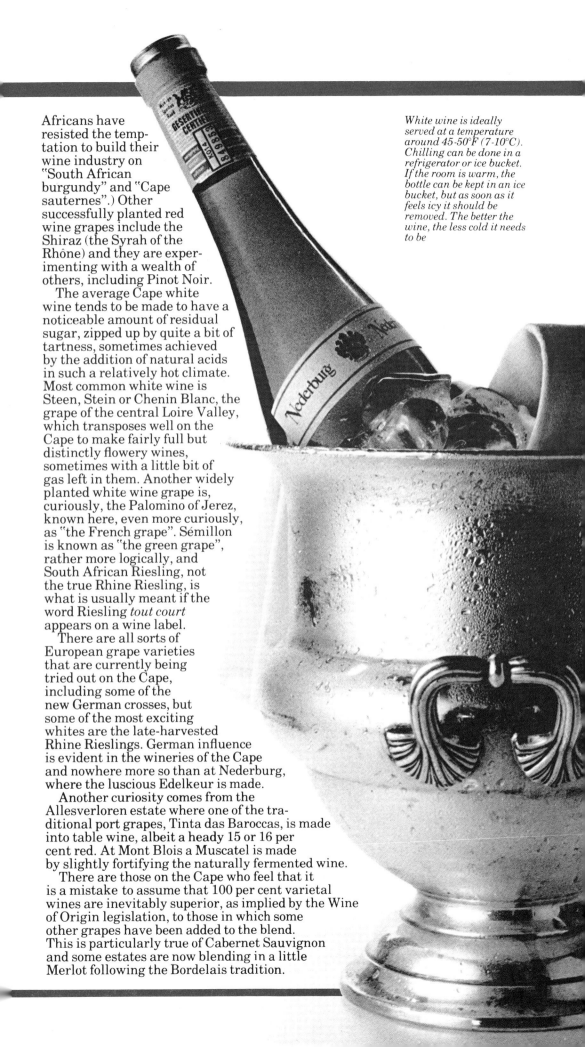

Africans have resisted the temptation to build their wine industry on "South African burgundy" and "Cape sauternes".) Other successfully planted red wine grapes include the Shiraz (the Syrah of the Rhône) and they are experimenting with a wealth of others, including Pinot Noir.

The average Cape white wine tends to be made to have a noticeable amount of residual sugar, zipped up by quite a bit of tartness, sometimes achieved by the addition of natural acids in such a relatively hot climate. Most common white wine is Steen, Stein or Chenin Blanc, the grape of the central Loire Valley, which transposes well on the Cape to make fairly full but distinctly flowery wines, sometimes with a little bit of gas left in them. Another widely planted white wine grape is, curiously, the Palomino of Jerez, known here, even more curiously, as "the French grape". Sémillon is known as "the green grape", rather more logically, and South African Riesling, not the true Rhine Riesling, is what is usually meant if the word Riesling *tout court* appears on a wine label.

There are all sorts of European grape varieties that are currently being tried out on the Cape, including some of the new German crosses, but some of the most exciting whites are the late-harvested Rhine Rieslings. German influence is evident in the wineries of the Cape and nowhere more so than at Nederburg, where the luscious Edelkeur is made.

Another curiosity comes from the Allesverloren estate where one of the traditional port grapes, Tinta das Baroccas, is made into table wine, albeit a heady 15 or 16 per cent red. At Mont Blois a Muscatel is made by slightly fortifying the naturally fermented wine.

There are those on the Cape who feel that it is a mistake to assume that 100 per cent varietal wines are inevitably superior, as implied by the Wine of Origin legislation, to those in which some other grapes have been added to the blend. This is particularly true of Cabernet Sauvignon and some estates are now blending in a little Merlot following the Bordelais tradition.

White wine is ideally served at a temperature around 45-50°F (7-10°C). Chilling can be done in a refrigerator or ice bucket. If the room is warm, the bottle can be kept in an ice bucket, but as soon as it feels icy it should be removed. The better the wine, the less cold it needs to be

NORTH AFRICA

Non-wine-drinking, much-wine-producing countries are in trouble when they lose their major customer and this is the position in which Algeria, and to a certain extent Tunisia and Morocco, found themselves in the early sixties when they established their independence from France. Since then there has been a resurgence of militant Islam with its strict prohibition of alcohol and France has found alternative sources of rich red wine in bulk.

This has caused problems, particularly for Algeria, who in 1961 was the world's sixth biggest wine producer with up to forty per cent of the population involved in the wine industry in some way.

More recently Algeria has found new markets, notably the Soviet Union and, to a lesser extent, Germany, but she has still to decide whether to continue to produce large quantities of wine of decreasing quality from badly tended vineyards on the plains or whether to switch to making less but better wine from vines planted further up the hillsides. Algeria, being one of the closest wine regions to the equator, has never found any difficulty in producing wines high in alcohol and colour, ideal for blending with lighter, more acid wines such as those of southern France. Her whites tend to be much too full-blown for north European tastes and her best wines are reds from the hills of Tlemcen, Mascara, Haut Dahra, Zacca and Ain-Bessem.

The Tunisian wine industry, though only one-tenth as big as that of Algeria, faces the same problems. Her wines are similar, but at least Tunisia has a tourist trade to absorb some of her (domestically) unwanted wines. There is also the Tunisian speciality, a sweet white wine made from Muscat grapes and the wine industry is centred on the coast around the Gulf of Tunis.

It is generally agreed that Morocco, aided by the cooling breezes of the Atlantic, has greater potential as a serious wine producer than either Algeria or Tunisia. Her particular speciality is *vin gris*, a light, dry *rosé* not unlike some Provence *rosés*. Sidi Larbi is usually a robust, vigorous red made near the coast between Rabat and Casablanca, but her best wine comes from the Atlas foothills between Meknes and Fes.

A little wine is also made in Egypt.

NEAR EAST

As in North Africa, most Near Eastern vineyards are tended by those not allowed to indulge in the alcoholic pleasure afforded by them. Today more grapes end up as dried fruit than as wine.

Turkey is trying to develop a wine export business and offers, for instance, the irresistibly-named Buzbag, which, like most of her wines with export potential, is a full-bodied red that is high on alcohol and low on subtlety.

Lebanon continues to produce some wine, perhaps as a result of French influence. There is some good, crisp *rosé* and the excellent "French" red Château Musar.

Israeli vineyards produce Kosher wine and much of it comes from wineries founded by Rothschilds.

AUSTRALIA

With California, Australia is our most exciting New World wine producer at the moment, though it is perhaps impertinent to use the word "new" in connection with a wine industry that is two centuries old. There are now sixth generation winemakers in Australia, but it has been only in recent years that there has been a receptive and enthusiastic public eager for top-class table wines to encourage the sort of innovation that has so improved the quality of wine being made. For years Australia had a "tonic burgundy" image and indeed many of her reds are still weighty and characterized by a taste that suggests a high mineral content. An increase in the acreage planted with subtler, classic grape varieties and in the installation of new, temperature-controlled winemaking equipment, has brought with it a range of much more elegant wines.

As in California, it is common for wine producers to make a wide variety of different wines, ranging perhaps from a top-class red with ageing potential down to the "cask wines" that have become so much a way of Australian life. The "casks" in question are cardboard boxes with self-deflating plastic bags inside holding two gallons of everyday wine; they live in Australian fridges.

Australian wine labelling can be confusing for those brought up on European wine. "Claret" can be any old red wine, not necessarily even containing any Cabernet Sauvignon. "Riesling", "hock", "sauternes" are other names bandied about without any necessary connection with their European models. There is a trend though towards careful varietal labelling which is particularly helpful when so many of the better Australian reds are blends of two grapes, often Shiraz with Cabernet or Pinot Noir.

Shiraz is Australia's staple red wine grape, related to the Syrah of the north Rhône valley and hence often called Hermitage. It makes full, slightly sweet and often very alcoholic wines so that blending with the more austere claret grape Cabernet Sauvignon can often produce good results. The white bordeaux grape Sémillon is also widely planted and makes fairly strong but not necessarily flabby wines that are sometimes confusingly called Riesling. "Real" German Riesling is called Rhine Riesling.

South Australia now produces the greatest quantity of wine in vineyards that encircle, and sometimes encroach on, Adelaide. In the Barossa Valley to the northeast the tradition of the German settlers lives on in some fine Rhine Rieslings which are much higher in alcohol than their German prototypes but can have a fragrance and firmness of their own. To the south of the city centre is the Southern Vales area with the big wine company Penfold's red wine star, Grange Hermitage, actually sited within the city limits. Way to the southeast, and hence in cooler conditions, is Coonawarra with its distinctive red soil best suited to red grapes. Hugh Johnson suggests that Coonawarra claret is Australia's nearest approach to Bordeaux. The irrigated Murray River and Clare/Watervale areas of South Australia make a variety of dessert and table wines, with Clare best known for Rieslings.

New South Wales' best-known wine area is the Hunter Valley, nearest sizeable good-quality wine district to Sydney's wine lovers, being just 200 miles (a mere stone's throw Down Under) to the north of the city. Its northerly latitude means hot summers and very full, concentrated

wines, the best of which need ageing to show the best advantage. Much of the soil is volcanic and the wines can have a strong vanillin flavour. Shiraz and now Cabernet produce the Hunter Valley's reds, Sémillon (here known as Riesling) and now Chardonnay the whites. Riverina is another NSW wine area, created by irrigation from the Murrumbidgee River.

Victoria includes wine areas upstream of South Australia's Murray River area at Mildura, but perhaps her best-known wines are the long-established Château Tahbilk and Seppelt's Great Western sparkling wine, Australia's answer to champagne.

Some wine is also made in Tasmania, Queensland and Western Australia, where they have high hopes of the Swan Valley area.

It is only relatively recently that Australian winemakers have put their chief emphasis on the production of table wines rather than the fortified "Australian port" and "Australian sherry" of the past. In 1970, fortified wines still made up forty per cent of the total amount of wine produced that year, though this proportion had dwindled to nearer twenty per cent by the end of the decade.

The dramatic increase in Australian interest in light wines is illustrated by the fact that per capita consumption of wine doubled in the seventies. White wine in particular has enjoyed enormous popularity and now outsells red wine by more than three to one. This must be connected with the relatively hot climate of many of Australia's more heavily populated areas, and shows how stubborn wine drinkers can be in their tastes. For the area of vineyards planted with red wine grape varieties Down Under is bigger by far than that planted with white grapes, and indeed the Australians have been in danger of suffering a red wine glut. This is particularly strange as many foreigners have a higher esteem for Australia's red wine than its white.

As yet Australia has no overall quality designation system on the lines of those in operation in Europe but an increasing number of wine-producing areas are adopting their own local wine certification scheme.

This is one of the few respects in which the Australian wine industry is lagging behind its counterparts elsewhere. In wine research its oenologists are acclaimed the world over.

NEW ZEALAND

Here is another instance of great winemaking progress in the Antipodes. The New Zealand dairy industry with its advanced technology has done its bit to help along the quality of wine produced, particularly whites. Müller-Thurgau is the most widely planted grape variety and makes sprightly whites with a touch of sweetness, but there is increasing experimentation with other "European" grape varieties, including Cabernet, which can make light but definitely Cabernet wines even here, this far from the equator.

Vineyards used to be concentrated around Auckland in the north of the North Island, but other more suitable parts of the North Island have been sought out and the north of the South Island shows particular promise. Cooks at Te Kauwhata, Montana and the ubiquitous Penfold's are names to look out for.

CHILE

Chile is undoubtedly the country with the best potential as a top-quality wine producer in South America, many of whose vineyards are situated too close to the equator to be capable of producing anything really fine.

Even Chile's best vineyards, around Santiago, have their problems and irrigation is widely used, but the temperate climate influenced by the Pacific Ocean is capable of producing excellent reds more like the wines of Bordeaux than anywhere else. Cabernet Sauvignon and Merlot's pre-eminence in the vineyards provide another part of the explanation for this similarity. Phylloxera has never reached Chile and so vines may be planted without being grafted on to phylloxera-resistant rootstock as in almost every other wine region of the world, and this may be a factor in enhancing the quality of her wines.

What has not helped is the political difficulties experienced in Chile, where there has been a chronic shortage of investment in both vineyards and particularly in vinification centres. Chile has not continued to improve the quality of its wines as its potential deserves. White wine technology in particular clearly has a long way to go and most of the whites, often made from Bordeaux white grapes Sauvignon and Sémillon, are flat and stale by the time they reach any export market. Wine producers who have exported good reds in the past include Cousiño of Macul, whose Reservas Antiguas has been excellent, and Concha y Toro.

ARGENTINA

Argentina is yet to show the world that it can produce wines with quite the same finesse as the best of Chile, but it is trying hard and, as one of the world's top five wine producers (with France, Italy, the Soviet Union and Spain), clearly cannot be ignored.

The Argentinians not only make an enormous amount of wine, they also drink an enormous amount of it. Only the French, the Italians and the Portuguese can rival the Argentinians for their wine-drinking capacity, which is one of the reasons why Argentine wines are not yet well known abroad. They are beginning to be very interested in

developing their wine exports, however, and increasingly have wines of a quality to warrant it.

Most of the Argentine's best vineyards are just over the Andes from the vineyards of Chile, just over 17,000 feet that is. The province of Mendoza is the centre of the Argentinian wine region and vineyards here are on a grand scale: row after row of well-tended vines geared to mechanization stretching out in irrigated orderliness with the snowy Andes in the distance. The Argentinians are improving their methods of vine growing and winemaking and are efficient in getting the most from their vines.

The Criolla was the most widely planted grape, a descendant of the vines brought by the Jesuits from Mexico in the sixteenth century, but the Malbec, one of Bordeaux's less illustrious red wine grapes, has been gaining ground, literally. Argentina's more recent wine history has been influenced more by Italians than Spaniards, however, and this is doubtless a factor in Argentina's casual but voracious attitude towards wine.

Today Malbec makes more good wine than any other variety, though plantings of classic varieties such as Cabernet and Pinot are on the increase. As in Chile, white wine can be disappointing, though there are some good Rieslings from cooler areas and some Chardonnays have stood up well in comparison with European counterparts.

Argentina must be looked on as an up-and-coming source of good value wine.

OTHER SOUTH AMERICAN COUNTRIES

Brazil also has potential, though it will be some time before she is exporting any great quantity of any great wine. The best wine is produced in the south of the country just north of Uruguay, where the climate is its least humid. In the most humid areas European vines are unhappy and hybrids are widely planted in Brazil. There is increasing experimentation with better-quality wines, however, notably under the auspices of foreign wine concerns such as Moët & Chandon, whose Brazilian sister makes not only "champagne" [*sic*] but also still red and white wines. Very little Brazilian wine finds its way out of the country. This is true of the Uruguay wine industry.

Much of Peru is either too high or too tropical for the vine, but a little ordinary table wine is made around Lima. A small amount of wine is made in Bolivia, but Mexico is the biggest wine producer south of the Rio Grande apart from Argentina, Chile and Brazil, with about the same area under vine as Austria. Mexico's vineyards were first planted with the Criolla grape, whose other name Mission, gives some clues as to how it found its way there, to such inhospitably hot vineyards. Mexico's best vine is produced, not surprisingly, in her coolest region, the Baja California in the north. Under skilled direction Mexico's wine industry is making great progress and is already exporting sound if unsubtle wines to North America.

NORTH AMERICA

When you have a large country inhabited by increasingly sophisticated and enthusiastic wine drinkers, much of it being ideally suited to the cultivation of the vine, then it is not surprising that it is producing some of the world's finest wine. What is perhaps unusual is that it has taken the United States so long to develop its wine industry. For this delay Prohibition must take the blame, and it took several decades even after its repeal for Americans to look for an alcoholic drink with a less vicious kick than their highballs and cocktails. The early seventies saw American interest in wine broaden from high-alcohol dessert wines and wines for the large Italian community to include all the world's finest table wines. This was accompanied by a dramatic increase in the number of intelligent enthusiasts anxious to show that North America's most promising wine region, California, could make wines to rank with the best in the world.

CALIFORNIA

Wine has been made on the West Coast since the Jesuits brought the vine along their "Mission Trail". Even during Prohibition, some California wineries survived by making communion wine. (It is believed that the number of communicants was impressive in the twenties and early thirties.) California's wine industry has grown steadily in the amount of wine produced, the volume made up largely by the enormous wineries of the hot Central Valley responsible for California's basic "jug" wines. But the excitement recently has been in the rapid increase in the number of smaller top-quality wineries, often established by "dropouts" from other professions.

The big wineries are still extremely important. Theirs is the territory in which "Chablis" is American for white wine just as "Burgundy" is for red. Creditably sound wines are made at this bottom level of quality, much of it sold in large flagons, hence the "jug wine". The biggest of these big wineries is E & J Gallo, a family-run company that produces more wine than any other winery in the world at their Modesto complex, which even includes a glass furnace in which their own bottles are made.

But even Gallo are trying to cash in on the "varietal" act. "Generics" such as chablis and burgundy or sauterne [sic] are now seen by the American public as less desirable then "varietals", wines named after the main grape variety in the wine (which from the 1982 vintage must constitute seventy-five per cent of the blend). This craze for varietal labelling has led to some interesting examples of wines made from a single grape variety, such as French Colombard for instance, about which most European wine drinkers have never heard. There are signs now, however, that some winemakers are seeing the value of judicious blending, that one hundred per cent Cabernet Sauvignon may not be quite as good as a Cabernet and Merlot blend,

FREEMARK ABBEY

1976
NAPA VALLEY

CHARDONNAY

Produced and Bottled by
FREEMARK ABBEY WINERY, ST. HELENA, CALIFORNIA
Alcohol 14.6% by volume

which has led to the appearance of the amazing term "multi-varietal generics".

American winemakers are nothing if not experimental. Unfettered by the centuries-old traditions which can sometimes hamper their counterparts in Europe, they are able to change their methods at each vintage, sometimes succeeding, sometimes failing, always admitting their mistakes. They are great travellers and have been able to draw on winemaking techniques from all over the world. Geisenheim is making its contribution to their Rieslings for example, Bordeaux to their Cabernets. The oenology departments at Davis and, increasingly, Fresno, are revered by all who care about the technical aspects of wine production throughout the world. Meticulous vineyardists have taken virus-free clones specially developed at Davis back to wine regions all over the world.

The greatest concentration of California's smaller, top-quality wineries (called "boutiques" if they're small enough) is in the Napa and Sonoma valleys to the north of San Francisco. The climate here, confusingly enough, gets hotter as one goes north and some of California's best areas for Burgundy vines Pinot Noir and Burgundy Chardonnay is in the south of the Napa Valley, famous too for some

superb Cabernets. This is beautiful country, the fertile valley floor covered in vines, contrary to the French belief in concentrating on the poorest soil available, craggy hills rising up on either side, perhaps the site of future vineyards? Americans, and some foreigners, have not been slow to invest large quantities of money in installing the best that it can buy for the vineyards and wineries of California. Mechanization is advanced, harvesters used commonly, especially at night, when the picked grapes are less likely to start fermentation before they get to the winery. There are wind machines, that look as though they belong more to aircraft wings than vineyards, and drip systems which can either irrigate the land or spray vines with water to protect them from frost damage. And in the wineries there is the most sophisticated equipment, not necessarily ignoring tradition, but constantly modifying it. An innovative winemaker such as Robert Mondavi is said to have experimented not just with the exact sort of oak in which to mature each grape variety, but also with different cask sizes, varying maturing times, and even different types of staves.

In Napa and Sonona it is impossible to give an up-to-date directory of the best winemakers, for reputations are being made all the time. Christian Brothers, under the direction of Brother Timothy, is one of the biggest producers there and its exports are considerable. Beaulieu Vineyards, or BV, have one of the oldest reputations for quality, especially for Private Reserve Cabernet Sauvignon.

CALIFORNIA
CHABLIS

PAUL MASSON.
RARE PREMIUM WINES

This is a dry white wine with zest and personality. Of light straw color, it has a crisp clarity that rewards the eye as well as the palate. The fresh bouquet of this Chablis is captured by fermentation at ideally cool temperatures – saving the essence of the grape. Chill Chablis well before serving. It brings added enjoyment to light cuisine and is a delightful compliment to snacks of fruits and cheeses. Made and Bottled by Paul Masson Vineyards, Saratoga, California · Alcohol 11.5% by Volume.

Further north there are also wineries in Mendocino and the Russian River areas, but it should be said at this point that the location of the winery has no necessary connection with the provenance of the grapes being brought there, nor with the types of wine produced. Many wineries still cling to the idea that they must produce the full range of varietals, wherever they are located, and at vintage time the grape haulage business is big business.

Some of California's most exciting wine is made from wineries south of San Francisco, with the Monterey region notably cooler than much of Napa. Two of the biggest wineries, Almaden and Paul Masson, whose wines are not difficult to find outside the US, are on the outskirts of San Jose, while there are some interesting wineries much further south of Santa Barbara and even south of Los Angeles towards the Mexican border.

So far Cabernet Sauvignon has proved California's most successful red grape and illustrates better than any other perhaps that California wines taste like their European counterparts, only more so. Pinot Noir is doing well in the cooler regions, while those who care to are making intense, rich wines from California's native, spicy grape Zinfandel. Petite Syrah is a popular wine for much lighter, everyday red wine and should not be confused with the Syrah of the Rhône, just as Gamay Beaujolais perversely has nothing to do with Beaujolais, though Napa Gamay has.

The American predilection for "a glass of white wine" has sent white wine prices above those of reds, and this is particularly true of Chardonnay, which is capable here of producing wines with the depth of flavour and staying power of good white burgundies. Chenin Blanc of the Loire is a widely planted grape making fresh, medium dry whites, while really top-class sweeter wines are being made from California's version of Germany's Riesling, known here either as Johannisberg, or White Riesling. Some good Gewürztraminers are being made, usually modelled on Alsace rather than Germany. Another great success story has been Sauvignon, in California given a new image with the name Fumé Blanc, or Blanc Fumé, and often a much more full-bodied style of winemaking than it is given in the Loire and Bordeaux.

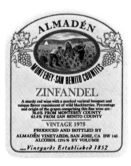

NEW YORK AND ELSEWHERE

The United States' other major wine-producing state is New York, up in the Finger Lakes region, where most of the wines grown are not the classy European varieties but the coarser and higher-yielding native American ones. The wines made from these non-*vinifera* vines can taste strange to those not brought up on them and there is a little experimentation with more widely acceptable varieties. This is also true of neighbouring Ohio and Ontario in Canada.

Such is the strength of the American's newfound enthusiasm for wine that there is hardly a state in the more temperate northern half of the US that is without at least one pioneer vineyard. Most successful so far have been those experimenting in Oregon, to the north of California.

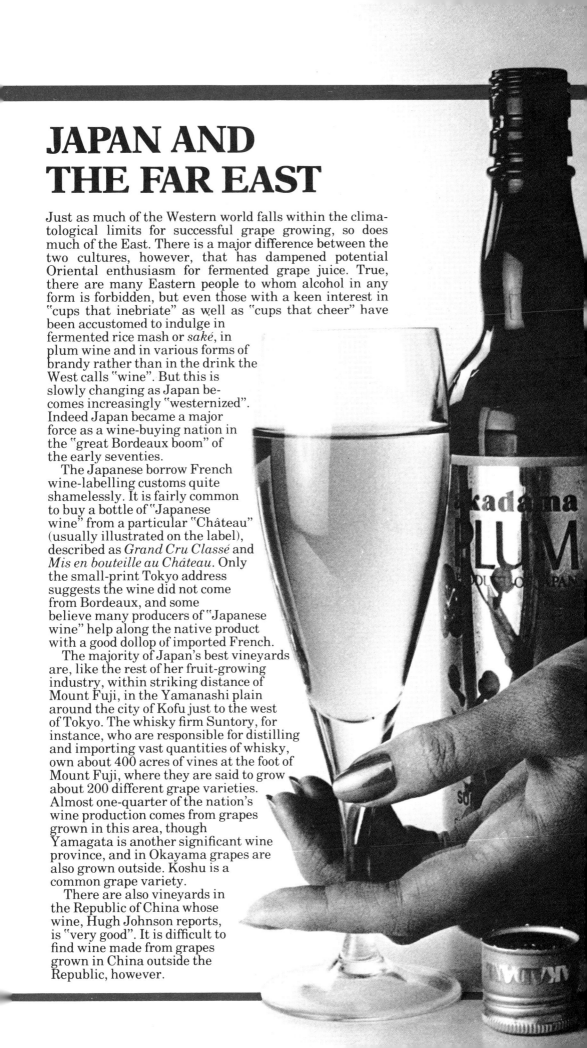

JAPAN AND THE FAR EAST

Just as much of the Western world falls within the climatological limits for successful grape growing, so does much of the East. There is a major difference between the two cultures, however, that has dampened potential Oriental enthusiasm for fermented grape juice. True, there are many Eastern people to whom alcohol in any form is forbidden, but even those with a keen interest in "cups that inebriate" as well as "cups that cheer" have been accustomed to indulge in fermented rice mash or *saké*, in plum wine and in various forms of brandy rather than in the drink the West calls "wine". But this is slowly changing as Japan becomes increasingly "westernized". Indeed Japan became a major force as a wine-buying nation in the "great Bordeaux boom" of the early seventies.

The Japanese borrow French wine-labelling customs quite shamelessly. It is fairly common to buy a bottle of "Japanese wine" from a particular "Château" (usually illustrated on the label), described as *Grand Cru Classé* and *Mis en bouteille au Château*. Only the small-print Tokyo address suggests the wine did not come from Bordeaux, and some believe many producers of "Japanese wine" help along the native product with a good dollop of imported French.

The majority of Japan's best vineyards are, like the rest of her fruit-growing industry, within striking distance of Mount Fuji, in the Yamanashi plain around the city of Kofu just to the west of Tokyo. The whisky firm Suntory, for instance, who are responsible for distilling and importing vast quantities of whisky, own about 400 acres of vines at the foot of Mount Fuji, where they are said to grow about 200 different grape varieties. Almost one-quarter of the nation's wine production comes from grapes grown in this area, though Yamagata is another significant wine province, and in Okayama grapes are also grown outside. Koshu is a common grape variety.

There are also vineyards in the Republic of China whose wine, Hugh Johnson reports, is "very good". It is difficult to find wine made from grapes grown in China outside the Republic, however.

The last drop of port. "Buzzing a Bottle of Croft's", 1820

FORTIFIED WINES

Fortified wines are, hardly surprisingly, those wines which have been fortified, or strengthened, by adding alcohol to ordinary table wines, or "light wines" in EEC parlance. They include all sorts of sherry, port, madeira, marsala, malaga, montilla, French and Italian vermouths and those proprietary brands made by mixing wine, spirits and whatever other ingredients are prescribed by the "recipe handed down for generations" on which the drink depends.

Ordinary unfortified table wines have an alcoholic strength of about eight per cent for the lightest of German wines to almost sixteen per cent for the heaviest of Italian wines, with the average wine being about eleven per cent.

Fortified wines vary in strength from about fifteen per cent for the lightest sherries or "sherry type" drinks, such as those made in Cyprus of the Montilla-Moriles region near Cordoba, to over twenty per cent for the headiest, richest port. Wines were initially fortified to make them more stable and better able to survive keeping and transportation. There was often nothing too sophisticated about the process of fortification, just the "dosing" of the light wine with spirit. Gradually, however, tradition and expertise has been built up in certain wine regions to the extent that these regions now produce the fortified wines ideal for their situation.

The two most famous of these regions are the sherry region around Jerez in southwest Spain and the port region in the Douro Valley upstream of Oporto in northern Portugal. The two different approaches to fortification practised in these two areas broadly determine the two styles of fortified wines made anywhere in the world. Sherry producers ferment their grapes out to produce dry wines that are strong but not necessarily sweet. Port producers, on the other hand, want their wines to retain a fairly high degree of sugar, so they add spirit, quite a lot of it, before the grapes are fully fermented.

The alcohol used for fortification is usually distilled wine: a fairly neutral, young, colourless spirit.

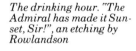

The drinking hour. "The Admiral has made it Sunset, Sir!", an etching by Rowlandson

SHERRY

There is Cyprus sherry, there is South African sherry, Australian sherry, Californian sherry even British sherry, but they are all poor relations of the best wines of the "proper" sherry region, the rolling sun-drenched country-side around Jerez in Andalucia.

Even the name sherry itself is a corruption of the word Jerez, pronounced, as Spanish speakers know, "hereth". In France, sherry is called "xérès".

Sherry is particularly appreciated in the cooler countries of northern Europe and historical trading links with Britain and the Netherlands in particular are maintained today by those who export vast quantities of sherry. The British, for instance, drink ten times as much sherry as the Spaniards. This may be partly a function of taxes and subsequent retail prices. A bottle of sherry in a Jerez supermarket costs about as much as a bottle of brandy, while in Britain sherry has been very cheap indeed relative to other alcoholic drinks.

Of all fortified aperitif wines, sherry has the noblest winemaking pedigree. Good sherry-making is a costly and lengthy process relying on careful slow maturation and critically skilful blending. The traditional process involving oxcarts in the vineyards, grapes on straw mats and casks "baking in the heat of the Andalusian sun" has been modernized rapidly over the last decade, though the same factors are important, if better understood.

Almost all the grapes grown in the sherry region are Palomino, of which the most suitable sort has been developed as Palomino Fino. In the past Moscatel and a local grape called Pedro Ximenez were grown quite extensively to make sweetening and colouring wines, but Palomino is being used more and more for these two purposes too.

The vines are planted in long, widely spaced rows on the pale, very hard-baked soil of the region. It is generally thought that the chalkier the soil the better the wine, and the region is divided into Albarizas, Barros and Arenas soils, getting progressively less chalky.

Most sherry vineyards today are situated on Albariza soil and the long hours of sunshine here in the southern tip of Spain, where the atmosphere can at times seem more North African than European, give winemakers grapes with a very high degree of ripeness.

The sherry companies have been subject to the same trend towards amalgamation, take-over and "rationalization" as any other business sector and the wines are being made in fewer and fewer wine centres, or *bodegas*, and on a bigger and bigger scale. Typically, the grapes will be taken to a huge receiving fermenting centre, either in the middle of vineyard country or in one of the three "sherry towns": Jerez, Sanlucar de Barrameda and Puerto de Santa Maria.

After fermentation, the wines are split into two quite different systems, *fino* and *oloroso criaderas* or "nurseries". The wines put into a *fino criadera* are destined to be lighter and drier than average, while the *oloroso criadera* is the place for richer, fuller wines. Their future is determined by just how much alcohol is added at this stage. If the wine is fortified to about 15° alcohol, then *flor*, a curious yeast indigenous to Jerez, will form on the top of the wine in cask, thus determining that it will develop *fino* characteristics. Potential *olorosos* on the other hand are fortified to a higher strength and *flor* will not form. The *flor*, a soggy thick layer of yeast, protects the lighter wine from oxidation and lends it that curious tang that characterizes a light, dry sherry. *Olorosos* are encouraged to oxidize, to "flatten out in flavour" to acquire that rich nuttiness of a good aged richer sherry.

From the *criaderas*, the wines are put into *fino* or *oloroso solaras*, systems of casks holding increasingly mature wine. Wine is moved from one rank to another, never emptying the cask of more than a third of its contents in any one operation, so that all sherry is, above all, a blend. A really fine sherry may go through a *solera* with as many as eight different ranks, each one slightly more mature than the other. It is impossible, therefore, to say exactly how old a particular cask of sherry is on this system, nor is it possible to have vintage-dated sherries made strictly adhering to this *solera* system.

When a batch of wine is being prepared for shipment it may be further fortified to bring it up to shipping strength (the *finos* sold in Jerez, for instance, tend to be slightly lower in alcohol than those exported) and will be blended with sweetening and colouring wines if necessary to match it to the type of wine required. The less blending that has been done to the wine, the better quality sherry it will usually be.

Lightest, driest sherries are sold as *finos* and these are the wines drunk with such relish, by the half bottle so they don't lose their freshness, in the *tapas* bars of Jerez. *Manzanillas* are very similar though they have been matured at Sanlucar on the coast and are thereby supposed to acquire a slightly salty tang. Both these sorts of sherry should be served chilled, and fast.

Amontillados are medium sherries, in sweetness and colour. A proper *amontillado* is an old wine from a *fino solera* that has gained richness with age. *Oloroso* sherries are one step up in terms of sweetness and are, classically, lovely nutty mature wines from *oloroso soleras*. Cream sherries are even sweeter and have great popularity in Britain and, increasingly, the United States. That they owe much to Britain for inspiration and consumption is evidenced by the fact that the most popular brand by far is Harvey's Bristol Cream. "Palo creams", with the sweetness but not the colour of the creams, are becoming popular too.

Commercial sherries have an average age of about three years, but the classic *oloroso* wines may be carefully aged for as many as a dozen years in the cathedral-like white-washed *bodegas* of Jerez.

PORT

That the wild, steep scrub that flanks the Douro river in northern Portugal should be cultivated at all strikes the visitor as surprising. The fact that this land produces a heady, rich dessert wine ideally suited to cool climate connoisseurs can strike the summertime visitor as positively absurd. But such were the effects of the Methuen Treaty of 1703 that Portugal started a tradition of sending wine from Oporto to England that has never ceased.

Port takes its name from *O porto* (the port), a slightly decaying but basically elegant city at the mouth of the Douro, where British influence is still very much in evidence. There is the eighteenth-century Factory House where the (British) port shippers meet for lunch every Wednesday, the Oporto Cricket and Lawn Tennis Club, and then there are the names: Croft, Cockburn, Dow, Graham, Sandeman and Taylor.

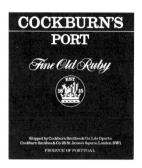

The famous port "lodges" where the wine is matured are long, low buildings by the river in Vila Nova de Gaia, just across the river from the commercial section of Oporto, but the wine is made many tortuous miles upriver, from grapes grown on the steeply terraced vineyards. The higher the vineyard the better. This is still very primitive country, with one bad road and one rarely used railway track forming the only communication link now that the Pinhão dam has put paid to river traffic. A wide range of local grape varieties are grown and brought to pretty, whitewashed, vine-shaded *quintas* for fermentation. They might also be taken to one of the bigger fermentation centres being set up by the port shippers in an attempt to bring port-making into the twentieth century. This is still almost barefoot country, in two senses. Not only are many of the local people still very poor, the practice of treading grapes is still alive in parts of the Douro.

As has already been outlined, the fermentation of port grapes is stopped midway by adding alcohol, or grape spirit, so that the mixture is too strong for the fermenting yeasts to work. This has the effect of making port a strong wine, and also a sweet one as only part of the sugar has been fermented out to form alcohol. But port wine has to have lots of colour, and it has to last if it is to be at all exciting, which means that a maximum amount of colour and tannin have to be extracted from the skins of the grapes during the relatively short fermentation. In the past this was achieved by treading the grapes in the fermentation vat. The gentle pressure was ideal to get the most out of the grapes without breaking the pips and releasing their bitter oils. Recent years have seen the introduction of a rather more prosaic but just as economic and dependable alternative, the special sealed fermentation vats. These are designed to keep the wine constantly churning through the "cap" of grapeskins that floats on top of the fermenting must. This is normally called "autovinification".

The partly fermented wine, after its generous dose of grape spirit, is a raw, tough, fruity wine that needs time to soften. In the spring after the vintage it is brought down from the Douro *quintas* to the lodges in Vila Nova to be assessed for quality so that the shippers may decide on its eventual destiny.

The crucial question is what sort of maturation it deserves. If it is a really very special wine, with great lasting potential, lots of tannin and fruit, then it might become a

"vintage port".
These are the ports of
gentlemen's clubs (or
rather they were, when
gentlemen could afford
to drink vintage port)
about which there is
so much discussion and
wager as to the exact
vintage and the shipper.
Vintage port is made only
in about one year in three,
depending on how kind the
weather has been. The shippers
"declare a vintage" only if the
wines of that year look capable
of developing great stature
if left to mature in bottle for
decades. Vintage port comprises
but a tiny fraction of all the port
produced, but is a vital part of
the romance of port as a whole.
It is usually bottled when it has

had only about two years to mature in wood. Because so much less air comes into contact with wine when it is sealed up inside a bottle than when it is in a constantly evaporating mass inside a cask, vintage port's maturation is an extremely slow process, and only those who can afford to pay for the holding of wine for twenty years and more can afford to drink vintage port. The old habit of laying down a pipe of port (the traditional measure of 115 gallons) for a godson has, understandably, disappeared.

Recent years have seen the introduction .of a form of vintage port that more people can afford to enjoy – late bottled vintage ports and "vintage character" ports. These are wines of superior but not necessarily the finest quality that are allowed to mature in wood for between four and a half and six years before being bottled. This means that they lack the concentration of a vintage port, but have the great advantage of being ready as soon as they are bottled.

Another fine old port, much favoured in Oporto itself, is a genuine old tawny port. This is a wine allowed to mature in cask for many years – sometimes ten, often twenty, and occasionally forty years (this figure refers to the average age of the blend). Instead of concentrating its richness, this sort of port will mellow and soften to a smooth, round treat and all that air will make its colour lighten to a lovely golden brown.

There is another sort of tawny that is considerably less subtle. All port is a rich ruby colour when young and first put into cask. These "wood ports" are the cheapest sort of ports available and are sold in two shades: ruby and tawny. This cheaper sort of tawny is made by simply mixing a young ruby with white port. Wood ports make up the commercial backbone of the port wine trade, particularly with France, port's biggest export market.

Sweet white port is the result of applying the port-making process to white grapes. Dry yet full white ports may be made by fermenting all the sugar out before fortification, as in the sherry process.

Decanting – pouring wine from its original bottle into another container – was originally a way of removing sediment before serving. Today, few wines except vintage port, fine bordeaux and older burgundies actually need decanting, but young wines can benefit from the exposure to air they receive during pouring, and gain in richness of scent and flavour

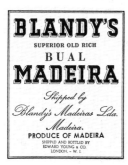

MADEIRA AND OTHER FORTIFIED WINES

Madeira is the world's third great classic fortified wine. It has seen more fashionable times, but since the amount of madeira wine that the island of Madeira can produce is strictly limited, it is perhaps just as well that demand is not greater.

Like that other great dessert wine made within Portuguese territory, madeira is made from grapes grown on very steep terraced vineyards, this time the volcanic slopes of this Atlantic island. Winemaking is controlled by an association of the major madeira shippers, but most of the vineyards are still in the hands of peasant farmers who have allowed a considerable proportion of the island's vineyards to be planted with high-yielding hybrid grape varieties rather than the traditional ones from which the various styles of madeira take their names. Sercial was the grape responsible for the lightest, driest madeira, the "fino of madeiras", while Verdelho made slightly rounder wines. Verdelho is not often seen, even as a style rather than a grape variety, outside Madeira itself. Bual is a rich, plummy sort of madeira, while Malmsey, supposedly made from the Malvasia grape of Monemvasia in Greece, is even richer in taste.

Madeira's special characteristic is a sort of "cooked" burnt flavour, the result of *estufagem*, the strictly controlled process of heating up the wine that is an integral part of madeira production. Many madeiras have a slightly green tinge, and the third distinguishing mark is longevity. What examples there are of most wines between 100 and 200 years old can best be described as interesting ancient relics. Not so madeira, which can still have life and health even at this age. And a bottle once opened (of better-than-everyday madeira) will retain its flavour and power for weeks.

Marsala is dark, rich, almost medicinal wine, popular in the kitchens of Italian cooks (French ones seem to favour madeira). It is made in a number of different styles and sweetnesses on the west coast of Sicily and it is rare to find one of sufficiently superb quality to drink on its own outside Italy.

It is still possible to find malaga, a liquid version of Christmas pudding, from the firm of Scholtz Hermanos, who still produce the wine in the Costa del Sol town of Malaga.

The Montilla-Moriles region near Cordoba produces wines very similar indeed to the sherry made just to the west in Jerez. Montilla tends to be lighter in alcohol than sherry and the very dry, light styles in particular will not withstand being kept in half-empty bottles for several weeks. Montilla gave rise initially to the term "amontillado".

Wines very similar to sherry are produced the world over. South African sherry, or Boberg, compares well as do some of Cyprus's lighter wines made in the sherry style. The Australian fortified wine trade is no longer as important as it was; ditto the North American one.

WINE-TYPE DRINKS

As well as South African sherry, Cyprus sherry and Australian sherry, there is also something called British sherry, but purists to whom wine is "the fermented juice of freshly gathered grapes, the fermentation taking place in the district of origin according to local tradition and practice" will not accept British sherry as a "proper" wine.

British sherry, indeed all British wine, is made from imported grape concentrate which is then reconstituted and made into wine with the help of specially developed yeasts and, often, fortifying alcohol. This is clearly quite different from English wine, which is light table wine made from grapes grown in the British Isles. British wines are made in all strengths – some still, some sparkling – and there are also some "tonic" wines to which medical properties are attributed.

In France too there are some very popular drinks which are called wines but which do not fall into the definition of "wine" as given above. One way of producing a drink that is both sweet and alcoholic is to take the port-making process to an extreme and add spirit to grape juice. This gives a liquid that has the fortifying effect of a wine, such as sherry or port, with the fruitiness of grape juice.

All around the Mediterranean coast are *vins doux naturels*, drinks that are made in this way to be drunk before meals (in France) or after (in Britain). Banyuls, Roussillon, Rivesaltes, Frontignan, Lunel and Beaumes de Venise all produce such a wine, usually of the scented Muscat grape. Rasteau just to the east of the Rhône valley is also responsible for a sweet dessert wine and this type has an equivalent in Cognac country known as Pineau des Charentes, usually a little stronger than most *vins doux naturels*. Champagne produces ratafia, a sweet aperitif.

The base product in all these cases is called *mistelle*, just as in Italy *mistella* is used as a base for many aperitifs.

Wines from "home wine kits" such as those sold in Britain are usually made in the same way as any other British wine, from imported grape concentrate, together

with sugar and yeast in the right quantity and quality.

Fruit wines such as elderberry wine and parsnip wine rely on the basic premise of all winemaking: that sugar and yeast react together to form alcohol. So long as yeast is added to any material that contains sugar, whether fruit or vegetable, then alcohol should form. Careful nurturing will ensure that an alcoholic liquid will be the end product. In this way wines can be made not only from fruit and vegetables but also from nuts, flowers and any other material that contains sugar.

As avid home winemakers know, it is easy to ferment honey – an obvious source of sugar with which yeast can react. In effect fermented honey is what was called mead in the Middle Ages. Four thousand years ago the ancient Babylonians decreed that "the wine of the bee" be provided as the drink for wedding banquets, the bride's father being dragooned into giving a month's supply to the bridegroom. The "honey month" gave rise to the term honeymoon or *lune de miel*. Today, mead is not commonly drunk, though there are producers still in the southwest of England and it is a popular and cheap way of supplying guests at "medieval banquets" with something stimulating to drink.

In the Far East, as has already been outlined, they call the fermented mash of rice, "rice wine" or *saké*. Its strength can vary between that of a strong table wine and that of a weak fortified wine (twelve to eighteen per cent alcohol). It is usually made by steaming rice, then mixing the mash with yeast mash, rice malt and water and leaving this to ferment for twenty-four hours or so. *Saké* is now big business in Japan, but the traditional custom of serving it warmed in special small porcelain cups lives on. *Saké* can taste strange and perhaps rather "sweaty" or "oily" to foreigners, but the continued tradition of serving it on any occasion in Japan is evidence of its appeal.

To many, the word toddy conjures up thoughts of a hot drink made from hot water, sugar, lemon, spices and spirit, often rum or whisky. The word can also apply, however, to an alcoholic drink that perhaps fits into the wine category better than any other: the cold, fermented sap of palms. According to John Doxat palm sap ferments very quickly and the result should be drunk as soon as possible, preferably on the same day as fermentation. An ingenious researcher in Singapore has managed to stabilize the product of fermentation at about six per cent alcohol.

In the same category is Maui Blanc, a dryish "wine" made from pineapple juice and produced on the Hawaiian island of Maui by a third-generation Californian.

Kava is described by Alexis Lichine as "a native wine of the South Sea Islands prepared from the root of the Polynesian kava shrub". In 1774, Captain Cook was the first to describe to Europeans the peculiarly disgusting production process: "Several people take some of the root, and chew it until it is soft and pulpy; they then spit it out into a platter or other vessel, everyone into the same: when a sufficient quantity is chewed more or less, water is put to it according as it is to be strong or weak: the juice thus diluted is strained through some fibrous stuff like fine shavings: after which it is fit for drinking". "Today", observes Lichine tartly, "kava is usually made in a screw-type press".

In the wilder parts of the southern Soviet Union, the milk of any sort of domestic animal is fermented to produce an alcoholic drink called *koumiss*. Though hardly similar to wine, *koumiss* is nearer in strength to it than to any other category of drink.

Wine is, above all, generous and accommodating.

SPIRITS
&
LIQUEURS

Aqua vitae, or water of life, is the Latin term for
spirits – drinks made by distillation. This
versatile process means that almost any type of
fruit or vegetable can be used to make alcohol,
producing drinks ranging from the classic grain
spirits to sweet fruit cordials. Almost every
country has its speciality. Some remain
curiosities of the region; others, like Scotch
whisky, are appreciated and copied all over the
world. Within this broad category of spirits, the
range of style, flavour and strength pays tribute
to a whole history of inventiveness.

SPIRITS

Alcohol, the quintessence of many of the world's most celebrated beverages, including wine, is manifest most powerfully in "the water of life" – *aqua vitae* or spirits. In these, regardless of flavour or strength, the arts of distillation play a significant if not total role.

Spirits, which may range from a little over twenty per cent alcohol up to a dangerously high level of 160 per cent, are produced legally or illicitly in nearly every country. They come from a huge variety of bases, in a vast array of brands, of every imaginable taste and in qualities from the superb to the noxious. They have been both prescribed and proscribed and, above all, they have been taxed. To paint a portrait of wine is to use a single palette with subtle gradations of colours; to depict the turbulent countenance of spirits one must combine the styles of Michelangelo and Matisse – and employ violently contrasting pigments.

Distillation

The role and presence of alcohol, at once elusive and potent, needs some defining. Wine holds alcohol – some also contain distilled spirits – yet it is a widespread custom to talk about "alcohol" as something separate from the natural vinous product and to reserve the term, in everyday speech, for distillates.

The word dates from early Arabic civilization. It derives from *al-koh'l* (kohl), a very fine metallic powder, often antimony, used as a cosmetic. The word attached itself to anything highly refined and hence to distillation, which is a form of refinement. The Arabic association was probably reinforced by Islamic alchemists, who were at an early date using forms of distillation to obtain perfumes from flowers and perhaps making alcohol for medicinal purposes.

However, little is known about the early history of dis-

The nineteenth-century French artist Raffaelli made this drawing of an absinthe drinker from life. It was a favourite subject of many artists and a drink their contemporaries enjoyed in the Bohemian cafes of Paris in the 1890s

A typical "absinthe drinkers" picture. It is notable that few, if any, of this genre of drawing ever showed the drinkers actually enjoying themselves. Serious imbibing (or post-inebriate gloom) are the impressions given to the onlooker

tilling or precisely who invented the process. Certainly it was being practised before the scientific principles underlying it were understood. The whole concept depends on the fact that alcohol evaporates at a lower temperature than water: 78.3°C, as against 100°C. It may be presumed that without possessing any technical knowledge of temperatures, experimenters in various parts of the world found they could, by heating wine and trapping the vapour, make a stronger beverage – just as they could similarly concentrate and refine perfumed oils from flowers. It is believed that the Chinese were performing some sort of distilling from rice 3000 or more years ago, and, by 800 BC, the practice had spread to India and Japan. All sorts of eras are given for the introduction of distilling – probably as crude a spirit as the dates are problematical – to Western Europe. There are semi-legendary tales of distilling in Ireland a thousand or more years ago. There are claims that the first proper separation of alcohol and water (*alcool vini*) took place in France around 1100. But real evidence does not emerge until 1519, when a fairly effective still was illustrated in *Das Buch zu Destillieren* by Hieronymous Braunschweig. European distillation probably antedated that by many years, but only during the last 400 years has distillation of spirits become a commercial proposition, gradually assuming its current importance socially and economically.

There are two basic types of alcohol, though several others are known to science: the one that matters is ethyl alcohol (ethanol). The other main group, methanol (colloquially called wood alcohol), is a poison.

Two general styles of still are in regular use for producing potable spirit: the pot-still, also known as the *alambic*, and the *patent* (continuous) still, sometimes also called the *Coffey* still, after Aeneas Coffey, who perfected it.

The pot-still has remained almost unaltered for centuries, apart from obvious refinements and with changes in detail for specific products: thus a Scotch whisky still is

A rather idealized picture of the type of agave plant whence eventually comes tequila, Mexico's native spirit

In an 1879 illustration (below left) to Zola's savage attack on alcoholism, "L'Assommoir" (The Grog Shop), two of the novel's characters enjoy a convivial noggin before succumbing to inebriation. It was to absinthe in particular that the blame for the evils of strong drink in France was attributed

In Tsarist Russia, artisans take tea from a communal samovar, which, according to the original caption, was liberally reinforced with vodka

By 1914, advertising was becoming quite sophisticated as this poster (top) for Dewar's Scotch whisky indicates. Earlier stages in the product's march to global fame were advertised naïvely, to the point of banality. Even the Union Jack flag – the Scots were eagerly wooing the English to drink Scotch – appears to be upside down in this example (below)

This detailed 1894 magazine advertisement for ever-popular Stone's ginger wine shows a brand that has retained its status for a century. Today, Stone's only has Crabbie's Green as a serious rival

not exactly the same as that used for cognac. The pot-still is used alike for primitive distillations and for the best whisky, brandy and special rum. It plays a part in the production of superior gin. It comes in a wide range of sizes, but whether a pot-still is making "moonshine" in Kentucky or the finest Highland malt, the principle – though by no means the practice – is essentially the same. In reality, it is a gigantic kettle. Into it goes an alcohol-bearing liquid. On the application of the right degree of heat the alcohol evaporates. This steam carries only a little water in it: it is mainly alcohol, in which flavourings inherent in the original liquid are suspended – wine or whatever. When the alcohol vapour cools in a condenser it is then spirit.

The continuous still is altogether different. It was patented in the 1830s by Aeneas Coffey, who improved on a system for continuous distillation evolved in Scotland by Robert Stein, a major figure in the early Lowland Scotch whisky industry. A virtue of this type of still is that it obviates the long delay for refilling which is required in the pot-still method. The continuous still is a much more complicated piece of equipment, lacking the glamour – visual or historical – of the traditional still. A modern distillery using only continuous stills is akin to an alcohol factory which possesses a flexibility of control beyond that of pot-stills. Continuous distillation constantly produces quantities of high-strength, high-quality alcohol.

Continuous distillation is not suitable for making fine malt whisky or for good brandy, but it is unsurpassed for mass production of basic unflavoured spirits which will eventually become gin or vodka. It can produce fairly heavily flavoured spirit, such as rum, and is specially excellent for lightly flavoured spirit, such as grain whisky, without which the tremendous global popularity of blended Scotch whisky could scarcely have happened.

However, these two contrasting methods are not in rivalry: they tend to complement each other in many directions, or are employed to produce distinctively different styles of spirit. Occasionally, a modified rectifier column, as used in continuous distillation, will work in conjunction with a pot-still: its function then will be to rectify (purify) completely spirit that is going to be transmuted into, say, a fine London Dry gin.

Preparatory to all distilling an alcoholic fluid must be made. The most common sources are wine, or grain "beer", or fermented molasses, though there are others, including potatoes, fruit and rice. During the manufacture of alcoholic washes (other than from wine) on the scale of modern industry, a great deal of carbon dioxide is given off. Where possible, this gas is trapped and liquefied. It forms a by-product almost as important as the subsequent distillates.

A matter of proof

Since the earliest introduction of spirits into the social – as distinct from the medical – arena, methods of assaying their strength have been sought. This became a matter of some urgency when alcohol came to be taxed and essential when and where tax was related to the proportion of alcoholic content. Finally there was the question of protecting the consumer, though this was not a high priority until quite recently.

Probably the earliest idea of how to assess what constituted *aqua vitae*, as contrasted with wine and beer, was to dip a rag into the liquid and ignite it. If the liquid was too watery the rag would not burn; if it contained sufficient

alcohol, the rag would catch fire. By the fifteenth century another method had become popular; that of pouring oil on to the fluid. If the oil sank, the spirit was strong enough; if it stayed on top, it was too weak. These gave little indication beyond establishing a vague minimum level.

The gunpowder treatment was a slight improvement. The liquid was mixed with the explosive, and a flame was applied. If there was no reaction the liquid was not strong enough. If the mixture flared, it was sufficiently ardent to be passed as "proved". If it exploded mildly, it was stronger still, or "over-proof". Here lies the origin of the British "proof" (analogous to that of "proving" gun barrels). Yet another old process of proving spirit was to burn of the alcohol: should the residual liquid be less than half the original quantity, the spirit content was satisfactory.

The first recorded use of taxation according to proof was in 1688, when, to encourage English distilling (see Gin), imported spirits were charged a duty of two shillings per gallon on "single-proof" and twice that sum for "double-proof" – what later might be described as under-proof and over-proof; though, in labelling, percentage (degrees) of proof spirit is now more usually employed.

Some very experienced distillers could, and maybe still can, determine strength with remarkable accuracy by partly filling a glass jar with spirit and, by striking the base, cause small bubbles to rise to the surface; the larger the bubbles and the longer they last, the stronger the alcoholic content.

The first scientific instrument to measure alcoholic strength was the areometer, working on a principle originally discovered by Archimedes. Known as the *mustimètre* in France, it is used there to test the specific gravity of grape "must" and thus to forecast the probable strength of the wine to be fermented from it. With spirits, broadly, the greater the specific gravity, the lower their strength.

The English scientist Robert Boyle laid the foundations

Travellers in Ireland in the mid-1800s refresh themselves with illicit poteen on their way to, or from, a fishing expedition. The spirit would probably have been distilled in the cottage dimly seen in the background, and it is probable that the potheen was matured for all of a week. It is unlikely that the drinkers would have looked quite so happy the following morning

Early seventeenth-century pirates sample captured rum, a spirit to which they were addicted and which they were prone to enliven with a few dashes of gunpowder – an early version of a Mickey Finn cocktail

Strega liqueur by Dudovich

for the introduction, in 1730, of the first practical hydrometer for measuring the specific gravity of liquids, but it was not until 1762 that "proof" was defined. It was another twenty-three years before an improved hydrometer was legally approved in England as an instrument for assessing the strength of spirits. Later developments resulted in the adoption of the system of proof measurement developed by a retired Collector of Excise Taxes, one Bartholomew Sikes (or Sykes) in 1816, which remained unchallenged for over 150 years.

The strength of alcohols is now assessed to the highest degree of accuracy, yet the methods and scales may vary nationally. The complexity of the subject for the layman is indicated by the American definition of proof spirit: that which "contains one-half its volume of pure alcohol of a specific gravity of 0.7939 at 60°F". (British proof spirit was 12/13 of an equal volume of water at 51°F.) The altogether more straightforward French (Gay-Lussac) system, now very widely employed, simply expresses alcoholic content in percentage of pure spirit: a bottle with, say, 45° on it means that the contents have forty-five per cent pure alcohol by volume. For practical purposes, the American system is easy to understand. Since proof spirit is represented by the figure 100 and pure alcohol by 200, halving the proof figure on the bottle will give the strength of the spirit in terms of percentage of pure alcohol. No such easy reference pertained to the long-lasting British proof system. British proof spirit was also represented by 100, but then came the joker; pure (absolute) alcohol was given the figure 175.25: in practice 175. No one seems to have got round to asking the system's inventor, Bartholomew Sikes, the reasons behind this peculiar arrangement, which vastly complicated the use of the admirable hydrometer he perfected.

A saner way of indicating alcoholic strength had eventually to come to the aid of historically perplexed British drinkers. In 1979 it was announced that, from 1980, Britain would conform with a recommendation of the International Organization of Legal Metrology, reinforced by an EEC

Gay-Lussac	Sikes (Britain)	USA
100 (% pure alcohol)	175	200
77.5	135.6	155
75	131.3	150
60	105	120
57.14	100 (proof)	114.29
52.5	91.9	105
50	87.5	100 (proof)
48	84	96
45	78.7	90
43	75.2	86
40	70	80
37.1	65	74.3
28.6	50	57.1
22.9	40	45.7
0 (water)	0	0

directive, and adopt assessment and announcement of alcoholic strengths by percentage of volume. The system is effectively the same as Gay-Lussac, with one minor difference that is solely of technical importance

The abbreviated table of strength comparisons shows the logicality of Gay-Lussac, the comprehensibility of the

American system and the whimsicality of the outdated British. It is included here because the alcohol-by-volume indications on bottles sold in Britain will not happen overnight: bottles marked by the supplanted Sikes proofing will be around for a considerable time.

It may be significant that whilst M. Gay-Lussac had a Parisian street named after him, Mr Sikes was not similarly honoured in London.

Aspects of alcohol
A book on drink is incomplete if it does not mention the effects of alcohol, its claimed merits and alleged dangers.

The best known by far of efforts to deprive people of alcohol was Prohibition – to give it its unpopular name – in the USA. Most social historians will agree that the effects of this "great experiment" were disastrous and totally counter-productive of the good intentions of its progenitors. However, since it is still often discussed and its history has become blurred, the salient features are worth recalling.

Aurum liqueur by Dudovich

The temperance movement in the USA dates from the early nineteenth century, though not until 1869 was it given political muscle in the Prohibition party. The militant Women's Christian Temperance Union was founded in 1874. There were other bodies such as the powerful Anti-Saloon League, but there was considerable inter-organizational dissent between advocates of total abstinence (TT) and the outlawing of all alcohol and those who sought only to control strong spirits. In 1846 Maine had gone "dry", followed by the District of Colombia and the states of Kansas and North Dakota: other states were largely "dry" – at least officially. Of course, it was impossible to stop transit of liquor from adjacent "wet" states. During the First World War, the Prohibition movement gained much impetus and by 1918 over half the states were "dry". A successful resolution to amend the Constitution meant that a year later Prohibition would become federal law in all States whether they ratified or not. The Volstead Act, overriding President Wilson's veto on Prohibition, was passed by Congress in October 1919, bringing into effect the 18th Amendment. America was dry.

What then happened is too well documented to need recapitulation here. Suffice to say that sanity eventually replaced hysteria, and on 20 February, 1933, Congress resolved to repeal the 18th Amendment and passed the 21st, which restored to the individual states their rights to control the liquor trade within their own boundaries. As a matter of urgency this amendment was submitted to the states the very next day and was ratified with such alacrity that, with modest local exceptions, most citizens of the USA were in December 1933 again at liberty to have a legal drink.

Prohibition, of course, has been by no means the perquisite of the USA. The Soviet Union had prohibition of spirits from 1914 to 1925 and Finland until later. There is total prohibition in many Moslem countries – with or without exceptions for expatriates; Pakistan has clamped down on public drinking and some Indian states have moved towards prohibition.

There will inevitably be criminals who will take any risks to reap the rich rewards of supplying the illicit demand. Prohibition brought to modern American history a chapter of crime which still scars the country and was the foundation of many a great Mafia fortune: now men gamble with almost certain death to run alcohol into Saudi Arabia.

Anti-drink campaigns seem to run in phases, and tem-

Courvoisier cognac, advertised as a drink for the fashionable and wealthy, has always been popular among the British upper classes

"The Barmaid", as depicted in 1894. The taverns which replaced the sordid gin palaces were welcome extravaganzas of decorative glass, brass and wood

perance propaganda waxes and wanes for no apparent reason. Alcohol is an extremely easy target and abstainers find it a convenient scapegoat for industrial absenteeism, growing divorce rates, road casualties, moral decline or any other pet aversion. No doubt excessive drinking may be one factor in a host of modern *malaises* – but it is nothing new, nor is there any evidence that legislation can do anything to halt abuses. Every nation has a drinking problem amongst sections of its population, just as it may have narcotic or gambling problems. Education must be the only answer. Repression never works.

The USSR, for example, admits to a widespread drink problem, and in recent years outlets for vodka have been reduced and the price increased. These moves do not seem to have had any effect: unknown quantities of home-made spirit (*samogon*) are made. But except where fatalities, injuries or crime result, the USSR takes the humane view that drunkenness is a social misdemeanour not, as in some countries, a criminal offence.

Norway, on the other hand, shows up very low on any list of national alcohol consumption. A majority of Norwegian Members of Parliament are staunchly abstentionist: it is a quirk of democracy that a hard-drinking electorate can vote them into power. Outlets for liquor are few and licensing laws rigid. So it is officially admitted that one-third of spirits consumed are illegally distilled.

In Scotland there are areas where, through church influence, outlets for alcohol are scattered or non-existent. In these exist *bothans* – illegal booze-dens – and dry parishes have a much higher proportion of alcoholics, and, worse, of juvenile alcoholics, than the national average.

As to the medical aspect, suffice it to say that medical opinion is sharply divided. At one extreme, the famous American student of alcoholism, Dr Maurice Chafetz, said that ninety-five per cent of regular drinkers have no problem He maintained that alcoholism is indeed a problem, but not liquor itself: "It relaxes you, it heightens pleasure, and makes you feel good. . . ." Dr Chafetz went so far as to say that good alcohol in almost any amount would induce

A 1909 advertisement for
Schnapps, describing it as
"A pure, wholesome spirit
containing all the charms
of a palatable stimulant
with the beneficial effects
of a health tonic"

no harm in a healthy human body. The emphasis is on
"healthy", meaning mentally as well as physically.

At the other end of the scale, many medical authorities
totally condemn all alcohols and can produce massive case
histories to prove their point. However, the preponderance
of physicians approve, and use, alcohol in moderation, and
even recommend it in certain instances. It is possible to
take the table which best suits your side of the argument,
select whatever "evidence" meets your proposition and
"prove" conclusively either that alcohol is a poison and a
social evil or that it is wholly beneficial.

Stringent licensing, rationing, taxation have no more
real effect on actual consumption than does legislation.
They only change its pattern. To research the various
national and parochial licensing regulations is a fascinating experience, producing such delightful items of useless
information as its being illegal in Natchez, Mississippi, to
offer beer to an elephant. . . .

A few words on intemperance seem here to be in order.
He who has never experienced excess cannot appreciate
the true meaning of moderation. Occasional social over-
indulgence in alcoholic beverages, a common enough hap-
pening, does induce a morning-after sickness, which in
Anglo-Saxon is called a *hangover*. Prevention is best taken
care of by not drinking much on an empty stomach, by not
mixing too many different types of drink and by giving
preference to spirits diluted only by ice or water.

White spirits – gin, vodka, white rum, tequila – are
mildly less harmful in quantity than whisky, brandy or
dark rum as they contain fewer congenerics (see Whisky),
and white wine is marginally preferable to red.

Nature alone provides a cure. The body is suffering from
dehydration, and from oxygen deficiency caused by slower
respiration. To combat the symptoms, drink plenty of
water, breathe deeply and go back to sleep if you can.
Alternatively, old wives' tales abound and if you have faith
in any of them they may do you good. Fernet, drunk as an
aperitif by the Italians, is an esteemed specific, as is the
German Underberg. Though it may seem ridiculous to add
alcohol to a physique already unduly filled with it, many
drinkers believe in the "hair of the dog" as being curative:
that is, to have a stiff drink, maybe champagne (which
bucks you up, at least for a time) or, traditionally, the same
drink that caused the trouble.

A seventeenth-century
engraving of Dutch
peasants enjoying a drink
– probably genever

WHISKY

A further instance of the art nouveau influence that crept into Scotch whisky advertising in the early twentieth century

Whisky, or whiskey, is produced in a great many countries. The basic word derives from *aqua vitae*: and then, in this instance, by translation into *uisge beatha* and *usque-baugh*, and thus to *uisge, usky, wusky* – and whisky. Current fashion is that Scotch and Canadian whisky is always written thus, without the "e", American and Irish as *whiskey*, and other whiskies according to local whim, with the burgeoning Japanese industry generally opting for no "e". The spelling is often discussed, but is of no importance.

The origins of whisky are not really known, though it seems most likely that it was the Irish who first began distilling from cereals. In the fifth century AD, they invaded Scotland and took their knowledge with them.

The distinctive character of whiskies from Scotland, Ireland or the USA derives from the difference in ways of production, the type of grains and the qualities of the water used. Scotch is inimitable because only in Scotland does the spring water rise through red granite and then pass through peat moss country, and in the USA the three principal distilling centres are located where there are springs rising through limestone rock.

The protection granted to whisky varies greatly, and in some countries what passes for the product verges on the poisonous. In others, such as Australia, Spain and the Netherlands, quite satisfactory whisky is produced, although it can never reach the standard of the "real stuff".

Scotch is the most favoured, successful and well-known whisky; it is also subject to perpetual imitation, counterfeiting of labels, adulteration and all ingenious – or ingenuous – faking known to commerce. There is never a time when the vigilant Scotch Whisky Association has not got a law case going somewhere in the world, for Scotch is so popular and carries such enormous prestige that the rewards of fraud inevitably tempt the unscrupulous.

Illegal distilling has, in the last hundred years or more, been much less prevalent in Scotland than in Ireland. However, this old illustration from Cassells Magazine *shows two Highlanders resting with a saucer of (apparently) tea while their illicit spirit flows from a primitive still*

SCOTCH WHISKY

Whisky came to Scotland from Northern Ireland – along with Christianity and bagpipes – and all three were to suffer considerable change from their original form. Irish colonization of Scotland commenced around AD 500, but whisky was not introduced for another half-century when the craft of distillation became established in Ulster. Then it was brought to Scotland by Irish missionary monks, who established monasteries in the wake of their compatriots, who were evicting the native Picts.

The earliest known mention of "malt" occurred in 1494. *Usque-baugh* was used at the Court of King James IV in 1500. The production of it must have been well established by then, for in 1505 supervision of spirit-making was vested, for the Edinburgh district, in the Royal College of Surgeons. Although spirits were clearly considered, as elsewhere, essentially medicinal, the necessity for control indicated a known social use. The reason for the growth of domestic distilling in Scotland was most likely the dampness of the climate, which made it difficult to dry grain after a wet harvest. The best thing to do with the fortuitously fermenting grain was to produce a beer from it and, as knowledge spread, to concentrate this into a primitive whisky. Hollinshed, in 1578, published in his *Chronicles* a celebrated eulogy on *uisge*, allocating to it many virtues: "It sloweth age . . . helpeth digestion . . . abandoneth melancholie. . . ." No modern whisky-lover could hope to improve on his panegyric.

Whisky received its first, inevitable, accolade in 1644: the Scottish Parliament attempted to tax it. When a product is first taxed it has arrived. Naturally, this tax – at the appalling rate of seven shillings and sixpence per gallon – was rarely paid: a considerable fillip was given to profitable illicit distilling, and insobriety increased.

The fateful year 1688 – which had lasting repercussions on English drinking habits – also saw the birth of what might be called the first "branded" whisky in Scotland. One Duncan Forbes of Ferintosh, Ross-shire, supported the new King William III against supporters of the deposed James II. The latter attacked Forbes's distillery, but if they thought to harm him they achieved exactly the opposite. Two years later Forbes was relieved of obligation to pay duty in reward for his loyalty (or, from a Jacobite viewpoint, disloyalty) and Ferintosh *wusky* became legally cheap and therefore popular.

The union between Scotland and England in 1707 meant that a department concerned with excise duties was established, but it would have been indeed a brave agent who tried to collect tax from the operators of stills proliferating in the remote and dangerous Highlands. The savage crushing of the final rebellion of 1745, at Culloden, was a turning point. In the train of the military, who, to subjugate the Highlanders, built the first roads to penetrate the previously inaccessible mountains, came a host of excisemen, known as "gaugers". Though the Lowlands and towns were easier to police, not even there did the authorities have much success, and in the Highlands their writ scarcely ran at all. In 1777 there were eight lawful whisky stills in the Edinburgh area, and an estimated four hundred unlicensed ones.

By 1823 the situation had become anarchic. Although 14,000 illegal stills, or parts of stills – mostly of trivial size

– were discovered, these represented a mere fraction of the total. So the government accepted with grateful haste a proposition from the Duke of Gordon that he and his fellow landowners would themselves suppress illegal distilling throughout their vast estates, in return for a practical licensing and taxation system.

Scotland, and its whisky, had some good publicity in 1822 when King George IV paid a state visit. In Edinburgh he drank a dram, to much acclaim and with apparent relish, not realizing that it was contraband spirit. Two years later the first licence under the new regulations was taken out by George Smith of Glenlivet, on Speyside. He was ostracized by his neighbours, who deplored this kow-towing to the state, and for some time carried pistols.

George Smith accepted that a £10 licence and a tax of two shillings and threepence per gallon were not an oner-ous burden and he built the first large commercial distil-lery in Glenlivet. It was thought that the area had about two hundred illegal stills in operation (of which Smith had owned one or more until he became licensed). He pros-pered, and as the turmoil surrounding the new laws settled down, Smith's rivals themselves accepted the new regu-lations, and sought to cash in on the great reputation achieved by Smith's Glenlivet Malt.

The year after George Smith joined the side of the law, a grandson of a Highland chief who fell at Culloden, the immensely tall "Long" John Macdonald, opened the second big legal distillery, in the wild Ben Nevis region: he is commemorated in a modern blend. Gradually, more dis-tillers recognized the profits in legitimacy.

Illegal distilling continued for a long time – widespread but on a declining scale – but was virtually killed by the explosive growth of a real Scotch whisky industry. Illegal distilling is rare in Scotland today, compared with Ireland or parts of the USA – to say nothing of other countries.

The 1860s were the turning point for Scotch whisky. Firstly, the prohibition on selling whisky in bottle to Eng-land was lifted, and, much more importantly, blending was introduced commercially.

Blended whisky could never have developed but for the aforementioned continuous still. Its story, in relation to Scotch whisky, began in 1824, when John Haig built a distillery at Cameron Bridge. In 1827, he experimented successfully with an invention by his cousin, Robert Stein, himself an important distiller: this was the original con-tinuous still. When it was improved upon and patented by Aeneas Coffey in 1832, the Steins and Haigs did not seem to have been put out. They accepted the new still and achieved in combination a near monopoly of Lowland dis-tilling. Straight grain whisky, as such, enjoyed a good sale in those days: it is now a rarity in retail commerce, repre-sented by a single, hard-to-obtain brand: Choice Old Cameron Brig. When blending started to come into fashion, Haig's were in a prime position to supply the essential grain. Patent distillation also benefited from the repeal of the Corn Laws in 1846, which cheapened maize.

Credit for the commercial exploitation of blended whisky goes to Andrew Usher, a grain-whisky distiller who was associated with the famous George Smith of Glenlivet. By adding the pungent malt he gave character to his simpler grain, producing the initial blend, Usher's Green Stripe.

So there were now three distinct types of Scotch whisky – malt, grain and blended. Everything favoured the indus-try's expansion: Queen Victoria was the champion of all things Scottish, Sir Walter Scott's novels were all the rage, and the new industrial and financial plutocracy, and the older rich English aristocracy, were following the Queen's lead in buying, restoring, enlarging or building neo-baronial castles and hunting lodges (mansions). Not a few were discovering the merits of whisky, too. Then came the scourge of the *phylloxera* louse, which, by wrecking the vineyards of the Charente, eventually reduced to a trickle the cognac which had long been the spirituous favourite of the English upper classes.

In the early 1850s it would have been a wise man indeed who could have forecast the meteoric rise of Scotch whisky. Take John Dewar, an inconspicuous grocer in Perth, where he set up his modest business in 1846. By the 1860s he was blending whisky and within a few years had the confidence to bottle and label a blend with his own name, the first famous bottled brand. In the 1880s his two sons went to London to sell Dewar's Scotch. Both became peers and died multi-millionaires. From small beginnings, too, came John Walker, an enterprising general grocer and wine and spirit merchant in Kilmarnock. His son Alexander recognized, from his father's success in selling to ships' chandlers in Glasgow, the export potential of whisky; he went to London and soon established a world-wide whisky empire. "Teacher's" started in young William Teacher's early nineteenth-century grog-shops in Glasgow. James Buchanan's story is different only in that he came to London in 1879 as factor for a whisky firm. He introduced his own Buchanan Blend (a name revived in 1978) and by the 1880s he had world-wide distribution; in 1904 he registered an early non-family brand-name, Black & White. He, too, joined the peerage and left an immense fortune.

This resumé of how some of the great whisky houses were born indicates how comparatively recent is the global march of Scotch whisky. What all the Scotch whisky pioneers had in common was energy, faith in their product, integrity, a firm belief in private enterprise – and a sincere desire to become rich.

The single greatest and most successful force in Scotch whisky today, which also controls the world's biggest gin companies and much else besides, is the Distillers Company. This was set up in 1877 to regulate the business of the leading distillers in Scotland, and was strongly instrumental in ensuring the prosperity of blended Scotch whisky, at times threatened by the disapproval of both the old malt distillers and English bureaucracy.

Another threat to the progress of Scotch whisky came during the First World War. The better traditional malt whiskies had for a long time been known to benefit from maturing, though there was no legal requirement to mature any malt whisky. During the First World War, it was thought that workers in British munitions factories, earning money on a scale unknown to their fathers, were spending an

Unless one wishes to announce a whisky's pedigree, it is socially attractive to transfer the spirit to a decanter, especially if it is adorned with an antique silver label. Whisky, as opposed to wine, decanters are customarily similar to the one below

WHISKY

unduly large proportion of their new wealth on whisky (largely grain whisky). Governmental reaction was to decree, illogically, that *no* Scotch whisky should be sold until it had been matured in bond for at least three years. This cut off the supply of unmatured whisky from Scotland – malt, grain or blended. Anyone in England who felt the deprivation, and was not prepared to pay for costlier matured Scotch, simply turned to cheaper gin. The Scotch whisky companies were momentarily glum, yet this apparently stupid regulation in fact did them a huge service: it improved enormously the general standard of Scotch whisky, particularly blended. The subsequent story is simply one of steady growth.

The nature of Scotch

For all that it is manufactured, whisky starts in a very natural way. Barley, steeped in the wonderful water from a burn or spring, which is the precious possession of each distillery, begins to sprout. It is constantly turned to aerate it. This used to be a laborious hand-process performed by rows of men with shovels – a picturesque sight. The malting floors of the distilleries have now, for all but show purposes, disappeared. Now automated "saladins" turn the sprouting grain with exactitude, and ease. When the sprout is about as long as a thumbnail the grain is dried by peat-fuelled fires, the smoke lending an important characteristic to the final product.

The production of malt has been largely centralized, individual distillers specifying the exact type of malt and treatment their style of whisky demands. No one who has been near a Scottish malting house will forget the "peat reek" – an aroma which is a delicious foretaste of the whisky to come.

The dried malt is ground and unwanted elements removed: hot water is added to the malt in great vats and the mixture agitated with huge mechanized stirrers. A sweetish liquid (wort) results. What has happened is that an enzyme present in sprouting cereals converts the starch in the malted barley into sugar.

The wort is run off and cooled and the process is repeated several times until it has yielded all its sugar. Next, in

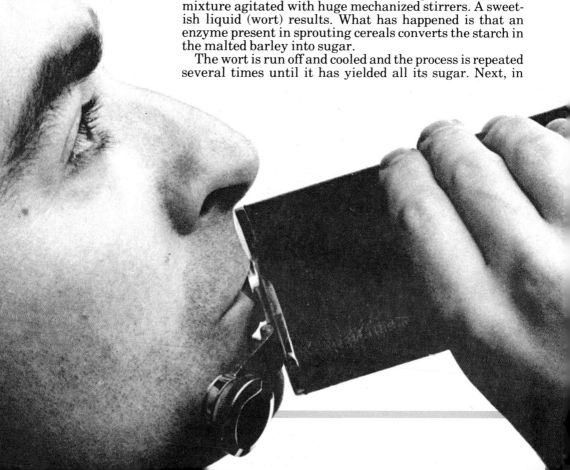

immense vessels, the wort receives yeast, composed of strains specially bred for the purpose. Violent fermentation commences which produces a sort of beer, the wash.

The next stage is to feed this alcohol-bearing fluid into a large pot-still – the "wash" still – whence comes a concentrate called by the ancient name "low wines", a weak and pungent spirit. This is charged into a second pot-still and the distillate from this is strong Scotch malt whisky.

The whisky has carried over from the wash the subtle flavours of burn-water, peat smoke, malted barley.... Each of well over a hundred malt distilleries has its distinctive style. A soft Lowland malt may be so different from a robust Islay that the untutored palate will instantly recognize the contrast, or the divergence of bouquets may be so slight that only an expert can tell them apart. Yet different they are, and it is the fact that there is such a unique range of whiskies with a single common factor that gives Scotch a lead over any other whisky.

Maturing

It was probably discovered at a fairly early stage that malt whisky improved in cask, for it was in cask that it was stored and transported, though served from flagons.

Distillations contain varying amounts of congenerics. These are strongly present in such products as Scotch malt whisky or cognac, produced by the pot-still; much less so, or almost non-existent, in the product of a continuous still (for example grain whisky). It is the congenerics that give the "natural" flavour and character to distillations.

Though grain whisky contains far fewer congenerics than malt, it, too, improves during the obligatory minimum of three years' maturing. Many malts – and some grains – are matured well beyond the minimum period. Opinions differ on the ideal age for a fine malt: perhaps fifteen years would represent a consensus of expert belief. Though a few would go for twenty years, or even longer, it is generally held that after that time the whisky would start to go downhill and tend to become "woody".

Whilst the character of Scotch rests in malts, it is on blends that the tremendous popularity of Scotch whisky relies. A good blend will contain around fifty-fifty malt and grain, but there are excellent whiskies with a higher proportion of grain. The number and age of malts employed in a blend is equally variable: twenty-five is about the norm. On the other hand, just one rather pungent malt could suffice. The blend with probably the highest number of constituent malts (Black & White) has over sixty.

A high number of malts does not itself make for quality, but it eases the task of maintaining an unchanging taste pattern. The blenders in whisky companies are immensely important. On their judgement and skill depend the quality and consistency of their houses' brands.

Malt whisky will have some natural colour, taken on during its sojourn in cask. Grain whisky has very little. If the age of a Scotch whisky appears on the label, it means the actual cask age in the case of a single malt, and the age of the youngest whisky in the instance of a vatted malt or a blend.

AMERICAN WHISKEY

For most people, the description "American whiskey" is virtually synonymous with Bourbon. It is protected by a 1964 Act of Congress as a "distinctive product of the United States". There are twenty-nine other legally defined styles of American whiskey – but they have not the same Congressional cachet, excellent as some are.

A foreigner is entitled to be curious as to why such an important whiskey should carry the name of a French monarchical dynasty. Bourbon's origins are in fact more clerical than regal. Its history is precisely and attractively coincident with that of the USA. In 1789, the year of George Washington's inauguration as first president, the Rev. Elijah Craig, a Baptist minister of seemingly very worldly pretensions for one of his calling, commenced distilling at Georgetown, Virginia (later Kentucky). So there was a kingly connection, the settlement being named for the English sovereign, the hated George III. However, more important in the event was Georgetown's situation in Bourbon county. It was that name which endured.

This was not the first, if it was the most lasting, distillation in the country: the Dutch were distilling well over a century earlier in their New Amsterdam (New York). It was later recorded that they made whiskey, but it seems more likely they would have tried to repeat in the New World the spirit they had given the Old – gin. Other early settlers were the Irish and the Scottish, who were certainly familiar with the art of distilling. The chances are they made good use of home-grown corn, rye, barley and wheat.

American whiskey was not to have an easy adolescence. The new nation, which had been born of dislike of alien taxation, was not slow to impose its own, and placed an impost on distillates: the legislators could have profited by a look at Scotland. This led to the "whiskey rebellion" of 1794. Troops had to be sent to quell this revolt, with the result that they were introduced to whiskey. The more enterprising distillers, who had no intention of paying a cent to Washington, upped stakes and moved on beyond the reach of the authorities, easy enough then, or retired with their stills into inaccessible mountain hideouts, where the troops or excisemen had little chance – rather as happened in Scotland. Thus was established a fine tradition of illicit distilling which has never died, particularly in Kentucky, which flourished under Prohibition and is still reasonably strong.

Bourbon's principal home remains Kentucky, although it is also produced in California, Georgia, Illinois, Indiana, Ohio and Pennsylvania. Its production is strictly controlled: Bourbon must be made from a mash containing not less than fifty-one per cent maize (corn), and the spirit must come from the still at not above 160 proof US (eighty per cent alcohol). It is usually distilled at a lower strength, and must be matured in new casks. (This helps Scotland by providing good casks only once used.) These factors, plus the character of the mash, make Bourbon a rather highly flavoured whiskey.

It was long considered that the manufacturing processes by which Bourbon has to be distilled and matured militated against its commercial growth, particularly overseas, and

in the domestic market caused it to suffer against lighter Scotch and Canadian whisky. After strenuous lobbying, the American Distilling Company obtained the right to distil a whiskey at over 160 (but under 190) proof and, particularly, to be able to mature it in used casks and still have the whiskey "bear a conventional age statement": that had not previously been permitted. In 1972, American straight "light whiskey", after four years' maturing, was introduced with a flourish of trumpets. But the subsequent sales were not music to the producers' ears. A great deal of the new whiskey had to go for blending. Bourbon drinkers stayed with the main line; those who preferred lighter styles with Scotch or Canadian; the rye drinkers remained faithful.

"Straight" Bourbon is the product of a single distillery in one year and is unblended with other distillations. That labelled as having been "bottled in bond" carries some extra status and the term may only be applied to straight whiskies. "Blended straight" Bourbon is all Bourbon, but from more than one distillery. "Blended" Bourbon (not "straight") must contain at least fifty per cent Bourbon: if the proportion is less, the word Bourbon may not be used.

Rye is another distinctive quality American whiskey; with rye substituted for maize. The regulations pertaining to it are similar to those for Bourbon, but rye is usually blended. Some confusion may be caused by the fact that colloquially "rye" is often used, particularly in eastern states, as a generic term for whiskey, and "Bourbon" may be equally loosely employed in the south and west.

For "sour mash" whiskey the fermentation comes from the residue of an initial fermentation, which includes malted barley along with corn and rye. This makes for a very full-flavoured and superior whiskey – and a costlier one. The most notable of this is the special Tennessee whiskey, which proudly disdains the Bourbon title. There are only two distilleries in the state, including the oldest in the USA, Jack Daniels's.

At the age of twelve, in 1860, Jack Daniels went to work at a local distillery owned by Dan Call: three years later he had been elevated to the position of Call's business partner. After the Civil War, Call decided to give up the whiskey business on religious grounds and the distillery was handed over to the young Jack Daniels.

One secret of Jack Daniels whiskey is the fresh spring water employed, which comes from a cave in

the limestone cliff nearby. Some of the production processes too, are the same now as they were over a hundred years ago. The "sour mash" from this distillery is uniquely filtered through sugar maple charcoal: a process which owes its origins, it is said, to the "moonshine" made in the mountains by slaves and purified by this method. In any event, as applied today, the filtration removes much of the "corny" taste and improves the spirit before maturing.

Corn whiskey is made from at least eighty per cent maize and must be matured for a minimum two years – against four years for true Bourbon or rye – and aged casks may be used. It is often sold at higher strength than the 100 proof US customary for Bourbons.

The largest-selling type of all is simple blended whiskey, without any other description (such as Bourbon, rye or corn). Though the better brands will have a higher proportion, this need contain no more than twenty per cent 100 proof two-year-old whiskey of any legal type. The remainder is neutral spirit which does not require maturing.

Seven Crowns American whiskey is the top selling spirit in the USA and has been the leading American brand for thirty years. It is a product of the Seagram Company – the largest producer and marketer of spirits in the world.

Production of illicit "moonshine" whiskey remains considerable, though it has declined in recent years. In 1968 the estimate by the American Distilled Spirit Council put the output of "moonshine" at thirty-six million gallons, or sixteen per cent of the spirit sold legally. This was far from the peak of illegal production. Owing to the increased affluence of the drinking public and the decrease in local rural "dry" areas – and possibly to more intensive action by the law officers – in the next decade "moonshining" fell dramatically and is now probably not above eight million gallons. However, these are mere estimates: bootleggers do not hasten to supply statistics. "Moonshine" can be good pot-still whiskey, just as Irish poteen can be, but both suffer from lack of maturation, a deficiency which usually has disastrous results on the consumer the following day. Also, some "moonshine" is deplorable stuff from the start and has lent its name to any legal whiskey which enjoys, deservedly or not, a low reputation. Colloquial words to describe "moonshine" include "panther sweat", "tarantula juice", "fighting soup" and "pop-skull".

The seamy side is best forgotten. After all, the USA has the largest spirits market, and industry, in the world and produces many noble, highly distinctive whiskies, worthy of a place in the pantheon of the finest spirits.

CANADIAN WHISKY

In Quebec towards the close of the eighteenth century, the only spirit that was being manufactured there was rum, and not very much of it. It was soon to dwindle and be superseded by whisky production. Thanks to the efforts of a handful of determined distillers in the opening decades of the nineteenth century it snowballed into a thriving industry. By the 1850s there were some hundreds of distillers throughout the country (let alone the profusion of illicit stills that always flourish in a pastoral and thirsty society). Two of the biggest names to emerge at this period were those of Hiram Walker and Joseph Seagram (the son of an English immigrant).

The most important grain used in making the mash for Canadian whisky is corn (maize). But some rye and malted barley are also employed, so that the final drink has "a little something for everyone". There are some of the qualities of Bourbon and of rye whiskey, together with a hint of Scotch and a memory of Irish. Elsewhere Canadian whisky has been described as a "compromise"; not, of course, in a perjorative sense but in an attempt to explain its character. Though not as heavy as Bourbon, it lacks the aroma of a well-blended Scotch. Quite often (but erroneously) it is described as rye whiskey. Canadian whisky is a distinctive product in its own right and, unlike some lesser American whiskey, is never of anything but consistently high quality. State supervision of production is remarkably rigorous.

Canadian whisky received a big bonus during the Prohibition era in the USA. It poured across the border and many Americans – particularly residents of states along the 49th Parallel – acquired a taste for Canadian whisky: at least one famous Canadian company owes much of its success to bootlegging. It now outsells Scotch in nearly half the USA and is a worldwide export. There are five leading distillers with over a century's experience and some fifteen of more recent origin.

The continuous distillation process predominates, which is another factor contributing to the lightness of Canadian whisky. Virtually all brands are well "married" blends. The distilling process ensures that the spirit is virtually free of the congenerics (or impurities) which form part of the character of Scotch, for example. Second rectification of the "high wine" (the alcohol left in the condenser at the end of the first distillation stage) renders the spirit so pure that it could almost be turned into vodka.

The new whisky is stored in old Bourbon barrels or new white oak barrels and matured for a minimum of three years. Because the whisky is so light and pale in colour, at the end of the maturing process a small percentage of rye whisky is added, for more volume, along with just enough caramel to darken it (these are the only legal additives allowed). The whisky is then ready for sale; some is put back into barrel and may be aged for up to eighteen years, though six or eight years is more usual.

Canadian whisky is peculiarly suited to mixed drinks, if a trifle bland taken neat. Most whisky is sold at 70° proof, and recently 65° proof spirit has appeared on the market. It appears particularly well attuned to growing modern taste for spirits without too marked a flavour.

IRISH WHISKEY

This is certainly the oldest of whiskies. Some 800 years ago, the Book of Leinster recorded that after a feast at Dundadheann, near Bushmills in the north, the guests, who had been imbibing the local *uisge beatha*, set out for Louth on the east coast. Staggering around, they came to their senses far south in County Limerick.

As in Scotland later, Irish distilling left the monasteries and became a cottage industry: anyone could make rough whiskey without interference. Henry VIII, not caring for this freedom of enterprise by his Irish subjects, promulgated a law to restrict distilling to licensed places only, whereupon his viceroy in Ulster promptly granted himself a monopoly. In 1661, a tax on whiskey was imposed: even at only fourpence a gallon there was not much chance of collection. A century later, when administration had improved, it was reckoned that at least a third of stills in use were still unlicensed. Gradually, as in Scotland, some order was established, and as the more powerful distilleries increased their hold on the market, smaller ones were absorbed or disappeared. Eventually, in Eire, only three great distilleries remained – John Jameson & Son (founded 1780), John Power & Son (1791) and Cork Distilleries Co. (an amalgamation formed in 1867). In 1966 they combined as United Distillers of Ireland.

Irish whiskey is made from a mash of malted and unmalted barley with some wheat, rye and, uniquely, oats. The wash is distilled three times by pot-still. It is a fairly pungent whiskey, and though the law requires only three years' maturation, by tradition it has at least seven.

At one time most whisky drunk in England was Irish. But in the past century it has been almost wholly superseded by Scotch. Yet Irish whiskey is still very much in the first league: it deserves to be, for its high quality and distinctive character, and because Ireland gave whiskey to the world.

Northern Ireland drinks much whiskey from the Republic but also has its own style and its own malt distillery. *Uisge beatha*, as mentioned above, was being made at Bushmills, in County Antrim, a very long time ago: in the thirteenth century a local chieftain gave it to his warriors before they went into battle. The malting process came into use at the Bushmills distillery in 1590, and a whiskey akin to that is made today. Old Bushmills was being sent to America and the West Indies by 1784. Old Bushmills de luxe ("Bush Black") is a remarkable "liqueur whiskey" (not to be confused with a whiskey liqueur).

Lastly, there is poteen – variously spelt *potheen*, *potsheen* and *potyen*, and usually pronounced "potcheen". This illicit spirit is widely produced, particularly in the west of the Republic of Ireland. Poteen can be excellent whiskey. Strong poteen stands beside the best of any immature whiskey. It is, however, this immaturity that is its fault. As with "moonshine", such distillations sometimes taste splendid – but the after-effects can be nauseating. An effort was once made to market a legal whiskey described as poteen. It was no great success: it lacked glamour.

JAPANESE WHISKY

Not long ago scant attention was given by whisky-drinkers to Japanese whisky. It is now very much a force to be reckoned with. Long gone are the days when such Japanese whisky as was sold was largely bottled to look – though it did not then taste – as much like Scotch as possible, with such marvellously naïve descriptions as "pressed from the finest Scottish grapes". Things are very different today. Though Scotch malt has been blended into some Japanese whisky, and production methods, materials and taste style are akin to those of Scotland, it is as *Japanese* whisky that brands are now clearly labelled and promoted. Japanese tastes changed dramatically after the Second World War, in emulation of American customs. They took to Scotch, less to the preferentially taxed Bourbon, and then to their own improving whisky. Immensely popular in Japan itself, Japanese whisky is increasing sales in the Far East and it is to be found in more outlets every year in the USA and throughout the world.

Whisky has been made in Japan since 1923, by a company (founded in 1899) which is now the giant Suntory organization – a family firm. Its only serious rival started distilling in 1934. Suntory has some sixty-five per cent of the growing Japanese market for whisky, selling well over 300 million bottles a year. There are over a dozen Suntory brands. The quality Suntory "Old" is the most popular, and The Whisky, at about $250 a bottle, the most prestigious.

An untutored palate may find it hard to differentiate between the best Japanese whisky and blended Scotch. What it still lacks are intangibles – tradition, imagery, world-famous names. It is heavily protected in its home market, which has given it a commercial base for export.

OTHER WHISKIES

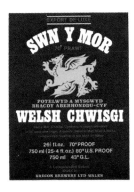

One oddity which deserves marks for trying has crept into the field. This is Welsh whisky (*Cymraeg chwisgi*). Whisky was produced in Wales in the last century, but then disappeared. A new version, with a small production for local consumption, was put on the market in 1978 under the brand-name Swn y don (Sound of Waves).

Less curious, and infinitely more viable commercially, are the whiskies of Australia. Whisky was first made there during the shortages of the First World War: during the Second it took on a much greater dimension. Australian whisky is an excellent spirit, produced principally in Victoria, in the Melbourne region, where the barley and water lend themselves to a whisky as akin to Scotch as any forbidden that proud label. New Zealand whisky is of much more recent origin, but is also of high quality.

The Netherlands makes good whisky which some people aver is closer in style to Irish than to Scotch: a long tradition of fine distilling ensures excellent quality. The same applies to the best of Spanish whisky, though the comparison here is more likely to be with American styles.

Portrait of a "typical" brandy drinker

BRANDY

The origin of the widely used word "brandy" to describe distillations from wine is almost certainly from the old Dutch *brandewijn* – "burned", that is to say, distilled wine – typically corrupted by the English to "brandywine" and subsequently shortened to brandy. Some authorities give the similar German *branntwein* (*weinbrand*) as the source.

In seventeenth-century Britain, any distillate was called brandy; even gin was included under that heading. Only later did the word come to refer almost exclusively to spirit from a wine base. In France, home of the two greatest grape distillates, brandy is well understood, though the product is technically just a division of the comprehensive description *eau de vie*. A great French house describes its product as the brandy, not the cognac, of Napoleon.

The most important by far of German distillers from wine call their spirit by the name brandy, and there are few parts of the world where, despite other linguistic descriptions, the term brandy is not recognized – though not necessarily as a wine-based alcohol. For brandy is colloquially used to cover distillations from a number of fruits other than the grape – and very good some of them are.

Indifferent, or frankly terrible, brandy is not necessarily the result of inefficient distillation but also comes from the use of bad wine, or the wrong type, and particularly from

An early twentieth-century advertisement for Courvoisier "Napoleon's Brandy". Even though the Emperor's patronage of cognac was never certain, the myth persists and many of the great cognac houses have a Napoleon grade – usually their most expensive

The heroic dogs of St Bernard, who rescued travellers lost in the snow, traditionally carried a small barrel of brandy round their necks

too short maturing – or none at all. No grape brandy will be attractive without adequate cask age: it may be positively harmful, or produce some unpleasant after-effects.

Sound, sometimes great, brandy is made in particular in France, Germany, Spain, Greece, Cyprus, Australia, the USA and South Africa. The best is often reserved for local consumption and does not find a world market; an obvious exception is France. There is an enormous production of grape spirit in South America, but standards vary greatly; that of Peru enjoys the highest reputation. The *ponche* (an all-purpose herb-flavoured brandy) of Spain is repeated in many forms in Latin America.

Inevitably, distillation from wine takes place wherever wine is made in quantity. In a few countries, such as Britain, brandy is legally defined – but in most it is not, and many cover various distillations or flavoured neutral spirits. We shall be dealing with many brandies; first must come the undisputed king amongst wine spirit.

COGNAC

The practice of condensing for shipment overseas the wine of the Charente region – popular but rather thin – by a primitive form of distillation became established as early as the fifteenth century. These would have been rough "low wines" with an alcohol content of around twenty-five per cent. The idea was not so much to produce a spirit as to save on casks and shipping space and to preserve the none-too-robust wine on long voyages. The addition of water at the receiving end would have restored the wine to something like its original state, but probably most of it was drunk as weak spirit. It would have been poor, feeble stuff by modern standards, almost certainly taken with some palatable additions such as honey or herbs.

Not until the seventeenth century, following the great improvements in commercial distilling initiated by the Dutch, did an unknown distiller in the Cognac region treat his "low wines" to a second distillation. By this means the "soul of the wine" was truly extracted and a strong wine spirit, redolent of the grape, first saw light in France: Cognac brandy was born. Incarceration in wood for export showed the benefits of maturing.

French brandy became enormously popular in England amongst those who could afford it, and neither wars nor taxes stopped its flow. It was the mainstay of the flourishing smuggling trade of the south and west of England. The Scots, traditional allies of France, also took to cognac, despite their own splendid native spirit. Of course, there was originally no definition of the Cognac region: it just happened that the best French brandy came from there and thus attracted the name of the central town. It would have been as viable to name it Jarnac brandy, after the more charming second town, which shelters three notable *grande marque* houses, but cognac it became and remains. The names of some other brandies – *coñac*, *kanyak*, and the like – pay tribute to cognac's supremacy. However, most countries, by law or tradition, reserve the word cognac for the genuine French product.

In the mid-nineteenth century, when cognac had established a worldwide reputation, it happened that two friends, a geologist and a spirit expert, visited the area to test a theory. The geologist believed that by analysis of soil he could say in which ground would grow grapes whose wine would be most suitable for distillation. The spirit expert was able to confirm his companion's findings. This was eventually the basis for the very strict demarcation of the carefully defined Cognac region's six divisions. These are, in descending order of prestige, the Grande Champagne, Petite Champagne, Borderies, Fins Bois, Bons Bois and Bois Ordinaires.

The use of the word *champagne* has caused a certain amount of confusion. It has absolutely nothing to do with the wine of the same name. People will sometimes refer to a "champagne cognac", as if conferring a special status on brandy: there is no such thing as a "champagne cognac". *Champagne* in a cognac context is a local derivation from the Latin *campania*, an open space, a field or a small district. It is a survival from Roman occupation of the region.

Though the Grande Champagne is rated more highly, the quality of wine from the Petite Champagne is virtually identical. A label carrying the words "Grand Champagne" denotes a cognac solely from that area. Unblended Petite Champagne wine is comparatively rare. Fine Champagne is not a zone: it is a cognac containing a mixture from both *champagnes* with not less than fifty per cent *grande*. To justify the word cognac, a brandy must be solely a product of the region, made in accordance with the strict regulations controlling size and type of stills and many other details.

The wine of Cognac is harsh and acid. One could make a general rule that good wine makes poor brandy. A little Cognac wine is drunk locally, but this must be from pride or hereditary taste. The harvest is fairly late. The newly made wine is run into stone, concrete or metal vats. Maturation is avoided: the wine must retain its original attributes, for it is these that give cognac its unique character. Distillation starts immediately and continues until the following spring. As with Scotch, cognac is double-distilled in much smaller copper pot-stills than those used in Scotland. The first distillation of "low wines", *brouilli*, contains about twenty-eight per cent alcohol. The *brouilli* may be made in stills containing as much as 100 hectolitres, but the second distillation, the *bonne chauffe*, must come from an *alambic charentais* (maximum 25 hectolitres) and must not contain more than seventy-two per cent alcohol.

The new cognac is put into casks of French oak. The main supply is traditionally from the Limousin forests, but the very different Troncais oak – a tall, comparatively slender tree – is much used nowadays.

The casks of cognac are stored in *chais*. The old *chais* – and some are very old – are low buildings with earthen floors, well ventilated. The idea is to keep them as cool and damp as possible. Modern *chais* are lofty, with casks stored on high racks (made possible by the use of fork-lift trucks). Both serve equally well, though romance is all on the side of the ancient *chais*, their roofs covered with a peculiar

moss that feeds on the evaporation of the spirit – the fabled "angels' share". The air is fairly dry and summer temperatures high, and evaporation is considerably greater than in Scotland. The holder of the biggest maturing stocks, Martell, estimates that it loses the equivalent of two million bottles a year – enough to make many angels happy!

At the annual stocktaking, evaporation is compensated for by the topping up of casks with spirit from newer ones, building up average age. Some fine cognac will be left to mature unblended, though usually "refreshed" with spirit of similar age and type to keep the cask full. Opinions vary, but fifty years may be taken as the maximum age for a brandy to rest in wood. Very old cognac is disgorged from cask and kept in glass containers in what brand-owners aptly called their *paradis*.

New casks are seasoned by being first filled with lesser grades and only when they are well impregnated with spirit, and are unlikely to impart excessive tannin to their contents, are they used.

Virtually all cognac sold is a blend of brandy of different ages and from several zones and distillers. Higher grades will be improved by the addition of a proportion of venerable spirit from the *paradis*: it is a virtue of such brandy that it can bring an almost miraculous change to a blend.

Under French law a cognac may not be sold with a date. However, some Grande Champagne — and occasionally Petite – from leading houses is shipped in cask to Britain a year or so after the vintage from which it was distilled. After long maturing – say fifteen years – a sample will be submitted to the shipper. If he approves, labels sufficient to cover the bottling of however much brandy remains in the casks will be issued, and this may then be sold as so-and-so's cognac of such-and-such vintage. It should also carry the name of the bottler, and the years it was landed and bottled. It is the difference between the last two dates which indicates the cask age. Like any other spirit, cognac cannot improve in bottle. By bottle age it may acquire

A glass of fine brandy – particularly cognac or armagnac – will benefit from being gently warmed by folding into the palm of one's hand. It should not be heated by flame. Lesser brandies scarcely deserve such treatment

rarity value: nothing more. It can quite easily deteriorate. Vintage (in trade terms "early-landed") cognac, almost exclusively a British phenomenon, attracts prestige.

The Napoleonic myth persists. A number of great brands of cognac include a "Napoleon" grade – usually, though not always, their costliest. The fickle public having attached special magic to the imperial title, the cognac-producer can hardly be blamed for pandering to it. Even Hine – whose English founder, Thomas Hine, suffered persecution during the Napoleonic wars – has had to succumb to the pressures of the market-place and introduce a "Napoleon" for certain sales areas. This aspect of the cognac business is wrapped in mystery. Napoleon was an abstemious man, though his native Corsica, and Burgundy, were to claim him as favouring their wines. The nearest there is to a source for the Bonaparte legend is the presentation to him of a cask of cognac, in 1811, to celebrate the birth of his son, the unfortunate King of Rome. After Napoleon's fall, a quantity of this appears to have been sent to England where it was later bottled as Fine Champagne Impériale 1811, with an embossed "N" on the shoulder of the bottle. Various editions of this, and also of "Napoleon" vintages 1805 and 1809, turn up. They may be truly antique – or counterfeits. In terms of commerce, there is no such thing as a Napoleon I cognac. It would be most certainly undrinkable.

There are several points to ponder when looking at a bottle of cognac, beyond those we have already mentioned. Some houses use three stars to signify their standard grade. This does not mean it is three years old – minimum age for the important British market – for the average age of a reputable cognac of this grade will be higher: it is simply a convention. If there are more stars on the label, that is a brand-owner's whim but of no actual meaning – though, perhaps, with hope that the untutored consumer will read it as indicating a greater age than a three-star. Some brands have rejected the stellar system in favour of invented names. The widely used VSOP title stands for "Very Special (or Superior) Old Pale" and stems from the time about a century ago when cognac changed from the heavier style – in flavour and colour – favoured by upper-class Englishmen to the paler type of today. It denotes a grade that is more aged than the same company's three-star or similar. It should contain no brandy that has been less than four years in wood. A number of other descriptions are employed, mostly peculiar to individual firms, and they must be learned by experience. Cognac-drinkers will also grow to prefer the products – in different grades – of the various *grandes marques*: there are not that many. These are the firms on whose traditions and reputation rest the integrity and quality of cognac.

Old cognac that has cork as a closure must be kept stored upright or the spirit will attack the cork and be ruined. It will over many years, even if the cork is sealed, lose some strength by evaporation, but without harmful effect.

When opened, an old cognac should not be kept indefinitely in bottle or decanter if there is a good deal of air space: the remainder should be transferred to a smaller vessel. These considerations do not apply to grades drunk with additives, which are probably going to be more quickly used: of "three-star" cognacs perhaps only Delamain and Hine deserve drinking neat.

It was certainly of cognac that Dr Johnson was thinking when he wrote: "Claret is the liquor for boys; port for men; but he who aspires to be a hero must drink brandy."

ARMAGNAC

In the Armagnac region, home of the second great French brandy, they cherish the creation of Alexandre Dumas: the immortal musketeer d'Artagnan, which character was based on a nobleman, Charles de Batz, born around 1615 at the Château de Castelmore, near Lupiac. He was a true Gascon hero and according to legend (though it seems unlikely) an early patron of armagnac brandy. Consequently, he remains the champion of armagnac; there is even an association of armagnac producers and supporters called La Compagnie des Mousequetaires de l'Armagnac.

Indeed, no Gascon admits to armagnac as second to cognac – except in quantity – and firmly believes his brandy to be the premier, with cognac a comparatively modern upstart. This is certainly true of the Marquis de Montesquiou, a descendant of de Batz, whose name pertains to a notable brand, and who has done much to promote armagnac.

Here, we are in wilder, more picturesque country than the calm Charente, and this is reflected in the quality of armagnac brandy. It is a more powerfully flavoured spirit and its makers are highly individualistic. The manufacture of armagnac remains largely a cottage-industry, less commercialized in modern terms than its successful rival to the north, less organized – and, to many, the product therefore retains a special charm.

A feature of armagnac is that it is distilled only once (cognac uses double distillation) and at a strength not exceeding sixty-three per cent alcohol, and usually considerably lower. This is achieved in a still which is halfway between a pot-still and a continuous still. Thus a great deal of flavour is carried over to the spirit, producing a brandy of strongly aromatic flavour and with a large quantity of congenerics. Therefore armagnac requires extra-long maturation – in casks of Gascon oak – and an average age in excess of ten years is common. As the late Jean Monnet, architect of the EEC and a very patient man, said: "To make brandy you need patience." That is very true of the finest armagnac, yet the distiller's patience is the drinker's reward: at its best, old armagnac need fear no adverse comparisons with any cognac and many connoisseurs will drink no other brandy.

In the Armagnac region can occasionally be seen the itinerant distiller, who moves from small farm to small farm distilling what wine has been grown there. The main grape variety for the armagnac base wine is St Emilion (which is also the preferred cognac grape), but cultivated in the sand and clay of Armagnac as compared with Cognac's chalky soil. By no means all of this wine will find its way to the market in the flat flask-shaped bottles which are a hallmark of armagnac: it will go to be made into the better liqueurs – to name but one, Trappistine, akin to better-known Bénédictine but based on armagnac rather than cognac.

The grade designations are similar to those used to describe cognacs, but the age of armagnac will in each case be markedly higher. Inevitably, armagnac is compared to cognac, but it is a distinctively different brandy – the noble product of a proud people whose comparative disdain for the exploitation inherent in modern marketing is admirable, and typical of the remote, *bon vivant*, friendly and historic land in which they dwell.

OTHER GRAPE BRANDIES

Frequently of commercial importance, though lacking the glamour or finesse attached to cognac or armagnac, lesser grape brandies are found throughout the world, for any country that produces wine in quantity also distils from it.

The issue has been confused, particularly in Britain, by the (quite legal) borrowing by other grape brandies of terms associated in the consumer's mind with cognac. One might therefore see on a supermarket's liquor store's shelves something like "Du Plex ***** Superior Rare Old VSOP Fine Napoleon de luxe Brandy, Produce of Ruritania", carrying a splendid portrait of the emperor and an attractive "N" seal. Standing beside it could be an excellent *** cognac of repute at a considerably higher price, *caveat emptor*. Many is the customer who will select the former and discover, to his chagrin, that he has purchased nothing better than a rough, coloured *eau de vie*.

The word *fine* itself presents difficulties. Clearly, in Fine Champagne it has a legal definition: if a sound cognac is described simply as *fine* it indicates a good grade but makes no exceptional claim. However, in a bistro, "*une fine*", colloquially, is an order for an *eau de vie* of any sort. On the other side of the coin, various French regions produce *eau de vie du vin* of quality; for example Fine de Champagne, Fine de la Marne. France produces a host of grape brandies ranging from the more than tolerable to the frankly terrible. Low on the scale comes *marc* (officially *eau de vie de marc*). Most of this is poor spirit, but to add to our semantic confusion, Marc de Bourgogne and Marc de Champagne enjoy the high regard of many.

German brandy, almost a monopoly of Asbach, is made from a variety of imported wines, for those of the country are too good and costly to turn into spirit. It may be drunk as a "liqueur", but is better in long, mixed drinks, being thin and faintly sweet. German brandy from wine residue is called *trester*: it is usually treated as a short, chilled schnapps drink.

Italian brandy has similar characteristics to that of Germany. Stock is the best known and is fairly popular in the USA. Spirit distilled from the residue of Italy's enormous wine production is called *grappa* (a word also used in California), and is very popular.

Spanish and Greek brandies are made in large quantities. Basically they share a touch of sweetness and tend to be well caramelized for smoothness. Greece resinates brandy to turn it into an aperitif called *mastika*.

South Africans are great brandy-makers and drinkers. It is a sound, dry spirit, excellent for long, cooling drinks and with a few aged specimens deserving respect. The industry is old-established, and its traditions of Dutch expertise provide firm foundations for fine distilling.

Mexico distils a great deal of brandy: it is even more popular than the national distillate tequila.

In South America's wine-producing countries an enormous amount of distillation from wine is done. The product attracts the overall title *pisco*. It comes in every sort of quality, the best coming from Peru.

California has a huge grape-brandy production. This includes some splendid spirit, on the delicate side, which is

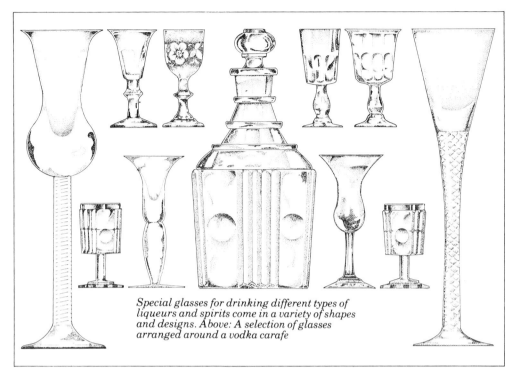

Special glasses for drinking different types of liqueurs and spirits come in a variety of shapes and designs. Above: A selection of glasses arranged around a vodka carafe

perfect for the mixed drinks in which Americans excel. If an American does relish an after-dinner brandy he will most likely turn to France. He is fortunate that for more commonplace occasions he has a comprehensive choice of excellent domestic grape distillations.

FRUIT BRANDIES

Apart from true grape brandies several well-known products, which have nothing to do with wine, attract the description "brandy". Calvados, Normandy's apple brandy, has strong affinities with the applejack of the USA. Distilled from cider, it tends to be rather tart and rough unless well aged. Thoroughly matured calvados is delicious — it has a smooth warming inner fire — and costly.

Often referred to as "plum brandy", *slivovitz* is the general spirit of central Europe and the Balkans: that of Yugoslavia is the best-known overseas.

Cherry brandy is a cordial liqueur and *kirsch* is sometimes confused with it. *Kirsch* is a proper distillate from cherries. This spirit comes from the Black Forest area of Germany and adjacent parts of France and from Switzerland.

There are many fruit brandies (*alcools blancs* in French terminology). These are of two types – those directly distilled from fermented juice (like *kirsch*) and those where an *eau de vie* has infused into it the essence of a particular fruit. Poire William is a much-esteemed variety of the pear brandies: one style has a pear grown in the bottle, a painstaking business. However, strawberry, bilberry, blackberry – in fact any berry – may be used, or a mixture of them. The oddest must be that from the holly-berry (*eau de vie de baie de houx*), otherwise considered poisonous.

GIN

This early nineteenth-century cartoon was entitled "The lure of the gin palace". The emaciated drinker is in marked contrast to the healthy appearance of the landlady – growing fat on the weakness of her customers

It is impossible to truly appreciate an important spirit without some knowledge of its historical background. Such information adds positively to the enjoyment of drinking. Gin itself is so bound up in social history that it would be easy to dwell at length on that aspect alone.

The introduction of gin as a commercial product may be dated with unusual precision, for it undoubtedly happened when Lucas Bols founded his distillery in Schiedam in 1575. The town's name became synonymous with gin, though "Schiedam" is not often used nowadays as a description of a Dutch gin, which is called *genever* in Holland, usually *geneva* elsewhere and sometimes "Hollands".

Gin was, of course, being produced in the Netherlands prior to the advent of Bols – now a name of global importance in spirits, liqueurs and related products. But until the second half of the sixteenth century distillation, or at least fine distillation of strong spirit, remained mostly confined to the monastery or the primitive medical world, which was still more involved with alchemy than science: a lot was known about herbs. The Dutch were well to the fore in producing ardent spirits and it is to Franciscus de la Boe – also known, confusingly, as Sylvius – that is attributed the invention of a medicinal compound of pure spirit and oil of juniper.

Juniper was an item in archaic pharmacology: the Latin *juniperus* literally means "youth-giving". The earlier

George Cruickshank, a reformed dipsomaniac, depicted many scenes in "gin palaces" (above), although in his day they were still closer to the grog shops of the eighteenth century than the splendid urban edifices they later became. Again we see "Old Tom" (right) now virtually a defunct type of gin, featured in this bar scene of 1887. In many English taverns, the gentlemen standing to the right would have been screened from other, more plebeian drinkers by a mahogany barrier. The child between these opposing social groups is probably buying a jug of gin to take home to her parents

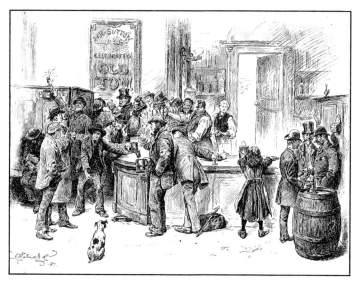

rough aquavits of the Low Countries were welcomed by soldiers fighting pointless campaigns in soggy conditions: the term "Dutch courage" stems from the use of raw spirits before battle. The new *jenever* or *genever* (juniper) – combining two beneficent ingredients – was altogether too good to be long reserved for the ailing. Distillers, following the example of the pioneer Mynheer Bols, started to sell *genever* to an eager public.

Today, wherever British and, to a lesser extent, Dutch influences have been historically strong, gin is made (notably in the USA). Australia and New Zealand produce good gin and so does South Africa, and Spain has been producing gin since Nelson's time.

LONDON DRY GIN

Although the English did not invent gin, their influence on the spirit – and *vice versa* – has been crucial.

English soldiers, sailors and traders were not slow to discover the merits of *genever* when it came into general sale. They quickly corrupted the word to "geneva" – giving rise to the misguided belief that it came from Switzerland – and then shortened it phonetically to the name by which the spirit has long been known the world over.

Gin from Holland found its way across the North Sea and achieved a small demand in ports such as Plymouth, Portsmouth and London. A few brewers turned to making it, though it was not considered a very proper activity. The mass of English mainly drank ale, or the newer beer, or cider where it was made, and the wealthier folk drank wine or brandy. Rum was the only spirit in general use. That was the situation during the seventeenth century until 1688. That year was to have a dramatic effect on gin.

With James II an exile in France and English relations with that country at low ebb, one of the first acts of Parliament in the new reign – the dual monarchy of William III and Queen Mary – granted farmers what they had long been demanding, protection for English grain for brewing and distilling and a ban on imports of, amongst other things, brandy. More importantly, the Act effectively granted anyone the right to distil from English grain. It was pure coincidence that King William came from the Netherlands, homeland of gin, and the only flavoured spirit of which the pioneer commercial distillers of England possessed any cognizance was gin (Hollands). A flood of gin commenced to inundate at least parts of the country, concentrating on London.

Two years after the Act in question was passed, consumption of gin was 500,000 gallons; by 1727 it was nearly

"Gin-and-tonic" – dry gin and iced Indian quinine water – is arguably the most popular of all gin mixes the world over. One brand name dominates the "tonic" field though there are many other makes, some tolerable, some very much less so

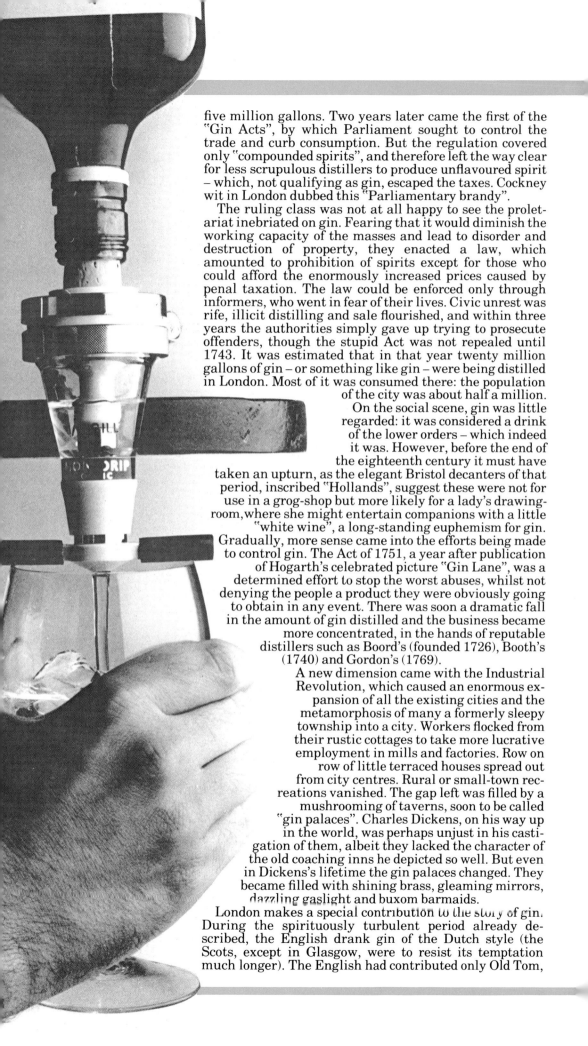

five million gallons. Two years later came the first of the "Gin Acts", by which Parliament sought to control the trade and curb consumption. But the regulation covered only "compounded spirits", and therefore left the way clear for less scrupulous distillers to produce unflavoured spirit – which, not qualifying as gin, escaped the taxes. Cockney wit in London dubbed this "Parliamentary brandy".

The ruling class was not at all happy to see the proletariat inebriated on gin. Fearing that it would diminish the working capacity of the masses and lead to disorder and destruction of property, they enacted a law, which amounted to prohibition of spirits except for those who could afford the enormously increased prices caused by penal taxation. The law could be enforced only through informers, who went in fear of their lives. Civic unrest was rife, illicit distilling and sale flourished, and within three years the authorities simply gave up trying to prosecute offenders, though the stupid Act was not repealed until 1743. It was estimated that in that year twenty million gallons of gin – or something like gin – were being distilled in London. Most of it was consumed there: the population of the city was about half a million.

On the social scene, gin was little regarded: it was considered a drink of the lower orders – which indeed it was. However, before the end of the eighteenth century it must have taken an upturn, as the elegant Bristol decanters of that period, inscribed "Hollands", suggest these were not for use in a grog-shop but more likely for a lady's drawing-room, where she might entertain companions with a little "white wine", a long-standing euphemism for gin.

Gradually, more sense came into the efforts being made to control gin. The Act of 1751, a year after publication of Hogarth's celebrated picture "Gin Lane", was a determined effort to stop the worst abuses, whilst not denying the people a product they were obviously going to obtain in any event. There was soon a dramatic fall in the amount of gin distilled and the business became more concentrated, in the hands of reputable distillers such as Boord's (founded 1726), Booth's (1740) and Gordon's (1769).

A new dimension came with the Industrial Revolution, which caused an enormous expansion of all the existing cities and the metamorphosis of many a formerly sleepy township into a city. Workers flocked from their rustic cottages to take more lucrative employment in mills and factories. Row on row of little terraced houses spread out from city centres. Rural or small-town recreations vanished. The gap left was filled by a mushrooming of taverns, soon to be called "gin palaces". Charles Dickens, on his way up in the world, was perhaps unjust in his castigation of them, albeit they lacked the character of the old coaching inns he depicted so well. But even in Dickens's lifetime the gin palaces changed. They became filled with shining brass, gleaming mirrors, dazzling gaslight and buxom barmaids.

London makes a special contribution to the story of gin. During the spirituously turbulent period already described, the English drank gin of the Dutch style (the Scots, except in Glasgow, were to resist its temptation much longer). The English had contributed only Old Tom, an artificially sweetened type, and the specially zestful Plymouth (beloved of the Royal Navy). Then, in the second half of the nineteenth century, London distillers started to make "unsweetened gin", advertised as "positively containing no sugar". It is not known who was the first distiller to make this much more lightly flavoured gin, destined to revolutionize the trade. Soon it was being called "Dry gin" and then "London Dry gin". It opened up entirely new markets, since this delicate spirit lent itself to the new mixed drinks that were being introduced from the USA, and it greatly helped the social upward movement of the product. In those parts of the vast British Empire where quinine was essential as a specific against malaria, it was found that gin made this bitter medicine – in the form of "Indian quinine (tonic) water" – easier and more attractive to take, and there began the gin-and-tonic habit. Brought back to the United Kingdom by those imperial proconsuls who survived to retire with wealth and honour to fashionable Cheltenham and Tunbridge Wells, the gin-and-tonic gave additional social acceptability to the once despised spirit. The cocktail age added fashion to respectability.

London Dry gin is based on neutral, highly rectified spirit, normally from either grain or cane (molasses). The difference is minimal, though some aver that from cane comes a distillate as near as possible to flavourless, whilst that from grain retains traces of its original mash. Methods of production vary, but quality gins are produced by redistilling the spirit with juniper berries, coriander, orris root, cassia bark and other botanicals, according to the formula of the brand-owner.

London Dry gin is usually accepted as a style – by far the most popular – and not as an indication that the product comes from London, though a few countries, particularly France, insist that only gin imported from Britain may carry the title.

After Prohibition ended, large-scale manufacture of their Dry gins by London companies commenced in the USA: today the largest-selling gin there – indeed, in the world – is Gordon's. Other companies, such as Booth's and Gilbey's, also produce their gins in many countries and direct export by Tanqueray and Burrough's (Beefeater) is very extensive. Such is London's reputation for Dry gin that numerous minor brands have sprung up boasting of a London provenance. This is not to deny that some London Dry gin is very satisfactorily made by foreign companies, notably in the USA and the Netherlands. But elsewhere there are many imitations of the labels of celebrated London brands, and some positively awful "London Dry gins" – especially in Africa, where "banana gins" (*waragi* or *moshi*), reminiscent of the "trade gin" of past eras, are sold. Gin became a potent force in African commerce with Europe – in places achieving a mystic status. To pour gin on a spot where an eminent foot was to be placed was an indication of signal respect.

Plymouth gin was previously an aromatic gin, distinctively different to London Dry and particularly associated with the pink gin favoured by Navy officers. Excellent as Plymouth gin is, it no longer has the old character associated with it; its naval image is dissipated.

The gin of the world is nowadays London Dry, described by the late great André Simon (who did not care for it) as "the purest of all spirits". The description, though not strictly accurate, has some truth in it. Good gin – be it Dutch or London Dry – is a singularly salubrious alcohol, and to London Dry pertains a remarkable versatility.

DUTCH GIN

The Dutch gin of today is substantially the same, in all probability, as that of four centuries ago, if more refined. It is based on malted, or partly malted, grain – distilled much as whisky – and is available in two different styles, "young" and "old", which are indicative of flavour rather than age. The botanical flavourings – juniper berries, coriander, citrus rind and so on – are added to the brand formula. This distillation may be repeated: each distiller has his own detail of method. The resultant spirit is aromatic, with a strong botanical taste. It has preserved a reputation as a healthful drink from its medical origins. Dutch gin is essentially for drinking iced, as schnapps, possibly with a "chaser" of lager. It is unsuitable for mixed drinks, though some experts claim that the cocktail John (or Tom) Collins should, correctly, be made with it.

Dutch gin has retained the affection of the people who invented it, accounting for over fifty per cent of spirits sales in the Netherlands, though dry gin has somewhat eroded this historic loyalty. Dutch *geneva* is popular in most of Scandinavia, in Belgium, and in Germany, where similar products – Steinhager is the best known – are distilled. Dutch gin is also a popular drink in Quebec province and some other parts of Canada, and also in New Zealand. The former demand for it in Britain has much decreased since the Second World War.

Drinkers of the world owe a very substantial debt to Franciscus de la Boe and the enterprising Dutch distillers.

Two celebrated old white spirits are pictured together – Schiedam gin and Vodka. It is fair to say that De Kuyper, famous as it is, must yield pride of place in seniority to Bols. Enormously successful Smirnoff recently reproduced their pre-Revolution pack (seen right) for a special celebration vodka

VODKA

Give a Russian, a Pole, a Finn – or a drinker
from another country where vodka is historically a national spirit – a glass of vodka of
the sort made in the West, and he will
doubtless toss it down. But if you were to
ask his candid opinion, and he were to give
it, he would doubtless say he found it a
weak and bland drink scarcely deserving
attention from a serious imbiber. That
shows the dichotomy attached to it: it is
different things to different nations.
By legend, vodka is said to have
been evolved in the twelfth century
in the Russian monastery-fort of
Viatka as *zhizennia voda* (water
of life), obviously a translation of
the universal *aqua vitae*, and it
would have been used for medicinal purposes. The word vodka
is an affectionate diminutive.
The spirit came into social use in
the sixteenth century: it was
then associated mainly with the
Ukraine, where grain was abun-
dant (it was also associated later
with St Petersburg and, later still,
with Moscow). It took some time
for vodka-drinking to penetrate
as far as the winelands of southern Russia, which is a big brandy-
producing region. Eventually,
vodka's domain stretched from
Lapland to Persia (now Iran) but
had not gained much of a hold
westwards beyond the Elbe.
Vodka blossomed from a local
product to a
major force in

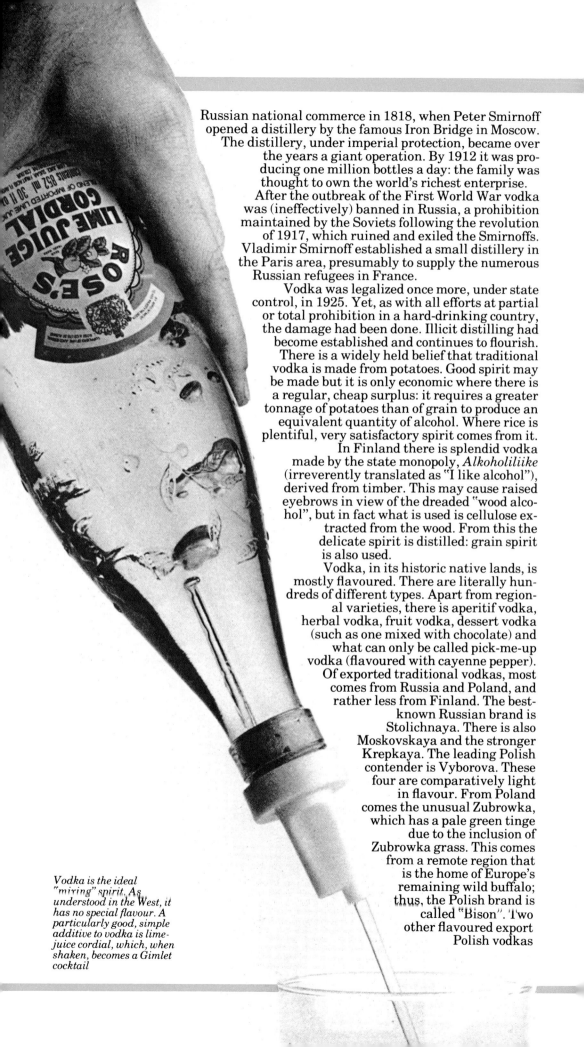

Russian national commerce in 1818, when Peter Smirnoff opened a distillery by the famous Iron Bridge in Moscow. The distillery, under imperial protection, became over the years a giant operation. By 1912 it was producing one million bottles a day: the family was thought to own the world's richest enterprise.

After the outbreak of the First World War vodka was (ineffectively) banned in Russia, a prohibition maintained by the Soviets following the revolution of 1917, which ruined and exiled the Smirnoffs. Vladimir Smirnoff established a small distillery in the Paris area, presumably to supply the numerous Russian refugees in France.

Vodka was legalized once more, under state control, in 1925. Yet, as with all efforts at partial or total prohibition in a hard-drinking country, the damage had been done. Illicit distilling had become established and continues to flourish.

There is a widely held belief that traditional vodka is made from potatoes. Good spirit may be made but it is only economic where there is a regular, cheap surplus: it requires a greater tonnage of potatoes than of grain to produce an equivalent quantity of alcohol. Where rice is plentiful, very satisfactory spirit comes from it.

In Finland there is splendid vodka made by the state monopoly, *Alkoholiliike* (irreverently translated as "I like alcohol"), derived from timber. This may cause raised eyebrows in view of the dreaded "wood alcohol", but in fact what is used is cellulose extracted from the wood. From this the delicate spirit is distilled: grain spirit is also used.

Vodka, in its historic native lands, is mostly flavoured. There are literally hundreds of different types. Apart from regional varieties, there is aperitif vodka, herbal vodka, fruit vodka, dessert vodka (such as one mixed with chocolate) and what can only be called pick-me-up vodka (flavoured with cayenne pepper).

Of exported traditional vodkas, most comes from Russia and Poland, and rather less from Finland. The best-known Russian brand is Stolichnaya. There is also Moskovskaya and the stronger Krepkaya. The leading Polish contender is Vyborova. These four are comparatively light in flavour. From Poland comes the unusual Zubrowka, which has a pale green tinge due to the inclusion of Zubrowka grass. This comes from a remote region that is the home of Europe's remaining wild buffalo; thus, the Polish brand is called "Bison". Two other flavoured export Polish vodkas

Vodka is the ideal "mixing" spirit. As understood in the West, it has no special flavour. A particularly good, simple additive to vodka is lime-juice cordial, which, when shaken, becomes a Gimlet cocktail

are the tart, cherry-flavoured Wisniowka and Jarzebiak, which owes its taste to the rowanberry. Polish pure spirit, a grain distillate of dangerous strength, unflavoured and containing eighty per cent alcohol is usually included in the vodka category. Home wine-makers find it useful for producing do-it-yourself cordials with high alcohol content.

These vodkas should be drunk cold, in small glasses and at a single gulp. The finest companion to true vodka is someone else's caviare.

Vodka made in the West is a very different product. The Smirnoff brand-name was brought to the USA by Rudoph Kunett in 1934. He was of Ukrainian extraction, and his father had sold grain and alcohol to Moscow's Iron Bridge distillery. Kunett set up in Bethel, Connecticut, an American branch of Société Pierre Smirnoff et Fils: it did not prosper. He happened to meet John G. Martin, the English-born president of the small, but long-respected, Hartford-based firm of Heublein. Against opposition, Martin arranged to retain Kunett, and in 1939 Heublein's took over the manufacture and sales of Smirnoff.

Shortly after the end of the war, Jack Martin was discussing the apparent failure of vodka with Jack Morgan in the latter's tavern, the Cock 'n' Bull, in Los Angeles. Morgan also had a difficulty: he held a stock of ginger-beer which he could not shift. The two men put the two problems together and added a touch of lime juice. The resultant Moscow Mule cocktail swept the city, the state and then the country. It was followed by the Screwdriver, and other special mixes, and soon vodka was usurping gin's supremacy in the white spirit market and even daring to invade the Dry Martini arena. Thanks to Jack Martin's faith, Heublein's were in a superb position to exploit this craze. In a short time, from a small company principally known for quality imported food and drink, Heublein's became a huge conglomerate.

The difference between Slav and Western vodkas is even more marked than that between Dutch and London Dry gins. Slav vodka encompasses a range of spirits: Western vodka is a specific product. It is as near as possible to being flavourless. A Russian (or Polish) brand-name is by no means a prerequisite, as has been illustrated by the success in the USA of "Gordon's Vodka", riding on the reputation of Gordon's in the gin market. Most American and British brands do, however, have Russian-style names.

After Smirnoff licensed production in Britain, the Distillers Company launched their Cossack vodka, and gradually a minor galaxy of brands joined the fray. British vodka is mainly weaker than other spirits.

Neutral Western vodka is made by filtering a highly rectified spirit (grain or cane) through charcoal: this further purifies the alcohol.

Western vodka (or similar) is being produced in more and more countries. Spain has turned to making it for the millions of tourists who regularly infest the country. In Australia, Smirnoff (under licence from the USA) leads the market, and vodka is also very popular in New Zealand. The Japanese equivalent to vodka is a rectified form of a more flavoured and traditional spirit, *shochu*, usually distilled from sake. China also produces a "vodka".

Vodka adds zest but no flavour to whatever is mixed with it. This appeals to people who like alcohol's effect but not the taste of spirits. Vodka is also said to be less fattening, not so easily detectable, less likely to cause a hangover. . . . Drinkers like to rationalize their preferences; and there is no harm in that.

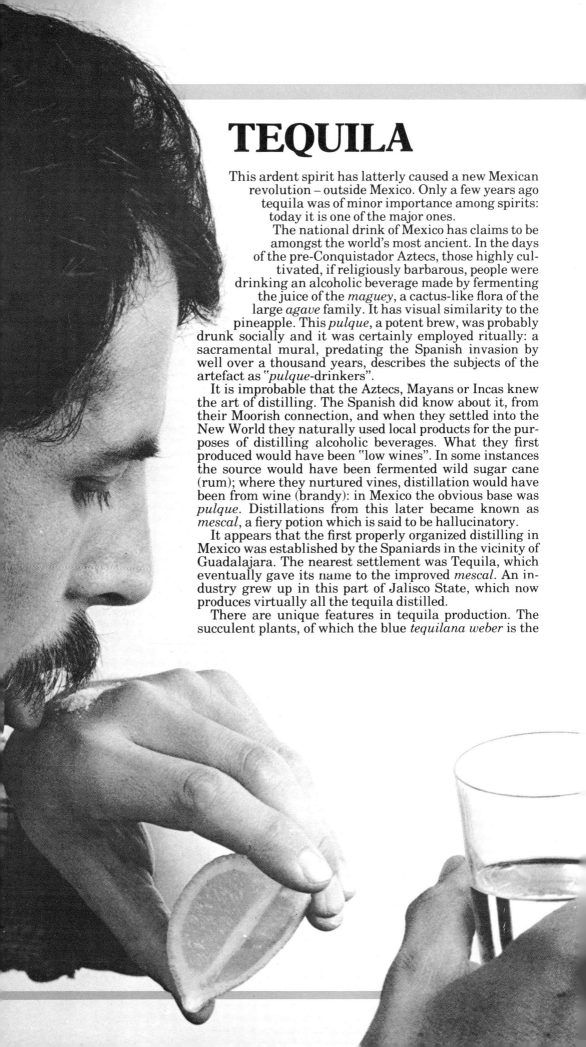

TEQUILA

This ardent spirit has latterly caused a new Mexican
revolution – outside Mexico. Only a few years ago
tequila was of minor importance among spirits:
today it is one of the major ones.

The national drink of Mexico has claims to be
amongst the world's most ancient. In the days
of the pre-Conquistador Aztecs, those highly cultivated, if religiously barbarous, people were
drinking an alcoholic beverage made by fermenting
the juice of the *maguey*, a cactus-like flora of the
large *agave* family. It has visual similarity to the
pineapple. This *pulque*, a potent brew, was probably
drunk socially and it was certainly employed ritually: a
sacramental mural, predating the Spanish invasion by
well over a thousand years, describes the subjects of the
artefact as "*pulque*-drinkers".

It is improbable that the Aztecs, Mayans or Incas knew
the art of distilling. The Spanish did know about it, from
their Moorish connection, and when they settled into the
New World they naturally used local products for the purposes of distilling alcoholic beverages. What they first
produced would have been "low wines". In some instances
the source would have been fermented wild sugar cane
(rum); where they nurtured vines, distillation would have
been from wine (brandy): in Mexico the obvious base was
pulque. Distillations from this later became known as
mescal, a fiery potion which is said to be hallucinatory.

It appears that the first properly organized distilling in
Mexico was established by the Spaniards in the vicinity of
Guadalajara. The nearest settlement was Tequila, which
eventually gave its name to the improved *mescal*. An industry grew up in this part of Jalisco State, which now
produces virtually all the tequila distilled.

There are unique features in tequila production. The
succulent plants, of which the blue *tequilana weber* is the

most usual, are planted as cuttings. They take up to thirteen years to reach maturity. The leaves are then removed and the single fruit (*cabeza*) taken to the distillery. Unlike wine, tequila comes from a plant which contributes but once to the product. In large ovens, the *cabezas* are cooked for several hours, then cooled and shredded, after which the juice is extracted. Natural fermentation lasts about four days. Double-distillation is used to produce tequila; the new spirit is matured in fifty-gallon casks. Two basic types result: *tequila nuevo*, between three and five years old, and *tequila maduro*, left for up to ten years in cask.

The slow growth of the *maguey* has caused problems because of tequila's recent vast increase in exports. Whilst introducing legislation to protect the quality of the export product and hence its reputation abroad, the Mexican government has permitted as much as forty-nine per cent of non-*maguey* spirit to be added to the domestic product. This is not quite true tequila, though it may carry the title, and it must be accepted that some tequila sold inside Mexico is not of prime quality.

Constant commerce between the southern United States and Mexico ensured that some Americans were familiar with tequila many years ago, but except in the border area it was little considered until the mid-1960s. Then things Mexican began to enjoy particular popularity – especially with the young, who are so often responsible for initiating changes in drinking patterns. Tequila started to move north in respectable quantities, most of it being drunk in Margarita cocktails, and very rarely in the Mexican manner. The traditional ritual is to moisten the base of the thumb, pour on some salt and hold a quarter of fresh lime between the forefinger and index finger of the same hand; then, licking the salt, you swallow a small glassful of the neat spirit in one go and immediately chew on the lime.

Sales of tequila in the USA rose by some 1500 per cent in the decade from 1965 and by the late 1970s over twenty million bottles of tequila were being drunk there annually, predominantly in the border states but elsewhere, too.

The taste of tequila is notoriously hard to describe. Take a top-quality export tequila and you have a spirit whose most obvious feature is a smooth sharpness: an apparent contradiction in terms that is fairly near the mark. The tart quality of tequila, more pronounced than that of vodka or Dry gin, make it an interesting spirit for mixing, and it is no longer wholly confined to a handful of special cocktails, but is making minor inroads into mixes dominated by gin, vodka and even white rum.

So, in the USA, tequila is established as decidedly more than one of those novelty drinks that appear from time to time in that volatile and enterprising market – some to be lasting, some ephemerally popular. Elsewhere it has yet to prove its acceptability. In Britain, serious importation did not start until 1974. It has attracted a little attention from trendy young metropolitan drinkers, but has made little serious impact. However, changes in drinking habits are slowly and cautiously wrought in the United Kingdom, as the vodka story illustrates. In Canada, prone to speedier adaptation of American fashion, there has been more interest. In West Germany and Australia there is apparent awareness of tequila.

Tequila has already been granted the major accolade of imitation. Undoubtedly, it is now set fair to take a reasonably significant place in the global drinking spectrum.

Outside Mexico, whence it comes, it is not usual to drink tequila in the traditional way: more likely the spirit – whose popularity in the USA especially is growing – will be part of a fashionable cocktail such as a Margarita. But if you want to drink according to the custom you will put a pinch of salt at the thumb's base, toss back the tequila and, after licking the salt, instantly bite into a quarter of fresh lime. Some people aver this makes straight tequila drinkable

RUM

Though distillation from sugar cane certainly started much earlier, not until the mid-seventeenth century was a special West Indian spirit heard of in Europe, and then under the appellation "kill-devil". It was described as "hot, hellish and terrible", and was given to the plantation slaves to ease their misery and keep them tolerably content during their appalling labours in the cane-fields. However, it may be assumed that plantation-owners also tried the stuff, if only when ships failed to bring supplies of more conventional stimulants from Europe or America.

How the spirit acquired the strange name of "rum" is not known. Some say it is a corruption of the Spanish *ron*, since probably the Spaniards were the first to distil in their colonies. Others claim the origin is to be sought in southwest England, from the Devon word *rumbullion*, a dialect form of *rumbustion* (an old English term for "uproar" or, later, "strong liquor"). The more scholarly may opt for derivation from the Latin *saccharum* (sugar). Be that as it may, half a century after the scathing soubriquet "kill-devil" first saw print, rum, under that new name, was being praised as " . . . very wholesome and therefore has lately supplied the place of brandy in punch".

During the eighteenth century rum achieved widespread popularity in England and in Britain's North American colonies. It is said that Paul Revere, during his celebrated ride, did not commence uttering his cry "The English are coming!" until after he had paused at a rum distillery for a few refreshing noggins. New England still produces a small quantity of rum from imported molasses. A traditional love of rum in the north-eastern USA was fittingly immortalized during Prohibition: the twelve-mile extent of territorial waters, in which bootleggers' craft had to dodge the sea-going forces of the law, was called not Gin Lane or Whisky Alley but Rum Row.

Old-time rum was all of the sweetish, heavy, pungent pot-stilled style often now called Navy rum – after "Nelson's Blood" of the British Royal Navy, the immensely strong daily rum issue. However, rum has changed with the times: the descendants of Boston privateers who quaffed draughts of rich, powerful New England rum now sip a white rum cocktail.

The principal centres of the rum trade are the West Indies, the Caribbean and the coast of South America. It is also made in many other countries – South Africa, Madagascar and the Philippines, for example – and there are distillates similar to rum that are known by other names.

Cuba, once so important, has recommenced export on a minor scale. However, in the West Indies, it is Puerto Rico, the largest producer, which supplies most of the US market. The French drink a lot of *rhum*: Martinique is their biggest source, Guadeloupe the second, and they also provide French *rhums* for export to other countries.

Further important rum producers include celebrated islands: Jamaica, Britain's biggest and oldest supplier; Barbados, historically noted for light rums; Trinidad, and Haiti, which has benefited by Cuba's decline. On the mainland, Guyana produces the famous Demerara, a luscious style of rum.

In Britain, the leading importers and brand-owners are United Rum Merchants. Seagram's Captain Morgan is a substantial seller and Bacardi looms large.

Rum may be distilled either from a wash of cane juice or from molasses (the sugar-rich residue of the conversion into cane-sugar). A second grade, rum-type spirit is also produced for cheap local markets and not exported, a sort of *marc de sucre*.

Though some of the greatest Caribbean rums are pot-stilled and usually matured and bottled at the place of manufacture, for the most part commercial rum is made by continuous distillation.

The almost flavourless, highly rectified rum produced from the continuous distillation process is then turned into "navy" or other style of dark rum by the addition of concentrated flavouring, and darkened according to demand. Conversely, white rum that picks up colour during maturing may require decolouring before bottling.

Like any other industry – and rum is a big industry – the product has had to adapt itself to a changing demand in the market. To a marked degree this has in recent years been a question of "follow the leader". The prime example is the emergence of white rum as a conquering force.

Bacardi

For a long time white rum, often direct from the still, was purely a local drink, employed to enliven coconut milk or whatever fruit juice was most available. As the Coca-Cola empire spread across the globe, that product was found to go admirably with the spirit. It is probable that white rum first came to the gen-

Rum and Coca-Cola, Bacardi-and-Coke, call it what you will. It is (with the addition of lime juice) a famous mix called, no longer so often as it once was, the Cuba Libre. It was, and remains, a title laced with irony. The name Bacardi is applied to the world's greatest white rum: it is not a generic term

Old pewter spirit tots (below) from the author's collection, pictured about two-thirds actual size

Also from the author's collection (opposite) is this Swedish aquavit decanter with silver-mounted cork stopper, dating from the 1930s. In front of this is another Swedish speciality – a "widow" – containing herbs in alcohol, a concentrate which may be added to unflavoured aquavit to give it any individually preferred taste

eral attention of the American public during Prohibition, when the Americans flocked to the Cuban capital of Havana, a city overflowing with booze and other delights denied the USA. There they discovered the merits of the Cuba Libre (white rum and Coca-Cola), a satirically named mix under an iron-heeled if socially permissive dictatorship. The Daiquiri cocktail likewise came to their notice and joined the ranks of great cocktails in the post-Prohibition American repertoire (to say nothing of the uncounted Daiquiris mixed in speakeasies). Much later – not until the 1960s – young Britons, influenced by Mediterranean holidays, took to Bacardi-and-Coke in a big way.

Ironically, the founders of Bacardi played a leading role in Cuba's fight for independence from Spain. Then, by a quirk of history, after another battle to gain freedom, this time from the Battista tyranny, a new dictatorial power (Castro's) expropriated the company. It had been founded in 1862 by Don Facundo Bacardi, who had the idea that from Cuba's copious and splendid molasses a new sort of rum could be produced – light, smooth, pure and low in flavour. Don Facundo's son Emilio was so successful, despite a couple of spells in exile for political activity, that by 1885 he was bringing actions for infringement of the copyright in his label design. In 1892, the heir to the Spanish throne fell gravely ill. He was given Bacardi rum, and his fever abated. On his recovery, the royal physician was authorized to write to Don Emilio praising the rum's apparent life-restoring qualities. The family sufficiently forgot their republican principles to add the Spanish royal arms to their label.

The more recent exile of Bacardi on corporate rather than personal grounds has only enhanced its prosperity. Its headquarters are in Nassau; the main distillery is in Puerto Rico, convenient for the huge American market. A distillery had been established in Barcelona in 1910. There are now Bacardi plants in Mexico and Brazil. It is possible that Bacardi *carta blanca*, colourless and very delicate, is the world's biggest-selling single brand of spirit (brand, as opposed to product group). The less well-known *carta oro* is faintly coloured and fractionally less dry.

Bacardi's immense growth has spawned a plethora of white rums of varying qualities. Some of these white rums are virtually impossible to distinguish from vodka when mixed with ice and citrus-flavoured additives. For those traditional rum drinks that have survived, such as the various punches, a dark rum is preferable, the degree of pungency being a matter of taste. Rum is a spirit that appeals, in its many forms and in the guise of many mixes, to an extraordinarily wide range of consumers. You can see it being drunk by career women in New York bars and sailors in Guadeloupe cafés. Over the centuries rum has shown resilience and adaptability worthy of its origins.

AQUAVIT

The generic spirit of Scandinavia and parts of Germany, aquavit (or *akvavit*), is obviously a derivative of the universal *aqua vitae*, and covers almost as broad a spectrum of spirits. Also referred to as schnapps (or *snaps*), these are, in the main, drunk the way the Russians drink vodka.

Potatoes and grains are the usual bases for aquavits, which are highly rectified. The range of flavourings is a wide one, mainly herbal, and with caraway seed predominating. The biggest producer is Sweden, and there are around a score of brands. There are only half that number in Denmark, the second largest distiller: Aalborg akvavit holds over ninety per cent of the market. In contrast, the Norwegians are moving away from aquavit towards vodka (Western-style). A Norwegian speciality is Line (*linie*) aquavit. This dates from the time when it was discovered it was beneficial to send some wines, such as madeira, across the Equator (the "Line") and back: the seafaring Norwegians adapted this practice to aquavit.

Into the aquavit schnapps class falls the popular *Kornbranntwein* of Germany, neutral grain spirit which is given a wide range of flavours.

78° PROOF PRODUCE OF FRANCE 34 FL OZS
Imported by J.R. PARKINGTON & Cº LTD. LONDON W.1

OTHER SPIRITS

Though it has been loosely so described, it takes a vivid imagination to classify arrack (*arak, raki*) as a brandy. Grape juice, rice, sugar cane, grains, milk – you name it, some type of arrack will be distilled from it.

Batavia *arak* from Indonesia is the basis for Swedish *punsch* (punch), which is difficult to classify: in this book it is categorized as a liqueur.

Caña, the very strong spirit (seventy-five per cent alcohol) of Majorca, almost defies classification. In 1979 a café was burnt out when some *caña* ignited while being poured – you have been warned.

Pastis is properly the name of anis aperitifs, particularly associated with Marseilles, but it is a convenient word to describe with reasonable accuracy a mass of aniseed-flavoured spirits, which include a number of arracks. Pastis itself was successor to the fabled absinthe that was outlawed in France the day the First World War broke out. Pernod's name then became synonymous with pastis; this was the product, tasting very much the same, that replaced the banned concoction. Pernod passed into the domain of a M. Ricard. Other members of the broad family are the *ojen* of Spain and Greek *ouzo*.

LIQUEURS

It is no easy task to draw precise lines of demarcation between categories of alcoholic drinks, and liqueurs present particular problems. The word "liqueur", shortened from *liqueur de dessert*, has become internationalized, though most Americans favour the good description "cordial". The name "liqueur" is generally held to cover sweetened and flavoured spiritous amalgams: some are based on fruits, some are of mainly herbal character. The sweet, usually low-strength creams (*crèmes*) are not always called liqueurs, but here they are so designated on social grounds (*sirops*, on the other hand, are excluded). To complicate the issue, English-speakers commonly speak of liqueur Scotch or liqueur cognac, merely to indicate a superior grade, suitable for drinking without dilution. However, it is quite correct to talk of a Scotch whisky liqueur (such as Drambuie) or a cognac liqueur, for several are based on good cognac. Some of the finest fruit brandies are sometimes classified as liqueurs, but are excluded here because they are not compounded.

The manufacture of liqueurs is almost as varied as their colours and tastes. They may be based on fine brandy, carefully redistilled with a wide spectrum of botanicals, or they may simply be a blending of concentrates into neutral spirit. Exact formulae are rarely divulged by the makers of proprietary liqueurs, but even if they were, knowledge of the technicalities could add nothing to the pleasure of drinking them. To savour one's preferred liqueur at the end of a good meal or to discover a little-known speciality, perhaps in a remote mountain hostelry in the Vosges, is one of the joys of good living.

The list of liqueurs is unending. In parts of Europe almost every village has its own or its version of a regional product. Below are listed some of the best-known liqueurs, plus a few oddities.

ABRICOTINE
A liqueur strongly flavoured with fresh apricot juice (but not to be confused with *eau de vie d'abricots* – apricot brandy)

ADVOCAAT
Made of sweetened egg yolks blended with brandy and other ingredients, this is a Dutch speciality. The name translates as "lawyer", and the origin is said to be that it makes those who drink it talk like one. Britain produces "egg flip", which has a not dissimilar taste but is weaker and usually wine-based. Advocaat or egg flip mixed with fizzy lemonade is known as a Snowball

AMARETTO
An attractive "classical" Italian liqueur with a legendary history, Amaretto is said to have been evolved in about 1525 by a young widow, beautiful but impoverished, as a present for Bernadino Luini, an artist of the Leonardo da Vinci school

ANISETTE
This is a sweetened form of pastis

AURUM
Brandy-based and golden, this bitter-sweet Italian liqueur has an orange after-taste

BAILEY'S IRISH CREAM
This is a cordial compound of coffee, chocolate, coconut, fresh cream and Irish whiskey, with sweeteners

BENEDICTINE
One of the world's truly great liqueurs, this is sold everywhere. It has been made since 1510 in the splendid monastery at Fécamp in Normandy. Ex-

cept that the spirit content is fine cognac, the ingredients are a closely guarded secret. To try to describe the taste of this nectar is impossible – except to say that its elusive flavour is sweet without being in the least cloying. It is supremely digestive. Quite a number of Bénédictine's admirers mix it half-and-half with cognac, and one can buy it so blended as "B & B". The initials D.O.M., virtually the trade-mark of Bénédictine, stand for *Deo Optimo Maximo* (To God, Most Good, Most Great), as befits a liqueur made by monks

CAPRICORNIA
This Australian liqueur, based on local spirit, is flavoured with various exotic fruits

CHARTREUSE
This was evolved for medicinal purposes by Carthusian monks in their great establishment in the vicinity of Grenoble in the seventeenth century. It was not commercialized until the mid-nineteenth century. Chartreuse is made according to extremely complex secret formulae and contains about 130 different herbs. The monks control distillation, while bottling and sales are conducted by a secular company. The considerable royalties accruing to the order finance much charitable work.

It is the green Chartreuse that is the strong one; the yellow is slightly weaker and marginally sweeter. There is also the rare *élixir végétal*, nearly eighty per cent alcohol, which is probably very close to the original medicinal compound

CHERRY BRANDY
A wine spirit strongly flavoured with cherry juice, this should not be confused with kirsch. Leading brands are Denmark's Cherry Heering, De Kuyper from Holland and Cherry Rocher from France. Grant's Morella is the British brand

COCORIBE
From the USA, this cordial liqueur is made from wild coconuts and Virgin Island rum

COINTREAU
For most drinkers, this is the greatest orange curaçao (*triple sec*). The Cointreau family placed their name on their brand to avoid confusion with other, lesser products

CONTICHINNO
This Australian liqueur, a companion to Conticream (below), is made of white rum, coffee and fresh cream

CONTICREAM
A companion product to Contichinno, this consists of Australian whisky blended with chocolate and cream

CRÈMES
There are many crèmes, of which *crème de cassis* (blackcurrant) is probably the best known internationally. Other important ones are *cacao* (chocolate-flavoured), *ananas* (pineapple) and *mandarine* (tangerine). Crèmes are made from almonds and other nuts, rose petals, tea... all very sweet, and more used in mixed drinks than taken on their own:
Crème de menthe (peppermint) stands in a category on its own. It comes in green or white varieties, the latter less sweet
Crème de myrtilles (bilberry) is an alternative to *cassis* for making Kir
Crème Yvette is a long-established American brand, strong and sweet with the colour and bouquet of Parma violets

CURAÇAO
Originally named after the island of Curaçao, whose oranges were the basis for its first production, the name is now generic. Now made from a variety of oranges, only the peel of the orange is used for curaçao. It may be based on any white spirit, though molasses (cane) or grape are the most likely, and it comes in a range of colours, including blue. *Triple sec* was the term for a second distillation.

DRAMBUIE
One of the world's great liqueurs, Drambuie is based on the finest Scotch whisky. To

use fifteen-year-old malts for turning into liqueur may seem like sacrilege, but in the case of Drambuie the end justifies the means. The name comes from the Gaelic *an dram buidbeach* ("the drink that satisfies"). Legend has it that the recipe was given to the Mackinnon family by Bonnie Prince Charlie, for saving his life after the collapse of the Scottish clans' rebellion of 1745

ELIXIR D'ANVERS
A celebrated Belgian liqueur known to contain thirty-two herbal ingredients, this has the colour of yellow Chartreuse and tastes like it

ELIXIR DE SPA
This was originally one of the classic liqueurs of the Low Countries, attributed to the Franciscan monastery founded in the vicinity of the town in the mid-seventeenth century. It might have taken the place of Elixir d'Anvers had the monks not been dispersed in 1797 in the wave of anti-clericalism. The formula was rediscovered in old archives much later. The recipe is a close secret, though the product is known to be brandy-based and flavoured with many, mainly local, herbs

FIOR D'ALPI
Based on grape spirit, the Fior d'Alpi ("Flower of the Alps") liqueurs are unusual in that they contain a twig on which the sugar in the drink crystallizes when the bottle is chilled. The most famous of the group is Mille Fiori, which is alleged to contain the essence of a thousand flowers and herbs

FORBIDDEN FRUIT
This long-established American cordial liqueur is apple and citrus-flavoured, with a predominating and distinctive taste of shaddock (a type of grapefruit), which is blended with orange and honey

GALLIANO
Established towards the end of the nineteenth century, this yellow herbal liqueur was named after an Italian military hero. Its popularity abroad, other than among Italian expatriates, is of quite recent origin, and is a remarkable example of the fortunes of a brand being founded on a single mix – the Harvey Wallbanger. From this has sprung a huge demand for Galliano as a straight liqueur, in mixed drinks and for cooking. The recipe is a total secret

GALLWEY'S IRISH COFFEE LIQUEUR
From Waterford, this is a matured liqueur of established quality, combining herbs, honey and Irish coffee

GET
Pronounced "jet", Peppermint Get is made by a subsidiary of Bénédictine and has a hottish, mint taste. It was created in 1797 by Jean Get

GINGER WINE
This attractive, distinctively British product is made from imported must, which is fermented then flavoured with ginger. The most popular brands are Stone's and Crabbie's Green

GLAYVA
This Scottish liqueur is whisky-based and has similarities to Drambuie

GLEN MIST
Another herbal and honey Scotch whisky liqueur, this one is peculiar in having been for a time made in Ireland, with Irish whiskey, during a shortage of ingredients in Britain

GOLDWASSER
This liqueur, a type of Kümmel (see below), was first produced in Danzig (now Gdansk) in the mid-sixteenth century. It was then fashionable to take gold as a medicine, hence the inclusion of flecks of gold dust, which would float around when the bottle was shaken. It is now made in West Berlin

GRAND MARNIER
A comparative newcomer among French liqueurs, this

one, first made in 1880, is a splendid curaçao-type based on quality cognac. It comes in two varieties: *cordon rouge* and a slightly weaker *cordon jaune*

GREEN TEA LIQUEUR
Part of the Hermes range of liqueurs from the great house of Suntory, this Japanese liqueur is a blend of delicate teas infused into brandy and subtly sweetened

IRISH MIST
This liqueur is said to resemble a legendary "heather wine" (a type of mead made from heather honey). It is made with old Irish whiskey at Tullamore Distillery

IRISH VELVET
In effect, this product is instant Irish coffee – a blend of Brazilian coffee, sugar and Jameson's whiskey. It is prepared by adding boiling water and topping with thick fresh cream

IZARRA
Based on armagnac, this aromatic liqueur from the French Basque country in the Pyrenean foothills is best known in its country of origin, where it has been produced since 1835

JÄGERMEISTER
This dark red German liqueur, flavoured with gentian, has a digestive reputation

KAHLUA
This splendid Mexican product, with a cane spirit base, is so strongly flavoured with coffee that it can make the perfect end to a meal

KÜMMEL
Flavoured with caraway, cumin and aniseed, kümmel is esteemed above other liqueurs as a specific against dyspepsia. The strong flavour may be lessened by adding white spirit: Dry gin is excellent for this

LAREDO
This whisky-based peach-flavoured product from Galliano International was devised to compete with Southern Comfort (see below)

MANDARINE
This is a generic term for the tangerine-flavoured French liqueur, not to be confused with *crème de mandarine*. Mandarine Napoleon is the best-known

MARASCHINO
Distilled from Marascha cherries, from Dalmatia, and usually sold in straw-covered bottles, this product is often copied in places where the correct fruit is not available. The leading brand-name is Drioli, a company that was founded in Zara in 1759. Maraschino Drioli became enormously popular throughout Europe, particularly with the British: the Prince Regent (George IV) was especially fond of it. Today it is perhaps more commonly found in mixed drinks

MULLIGAN
This is a new Irish liqueur, whiskey-based, designed to be taken with mixers and to compete in the British market with Southern Comfort

NASSAU ROYALE
Made in Nassau, by an American for Americans, this excellent liqueur is predominantly citrus-flavoured, with undertones of coffee, and based on cane spirit. Invented in the 1950s it was originally sold only in the Bahamas, as a tourist souvenir, but gradually acquired a reputation that justified distribution to some of the USA. Its memorable trademark is one of the island's spectacularly uniformed policemen

O CHA
This is Japanese tea liqueur (see Green Tea Liqueur)

PARFAIT AMOUR
Said to have originated in Lorraine (France), this is generically a very old *liqueur de dessert* – a digestive. It became rather a joke in late-Victorian times when it was reputed to be a "prostitute's preference", though it still enjoys some demand. It is a concoction of peculiar sweetness, usually violet in colour, flavoured with almond and highly scented

PEACEMAKER

This is a Canadian whisky liqueur (J. Carnegie's), now also blended and bottled outside Canada

ROYAL MINT CHOCOLATE LIQUEUR

Combining the taste of mint and chocolate, this product is the most successful British contribution to the range of liqueurs for many years. It was evolved after patient trial and error by Peter Hallgarten of the family firm of that name

SABRA

A fairly new and distinctive Israeli liqueur, with an orange-chocolate flavour, this first saw light (via Seagram's) in 1967. Its distinctive bottle is based on a 2000-year-old Phoenician wine flask (which may be seen in the ceramics museum in Tel-Aviv). Sabra has been particularly successful in West Germany. The name (meaning cactus) is proudly borne by native-born Israeli citizens

SAMBUCA

This has an aniseed-type flavour. The Italian habit of floating coffee beans on a glass of Sambuca and setting fire to them is described as *con mosche* ("with flies"), and has spread to restaurants everywhere. This picturesque activity in fact serves to burn off the alcohol in the drink at the same time as roasting the beans

SLOE GIN

This excellent English cordial may be bought commercially, but is much better made at home when there is a good sloe harvest (sloe harvests are highly variable). To make your own, third-fill a standard-size gin or wine bottle with individually picked sloes, add white sugar, to a depth of 5 cm, fill the bottle with dry gin, and shake. Leave for about three months, shaking regularly. Then, preferably, leave for several more months, though you can drink it earlier. Before doing so, decant carefully through a muslin cloth

SOUMUURAIN

This is a Finnish liqueur, rarely found outside that country, with the unusual flavouring of cloudberries

SOUTHERN COMFORT

This powerful and delicious American cordial liqueur originated in New Orleans, but is now made in St Louis. It has an elusive peach flavour. Outside the USA, its principal adherents are younger drinkers. It is rarely drunk straight, but it is taken with conventional mixers, as a substitute for whisky in cocktails

STREGA

The word means "witch": probably the most popular of generic Italian liqueurs, Strega is citrus-flavoured

SWEDISH PUNSCH

This spiced spirit is drunk either as an after-dinner drink, with coffee, or may be the basis of an exhilarating hot toddy

TIA MARIA

This successful coffee-flavoured liqueur originates from Jamaica and has a neutral spirit base derived from molasses

TRAPPISTINE

From the Doubs department of France (north-east of the Jura), this liqueur is not unlike Bénédictine, but is founded on armagnac. The recipe belongs to the Trappist order at the Abbey de Grace Dieu

VAN DER HUM

The title of this tangerine-flavoured South African liqueur translates roughly as "what's his name?" It is almost certainly grape-based, and is often drunk with a good local brandy as "brandy Hum"

VIEILLE CURE

A fine blending of local herbs with both cognac and armagnac brandies, the name means "Old Rectory" – a reference to the product's monastic origins near Bordeaux. It has been commercially produced in this area since the end of the nineteenth century

BEERS
ALES
&
CIDER

Beer, always the drink of the common people,
has lately regained its appeal for the
connoisseur. Travel has exposed drinkers to the
exotic brews of other countries, while the
campaign for "real ale" has resulted in the
launching of new brands and the wider
availability of interesting examples of various
brewing styles. Guinness, Carlsberg, Budweiser
or Löwenbräu; stout, pilsner, bitter or mild:
beers are brewed to suit every taste and
consumed enthusiastically all over the world.

BEER

The beer-garden remains typical of Germany's south, where the weather can be mild and the brew a strong Märzen or bock, especially if it is served in a stoneware stein. These can contain a litre, and sometimes two or three. Glass is more common today, and smaller sizes for everyday beers

The ale-drinking Englishman, with his preferred pint, has a unique institution in the shape of the pub. Originally, it was a family house which opened its doors for public refreshment. Some country pubs have no bar counter

It is unjust that the hauteur which rightly attends wine should so often be permitted to overshadow beer. The two ought to be companions of honour as the principal types of fermented drink: made in the first case from the grape (or other fruits) and in the second from grain (usually barley). Both are capable of great delicacy, and it is to the drinker's disadvantage that beer is not always explored in its great and exotic variety.

Of the two drinks, beer is the more complicated to make, since the barley has first to be malted and mashed, the enigmatic hop added as an agent of flavouring and preservation, and the whole brewed before it can be fermented. "Only recently have we begun to understand what a remarkable art it really is," wrote microbiologist Professor Anthony Rose in the *Scientific American* in 1959. "The brewmaster, by trial and error, has been manipulating some of the subtlest processes of life." The complicated chemistry of hop resins has been described as "an organic chemist's dream – or nightmare, according to one's point of view," by Professor Anna M. Macleod, of the Department of Brewing and Biological Sciences at Edinburgh's Heriot-Watt University.

That brewing is a great art has generally been appreciated in Czechoslovakia, Germany (itself a great wine-producing nation) and in Belgium. It was in danger of being forgotten elsewhere until the renaissance of interest in beer in the late 1970s. This renaissance was evident in several countries, including The Netherlands and Denmark, but was most dramatic in Britain, where the Campaign for Real Ale (CAMRA) brought about drastic changes in the policies of large, powerful brewery companies.

After decades of often damaging neglect, a new appreciation was accorded in several countries to the craftsman brewer. He benefited from the growing awareness throughout the Western world that a heritage is worthy of conser-

vation; from the reawakening of a taste for pure and natural products; and in many instances from the "small is beautiful" philosophy propounded in the celebrated contemporary work of that name by E. F. Schumacher.

While improvements in communications have often been an influence for uniformity through the means of mass marketing, the increase in travel abroad in the 1960s and 1970s exposed many drinkers to the specialities of other lands. And in the United States especially, imported beers introduced drinkers to less bland tastes, and encouraged a number of American brewers to revive characterful styles from the past.

Just as wines may be categorized as red, *rosé* and white; dry and sweet; sparkling and still; and then according to region; so beers divide into definite styles. The most important distinction is based on the method of fermentation, during which some species of yeast rise to the top of the brew and others sink to the bottom. Top and bottom fermentation are two distinct techniques, each classically preceded at the earlier stage of production by its own method of mashing, and succeeded by different styles of maturation. Like red wines, beers made by top fermentation are very full in flavour, and their palates are in many cases best expressed at room or cellar temperature; like white wines, beers made by bottom fermentation often have a lighter and more refreshing character, and are usually served chilled, though excessive refrigeration destroys their flavour.

Among the top-fermenting brews are all the genuine manifestations of porter and its brother stout, whether of the Irish dry or English sweet style; all genuine ales, whether pale or dark, bitter or mild, light or strong, whether of the well-fermented English style made famous in Burton or the fuller-bodied Scottish mode, or of some other provenance; many Belgian specialities, including the abbey brews and the *lambic* wheat beers of the Brussels area; and in Germany the *Alt* beers of the Rhineland and Westphalia, the *Kölsch* beers of Cologne, and the two distinctive wheat beer styles, the *Weizenbier* of the south

The Germans are the world's biggest beer-drinkers. In the south, steins are still delivered by the ambitious handful, but licence to spill so lavishly is extended only to artists

A stemmed ballon *glass is still favoured for special brews in the cafés of Belgium. Such beers may be strong ales, Trappist brews, or "Scotch" specialities. Potent beers flourish in Belgium, where the serving of spirits in cafés was made illegal by a measure passed during the worldwide temperance activity of the early 20th century. Many cafés are more basic than this*

El Greco's monks probably brewed their own beer, as holy orders have done ever since their abbeys served as hotels for passing pilgrims. Though their strong brews may have turned a few saints into sinners, the pianist in the New York "lager beer saloon" of 1864 shown above right seems to have led a life of lonely intensity

Good beer is made from malted barley, water, hops and nothing else, according to the German purity law, and the message has been enshrined in many an appreciative rhyme

Der Bierbreuwer.

Auß Gersten sied ich guten Bier/
Feißt vnd Süß/auch bitter monier/
In ein Breuwkessel weit vnd groß/
Darein ich denn den Hopffen stoß/
Laß den inBrennten Külen baß/
Damit füll ich darnach die Faß
Wol gebunden vnd wol gebicht/
Denn giert er vnd ist zugericht.

and the *Berliner Weissebier* brewed in the north.

Top fermentation predates the work of Pasteur, who helped brewers understand the behaviour of yeast. It has thrived as the principal national mode only where traditionalism has been protected by island geography – in Britain and Ireland.

The many bottom-fermenting styles are together known as lagers, after the German word meaning "store". This is because a properly-made bottom-fermenting beer is stored for not less than four weeks, and ideally for much longer, so that it can mature very slowly.

"Lagering" is carried on at low temperatures, and it was probably first practised in caves in the Bavarian Alps. The first mention of the technique seems to be in Bavaria, in the minutes of a Munich city council meeting in 1420. It was first employed in large-scale production in the 1840s, in Munich and by friendly brewers across the Austrian border in Vienna and in Pilsen in Bohemia (now Czechoslovakia). The technique was subsequently popularized in northern Germany by the brewers of Dortmund.

The Pilsener lagers are pale, hoppy and dry. Those of Munich are malty (Müncheners come in both the traditional dark *dunkel* and the later pale *hell* varieties). Between the Pilseners and the Müncheners in palate are the Dortmunders, pale and slightly stronger. The Vienna-style lager, amber, malty and stronger still, is most commonly found today in Munich, where it is described as *Märzenbier*. The brewers of Munich also perfected the strong *bock* lager, which originates from the town of Einbeck, in Lower Saxony, and the extra-strong *doppel* (double) *bock*.

The lager technique became popular because it produced a much more stable, and clearer, beer than could be made at the time by any other method. The building of economic unity in the German-speaking world during the same period, the industrialization of production through the use of steam power, and the spread of railways, helped the innovative brewers of Munich, Vienna and Pilsen to make a name throughout Europe for their lager beers. The Heineken and Carlsberg breweries pioneered lager brewing in The Netherlands and Denmark respectively, and the wave of emigrants from Europe after the 1840s – the Hungry Forties – took the technique, along with their knowledge of cattle-rearing and dairying, to the Mid-West of the United States. Messrs Anheuser and Busch went to

St Louis; Schlitz and Pabst to Milwaukee; the first Adolph Coors to Colorado.

In Germany, a Bavarian law dating back to 1516 demands that beer for the domestic market, with the exception of wheat specialities, be made exclusively from barley. Similar laws exist in Switzerland and Norway. In Finland and the Isle of Man (a self-governing dependency of Britain), barley is the only grain permitted, but sugars may be added. The use of sugar as a fermentable material, and to influence flavour and colour, was legalized in Britain in 1847, after pressure from growers and traders in the Caribbean colonies. Barley is the basis of all true beers, and its exclusive use is favoured not only by tradition but also because it provides a fuller flavour and cleaner taste than any other grain. Lack of availability in some parts of the world, cost, and a tendency of some barleys to produce hazy beers mean that the traditional grain in many countries is augmented with other fermentable materials.

In holding out for an all-barley beer, the purist can point out that even the most commercially minded of breweries retreat from the excessive use of cheaper adjuncts when they set out to make a "super-premium" brand. These same brewers then justify their use of adjuncts in lesser brands by saying, quite truthfully, that these cheaper grains produce lighter-bodied beers.

In the United States, corn (maize), the staple of the Bourbon whiskey industry, is widely used as an adjunct in brewing. It is against that background that Budweiser takes pride not only in its high proportion of barley, but also in its preference for rice as an adjunct. This ingredient is announced with a flourish on the label or can, and the brewery claims that rice contributes to the "distinctly crisp taste" of the world's biggest-selling beer.

Barley has been the preferred grain throughout history; Babylonian texts discuss the suitability of different types for various styles of beers. (Like wine, beer is at least as old as recorded history.) It was also noted in Babylon that hops were used in the production of a beverage which the captive Jews drank as a precaution against leprosy, though it is not clear whether this was a beer.

Although the stickiness of barley had to be offset by the use of some fragrant ingredient, the first evidence that the hop was the most favoured does not emerge, and then sketchily, until the ninth century AD, in Bohemia, Bavaria and northern Germany. The northern Germans may have brought the hop from Picardy in France, and the Flemings took it to Britain, in face of some resistance, in the sixteenth century.

The hop, superficially resembling the vine, and a cousin of cannabis, has an almost mystical impenetrability of character. It is some measure of this that the plant should have become universally accepted by brewers as a flavouring agent. Its early rivals included the juniper, still used by home-brewers in Finland and Norway, angelica, once employed in Sweden, and coriander. All three were used to the same purpose in distilled grain by the Dutch and English in the creation of gin. Another one-time flavouring agent, alder twigs, imparted to Nordic beers the same resinous, sappy quality that wooden casks give to some spirits, notably armagnac. Herbs, spices, barks and resins have also been employed since Roman times to aromatize wines, and eventually gave us today's vermouths and patent aperitifs. In them, and likewise in beer, a delicate bitterness is a prized characteristic, and a great stimulus to the appetite.

La Servance des Bocks is but one of Manet's works on a beery theme. Another famous example is his painting of the bar at the Folies Bergères, in which two bottles of Bass Pale Ale are clearly identifiable

In medieval times, the husband baked the bread while the wife brewed the beer. This ale-wife was portrayed as a hard-faced and grasping harridan, though there is no evidence that such a view was widely held

The thirsty drayman is a figure who has changed little since he was depicted in 1827 by the English caricaturist George Cruikshank. Twenty years later, the artist had become famous as a campaigner against drink

EASTERN EUROPE

All over the world, there are brewers who presume to style their beers "Pils", "Pilsener" or "Pilsner". No soubriquet is so widely used, or persistently misused. It has come to mean, quite wrongly, nothing more than a pale, golden-coloured lager of around four per cent alcohol by weight and five per cent by volume (the two figures differ because alcohol is lighter than water; some beers of this strength have a figure 12 on the label, but that refers to their original density). A brew of no particular quality, but produced to this standard Pilsener lager style and specification, has become a sort of international standard beer.

True, five per cent seems to be an optimum strength for beer (strong enough to taste, but not to intoxicate too quickly); true, pale beers have been popular ever since opaque drinking vessels of pewter and china were replaced by transparent glasses; but every lager which meets those requirements is not necessarily a Pilsener.

A handful of brewers internationally, and a good many more than that in Germany, know that a pale lager of this strength can seriously be regarded as being of the Pilsener type only if it is very well hopped, with the consequent flowery bouquet and dryness of palate. Indeed, in the latter respect, many German brewers outdo the original, perhaps because it presents itself as a competitor, being the biggest imported brand by far in their market. These bone-dry Pilsener-type beers of north Germany are almost a style in themselves.

The original Czech Pilsener has an altogether softer palate, and a Perrier-like *digestif* quality, deriving from the slightly alkaline spring water with which it is made. It is not only the superb Bohemian hops and the local water that have made this beer so famous, but also the geology of the Pilsen area. The last two go hand in hand, and together they helped the brewers of Pilsen to produce in 1842 a lager of a paleness, clarity and sparkle which was at the time without precedent; hence its celebrity.

The local sandy rock lent itself perfectly to the cutting of lagering cellars, which today stretch for six miles, and where the beer is still brought to maturity in oak casks.

Having inspired such imitation, the world's first pale, golden lager has to be sure to identify itself clearly as the original. In most parts of the world, it is labelled Pilsner Urquell ("Urquell" meaning "original source of" in German, the language of Bohemia in the days of the Austro-Hungarian Empire, when the beer was first brewed). In Czech, it is called Plzeňský Prazdroj.

Pilsen has a second brewery, named after Gambrinus, the legendary King of Beer, and founded in 1869. Gambrinus numbers among its products a well liked lower-density beer of 10 degrees (4.5 per cent by volume). Like most knowing beer-drinkers, the Czech manual worker opts for a relatively weak brew when he has a big thirst to quench.

While the rest of the world seized upon the name Pilsener to indicate a pale, golden lager, one inspired

brewer from the United States transplanted into Americana
the name of another Bohemian town which was enjoying
particular success in the new mode: Budweis. In 1876, a
wholly-American beer with the brand-name "Budweiser"
was produced in St Louis, Missouri. Its objective was to
popularize pale lager throughout the United States, and to
become a national brand. Today, American Budweiser is
the world's biggest-selling beer brand.

Meanwhile, the Czech original Budweiser beer is still
produced, its own sales increasing impressively, by the
Budvar brewery in what is now known as České Budějovice.
The original Czech Budweiser is an outstanding pale lager,
light in palate, clean-tasting, bitter-sweet, but without the
spring-water character of its famous cousin.

Because it lacks that *digestif* softness, and because it has
such a markedly clean palate, the Czech Budweiser is in
some respects a truer parent of the derivative pale lagers
produced elsewhere in the world. None the less, its all-
barley body, fermented to such lightness by four months of
maturation, leaves few rivals outside Czechoslovakia.

Budweis, or České Budějovice, also has the Samson
brewery, founded in 1795, the products of which include an
excellent 10-degree dark lager. Budweis and Pilsen were
brewing towns six hundred years before the lager revolution. So were other Bohemian towns like Žatec, which
gave its name to the famous Czech variety of hop, and
Prague. The capital has four breweries, the smallest being U Fleků, a home-brew beerhouse dating back to 1499.

The country has more than one hundred breweries, with
a good spread in Slovakia and Moravia as well as Bohemia.

Czechoslovakia's selection of pale and dark lagers
and "porters", ranging in strength from 3 to 8.5 per cent,
is to varying degrees mirrored in each of the other
Eastern bloc countries, depending upon their brewing
traditions. None of these countries can match
Czech quality, though Hungary and Poland
produce beers worth a second glass.

In Hungary, the quarrying of stone to build
Buda's twin town of Pest left behind caverns which
were ideally suited to the purpose of lagering, and
these were eagerly snapped up by Dreher, who
built his second biggest brewery there in 1854.
The brewery still exists, under the name of
Köbánya, and is well known for a 12-degree beer
known as Rocky Cellar. There is another famous
brewery at Pécs, in an area equally well known
for its wines.

In Poland, German influence has left a considerable brewing tradition in Silesia. There are
three breweries in Wroclaw (formerly Breslau),
and two near Katowice, one of which is the
country's biggest. Galicia's most famous brewery,
at Zywiec, near Cracow, exports quite widely.

The Soviet Union is the world's third or fourth
largest producer of beer, though consumption per
head is relatively low. Because of the problem of
alcoholism among vodka drinkers, beer is, like
wine, officially encouraged as a beverage of moderation. There are 62 brands, including an interesting dark "Ukrainian-style" beer of 13 degrees (5.5
per cent), a well-matured 19-degree (8.25)
"Amber", and the very occasional small-scale survivor of the top-fermenting ales once popular in
Russia. Supply of all beers can, though, be very localized,
and in some places *kvass* or *koumyss* are more accessible.

GERMAN-SPEAKING WORLD

Each of the great brewing nations has its own claim to primacy, but Germany has a whole portfolio of them. Although there is some evidence that the brewing arts of the ancients came West in an arc through the Slavonic and Teutonic worlds (Tacitus noted that the Germans drank beer), Germany's reputation relies on more than history.

In the modern world, West Germany alone not only has more breweries than any other country, but as many as all the other nations put together. The West Germans boast nearly 1,500 breweries, of which almost 1,000 are in Bavaria, home of the *Reinheitsgebot* (Pure Beer Law) and of the world's largest hop-growing industry. Even East Germany, with a population less than a third that of its far larger neighbour, has 225 breweries. Beer continues to be an important part of the social culture in the East, though the overall quality of the product is lower, and consumption less, for whatever reasons.

With a handful of notable and interesting exceptions, most countries of the world today brew in a broadly Teutonic mode, but there are more subtle influences in linguistically-linked countries like Austria and Switzerland.

Most years, the West Germans drink more beer than the people of any other country, though they are customarily challenged by the Czechs, Belgians and Luxemburgers, and Australasians. Other important brewing nations like Britain and the United States stand far down the consumption league.

In Germany, the average consumption per head is usually around 150 litres per year, which equals 264 of the Briton's beloved pints or 422.5 American bottles of beer. This figure is derived from the entire population, including women, children and non-drinkers.

German brewers largely agree that pasteurization damages the life and hop-character of beer, and seldom employ the technique in the home market, where turnover is fast enough to prevent any deterioration of the product. This is true even of bottled beer, and it is one of the reasons why cans are rarely used in Germany. Further fermentation in the bottle might blow off the top, but a can would explode.

The popularity of "fresh", unpasteurized beer has helped Germany avoid the centralization and concentration which has, to the great detriment of variety and individuality, affected the brewing industries of several other countries. A further factor is the decentralized nature of the country itself. With no single dominant city or region, each has at least to some extent been able to retain its own tastes, traditions and local pride.

None the less, many brewery companies have strings of subsidiaries, and some of the giants share the backing of the same banks or holding groups. Such a link joins Germany's biggest brewing company, Schultheiss, of Berlin, with two other giants. They are the Dortmunder Union Brewery, one of half a dozen or so major breweries in the city of Dortmund; and Löwenbräu, internationally famous, but at home just one among the Munich Big Six.

(Löwenbräu has no connection with the excellent Swiss brewing company of the same name; in whatever language, the world is full of Lion Breweries.)

The other members of the Munich Big Six are Augustiner, Hacker-Pschorr, Hofbräuhaus, Paulaner-Thomas and Spatenbräu. Each has its claims to fame, but none more than Spatenbräu, the home of the great innovator Gabriel Sedlmayr in the 1800s. Over the years, Sedlmayr drew on the work of Liebig, von Linde and Pasteur, and he is especially remembered as having paved the way for the brewing of the first modern lager by his contemporary Anton Dreher at the Klein-Schwechat brewery in Vienna in 1841. (Schwechat still functions, and is now owned by the Österreichische Brau group, Austria's biggest brewers.)

While the Munich lagers were a dark brown in colour, it seems likely that the Vienna brew was a translucent amber. A year later came the clear, golden beer of Pilsen.

In some parts of the world, a brown lager of modest strength which is malty without being excessively sweet is still described as a *Münchener*. In its home city, this type of brew is identified as *dunkel* (dark) to distinguish it from the pale (*hell*) version of the Munich style which emerged in the 1920s and became the everyday beer of Germany. Beers in style have an alcohol content ranging from just under 4 per cent by volume to something over 4.5, and a mild, malty palate. Neither strong nor dry, they may be drunk in reasonable quantity, as suits the local custom.

There is some doubt as to which of the big Munich brewers first produced a *hell* beer, with Spaten, Paulaner-Thomas, and by implication Hofbräuhaus among the claimants.

Whatever the historical claims of Munich and the south, a greater quantity of beer, city for city, is now produced in the northern brewing capital of Dortmund. Lager-brewing did not take long to arrive

The lid may help keep the drink cool, but cannot contain the dense head favoured by drinkers in most parts of Germany. Decorated stoneware is also used for serving Frankfurt Apfelwein

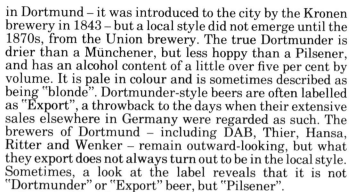

in Dortmund – it was introduced to the city by the Kronen brewery in 1843 – but a local style did not emerge until the 1870s, from the Union brewery. The true Dortmunder is drier than a Münchener, but less hoppy than a Pilsener, and has an alcohol content of a little over five per cent by volume. It is pale in colour and is sometimes described as being "blonde". Dortmunder-style beers are often labelled as "Export", a throwback to the days when their extensive sales elsewhere in Germany were regarded as such. The brewers of Dortmund – including DAB, Thier, Hansa, Ritter and Wenker – remain outward-looking, but what they export does not always turn out to be in the local style. Sometimes, a look at the label reveals that it is not "Dortmunder" or "Export" beer, but "Pilsener".

Back in Munich, the southern brewers have an equally catholic attitude. At Spatenbräu, the great Sedlmayr was so inspired by Dreher's Vienna beer, that he produced something similar, and called it *Märzenbier*, to commemorate the days before his own work on refrigeration rendered seasonable brewing unnecessary. At that time, it was impossible to brew in the heat of the summer. The last brew of the winter, made in March (*März*), was stored in lagering caves until the end of September, then ceremonially enjoyed.

Today's *Märzenbier* is still a seasonal brew, being notably enjoyed at the Munich *Oktoberfest* and Stuttgart's similar *Canstatter Wasen*. In consequence it is sometimes known colloquially as a *Wasen* or *Wiesen* beer, a term which to the outsider is confusingly similar to *Weizen* (wheat) or *Weisse* (white), but which indicates neither. A German *Märzenbier* is a conventional lager, but with a typical amber colour, a full body and malty palate, and an above-average alcohol content of 5.5 per cent by volume.

Although this style is not widely produced elsewhere in the world, it can be found here and there. Sometimes, in acknowledgement of its Austrian inspiration, it is known as a Vienna-style beer. In Mexico, once a part of the Hapsburg empire, the Dos Equis brand is a well-known example. Confusingly, the Austrians themselves today use the term *Märzen* to describe some rather ordinary beers. Although the Austrians still produce beers of very acceptable quality, the nearest they get to the classic style of Dreher is in their *spezial* brews.

Another inspiration for the brewers of Munich was the strong beer produced further north in Einbeck, Lower Saxony, during the thirteenth century. Einbeck was the most important brewing town in the Hanseatic League, and it produced beers of a very high original density, so that they could slowly ferment-out on their journeys to the fringes of Europe and beyond, in those pre-pasteurization days. Einbeck beer was given to Martin Luther as a wedding present, and to sustain him during the Diet of Worms.

Although the original Einbeck beers would have been produced by top-fermentation, their high alcohol content is remembered today in the very strongest of lagers. "Einbeck" was over the years abbreviated and corrupted until it became "Bock". Since that is the German word for a billy-goat, the beer is sometimes linked with the astrological sign of Capricorn, though the two can hardly be said to coincide. The astrological sign belongs to December and January, while the beer is usually drunk at the beginning of the traditional winter brewing season (in October or November) or at the end (March, April, May). In these months, there are celebrations in parts of Germany.

The beers themselves come in both pale (bronze) and

dark brown versions and they are usually more heavily hopped and less sickly-sweet than might be expected of a brew so strong. German *bock* beers normally have an alcohol content in excess of 6 per cent, and a *doppel* (double) *bock* has at least 7.5. Other countries affect these styles with varying degrees of fidelity, though in the French-speaking world the term *bock* is perversely used to indicate a weak beer. This probably derives from the Gallic custom of using a large "German-style" glass from which to drink a long, weak, thirst-quenching beer.

The local brewery in Einbeck still produces an excellent *bock*. With the prefix to proclaim its originality, this is labelled Einbecker Ur-Bock. A good few miles to the south, through Hesse and into Bavaria, the EKU brewery of Kulmbach, not far from Bayreuth, produces a *doppelbock* of 13.2 per cent, which is the world's strongest beer.

This is no mean feat, since an alcohol concentration of much over 11 per cent kills even the most patiently tenacious of brewing yeasts and thus arrests fermentation. The EKU brewery's answer to this is to refrigerate the beer until ice starts to appear. Since water freezes before alcohol, the removal of some ice strengthens the beer by concentration. The result is astonishingly potent but too thick to be very agreeable, even when its syrupy quality is offset by chilling.

EKU's famous "fortified" beer is known by the brand-name of Kulminator, and it shares its suffix with a great many other more conventional *doppelbock* brews. The tradition began with the first "double" *bock*, produced under the name of Salvator by the monks of St Paul, in Munich. Their brewery eventually fell into secular hands, but both the business and the *doppelbock* brand survive under the Paulaner-Thomas name.

Germany still has several active abbey breweries, especially in Bavaria, where two of the most famous are Andechs (inspiration for the American Andeker brand-name) and Mallersorf (where the brewmaster is a nun). There are also a couple of abbey breweries in Austria.

When the tide of lager-brewing swept through Germany, one or two proud and independent towns held out for their own traditional top-fermenting styles. The most precisely defined of civic styles is that of Cologne, in that the term *Kölsch*, the adjective formed from the name of the city, is in the matter of beer an *appellation contrôlée*.

This distinctive and distinguished *Kölsch* beer is one of the few top-fermenting styles to be produced in a truly pale colour. It is very pale indeed, a brassy colour, unusually gentle in its natural carbonation, with an agreeable lactic-acid quality as well as a delicate hop character, making it an excellent aperitif (though it is also an excellent *digestif*). Its alcohol content by volume is around 4.5 per cent. *Kölsch* is tapped straight from wooden casks in typical Cologne taverns like P.J. Fruh or Sion, which are both supplied by their own breweries, and at the Päffgen home-brew house. It is usually served in very narrow, tall cylindrical glasses, with snacks like *Mettwurst*, *Blutwurst* or cheese.

A more widely available top-fermenting beer is the type known simply as *alt* ("old") in recognition of the fact that this style of brewing predates the lager method. *Altbier* is the traditional brew of North Rhineland and Westphalia and, having stubbornly survived, it began during the 1970s to gain a wider popularity in Germany.

Although the *Alt* produced at the famous Munster home-brew house of Pinkus Muller is "blonde" (a pale, golden colour), most examples of this style have a deep, copper

hue. *Alt* has a full, malty palate but also an excellent hop bitterness, and its alcohol content by volume is usually just over 4 per cent. It is traditionally served in short, wide cylindrical glasses, and has a dense head. Its heartland is Düsseldorf, which has three home-brew houses: Im Füchschen, Zum Üerige, and Ferdinand Schuhmacher.

The even older wheat beer styles, which predate the universal acceptance of barley as the brewer's grain, are both still made by top-fermentation.

In its apparently infinite variety and sophistication, the South German version, known simply as *Weizenbier* (wheat beer), surely represents the baroque wing of craftsman brewing. Although the basic *Weizenbier* has an alcoholic content of around five per cent, many of the permutations are much stronger, and some are bottled with a *dosage* of yeast to send them on their way. Among the several breweries which specialize in this type of beer are Sanwald, in Stuttgart, and Weihenstephan, not far from Munich. These beers are usually served in a tall, vase-shaped glass, with lemon to sharpen their grainy palate.

The South German versions are made from a mash comprising between one-third, and two-thirds wheat, and the rest barley. The North German *Berliner Weisse* ("white") has only one part of wheat to three of barley, and is also characterized by a lactic-acid secondary fermentation in the bottle. The result is a very light, sparkling summer brew which has been dubbed "the Champagne of the Spree". This individualistic classic, brewed on both sides of the border, is traditionally served in enormous bowl-shaped glasses, and flavoured with essence of woodruff or raspberry. It has an alcohol content of only 2.5 to 3 per cent.

While such exotica flourishes far beyond Berlin, some other local specialities now have a more limited local existence. In the civic shadow of the famous Beck's beer, an excellent German lager but undistinctive in style, there still exists Bremen's sedimented *Kreusenbier*, albeit served in only a few selected taverns. Nürnberg has its roasty "copper" beer, and the Bavarian town of Bamberg a "smoked" beer. Among the many malt-extract brews there are two ancient versions, still produced in Brunswick, Lower Saxony, and Bad Kostritz, East Germany. Vestigial they may be, but individuality counts for a lot.

THE AMERICAS

The diversity of beers produced in the Americas is far greater than is commonly realized, and this is true even of the United States, which superficially might seem committed wholly to quantity at the expense of character.

Though the people of the United States drink relatively little per head, and have not always appreciated fine beers as they might, their country is by far the world's biggest producer in volume due to the sheer size of the population.

Christopher Columbus observed that the American Indians brewed a drink from maize, using birch sap for flavour; the Pilgrim Fathers cut their journey short at Plymouth Rock because they had run out of beer (having landed, they presumably set about brewing some more); and the first commercial brewery was opened by the Dutch West India Company in 1632 on Manhattan Island.

It is as a legacy of the early settlers that the old styles of beer, the ales, porters and stouts, are still most likely to be found in the East, from Quebec and the Maritime Provinces of Canada to New York State and Pennsylvania. These are all in their own way interesting beers: some because they are, indeed, authentically top-fermented products of a traditional character; others because they

are curious hybrids. In some instances, an ale mash is combined with bottom fermentation. In other cases, the term "ale" is used to indicate a bottom-fermenting beer which is, by North American standards, unusually well hopped, and probably of above-average strength.

In Canada, the overwhelming majority of brands turn out to belong to one of the country's Big Three – Carling, Molson and Labatt – though the Maritimes are proud of their independent Moosehead Breweries.

In upstate New York, a couple of relatively small brewing companies have won reputations for their interesting products. In Rochester, the Genesee brewery is especially well known for its Twelve Horse Ale and its Cream Ale. Another well-regarded Cream Ale is produced not far away by the local brewery at Utica. "Cream Ale" has long been a recognized term in American brewing, and seems to have first been used in this part of the country. There is not much evidence to support claims that the description is Irish in origin. Nor is there anything particularly creamy about beers described in this way. They are a compromise between a true ale and a lager, often bottom-fermenting.

The most famous Eastern ales are the Ballantine range, which were first brewed in New York State, then in Newark, and now at the Narragansett brewery at Cranston, Rhode Island. All three of them are top-fermented, and each has a powerful aroma of Brewer's Gold hops. The basic product is called simply Ballantine's Ale. A premium ale is known as Brewer's Gold, and the patriarch of the family is the superb India Pale Ale, aged for five months in wood, and with an alcohol content of more than 7.5 per cent by volume.

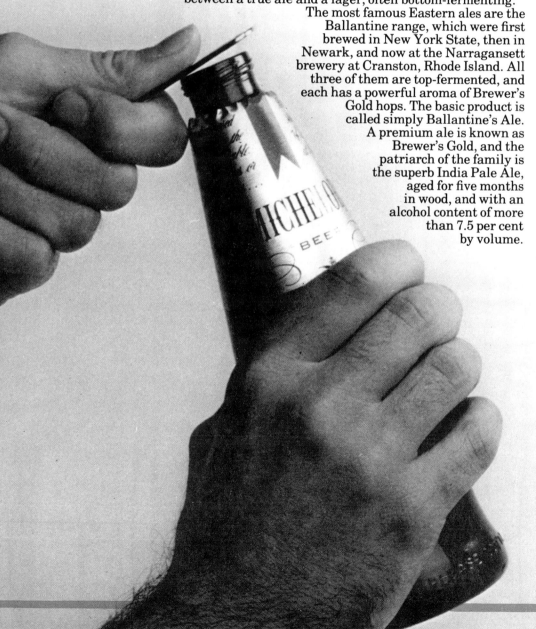

Ever since William Penn opened the first brewery there, the state which bears his name has done its best to look after the drinker. Today, it has a dozen breweries, which is more than can be offered by any other state. Philadelphia has two, Schmidt and Ortlieb, the latter long ago well known for its *Weissebier*, and more recently for McSorley's Cream Ale; the small town of St Mary's has the excellent Straub brewery; and Pottsville has Yuengling, the oldest brewing company in the United States.

Yuengling produces a colourful range of beers, among which are a lively, sweetish and well-hopped though bottom-fermenting ale called Lord Chesterfield (4.5 per cent) and The Celebrated Pottsville Porter, at a similar strength. The brewery, which was founded in 1829, also produces a *bock* beer.

Even the Eastern states become richest in breweries where they cling to the Great Lakes, and it is middle America which is today more popularly associated with the production of beer. Just as those early British and Dutch brought their brewing traditions to the East, so a subsequent wave of immigrants added theirs. Coming later, going further, to what are now the great cattle-rearing and dairying lands of the Mid-West, the Germans who fled European hunger in the mid-1800s also implanted lager-brewing in the United States.

The great beer-producing state of the mid-West is Wisconsin, with tiny but celebrated breweries like Huber, of Monroe, the Stevens Point Beverage Company, Leinenkugel, of Chippewa Falls, and Walter, of Eau Claire. Much as these small firms mean to the cognoscenti, the state is more widely known for the great brewing city of Milwaukee. In the 1840s and 1850s, Milwaukee gave birth to three brewing companies which are today national giants: Pabst, Schlitz and Miller.

Pabst, which has Andeker as its super-premium brand and also owns the estimable Blitz-Weinhard brewery in Oregon, is probably the most conservative of the three. Schlitz was at one stage the biggest-selling beer in the United States, but the company's desire for volume led to short lagering periods, the introduction of agitated fermentation, and in consequence a product rather lacking in finesse. Miller, once famous for its socially-aspirant High Life brand, took an ascetic turn in the 1970s. Despite its being owned by a cigarette company (Philip Morris), Miller won the waistlines of health-conscious Americans with its Lite beer. Although it was not the first company to market this type of beer Miller was the most successful, and its influence had a dramatic effect on the policies of brewers throughout the United States. American "light" beers are extremely watery, and quite different in style from the strong, dry, well-attenuated "diet" beers made in some European countries. The strength of nationally marketed American beers varies according to state laws, but is usually in a band of 4-5 per cent by volume.

The other great brewing city of middle America is St Louis. It may be a one-company town, but Anheuser-Busch is the world's biggest brewing firm. Run by the great-grandson of its founder, August Busch III, the company has a markedly more traditionalist approach than its immediate rivals. It was made famous not by its basic Busch brand but by its "premium" beer, Budweiser. When Anheuser-Busch first produced Budweiser, in 1876, the notion of a "premium" brand to be marketed nationally rather than locally was new. The idea of nationally mar-

keted brands soon became commonplace, and Anheuser-Busch found it necessary to reach higher for a luxury beer and invent the "super-premium" category, Michelob.

Both Budweiser and the fuller-bodied Michelob have a higher barley content than is usual in American beer, are made with hops rather than hop extract, and are aged for more than a month. They are also *krausened*. This means that a little unbrewed beer is added during lagering to produce a secondary fermentation and an added sparkle. Finally, the brew is filtered through porous beechwood chips. Commonplace "Bud" may be, but it is better than the average mass-produced beer.

Such judgements have to be made in the context of everyday American beers, which are characterized by an ability to refresh rather than to surprise. The other great example in this respect is Coors, a beer of such refreshing qualities that it is difficult to see why the brewery went on to produce a "light" version. Unlike the other giants, which have branch breweries all over the country, Coors has only one, in Golden, Colorado. This is the world's biggest single brewery, and its product for some years enjoyed a great chic partly because it was readily available in unpasteurized form; Coors pioneered the use of fine-filtration in the United States, so that even in cans the beer could be left unpasteurized. Fine-filtration does remove some of the character from beer, but less than pasteurization does.

As it became more widely available, Coors lost some of its mystique, and the publicly right wing stances of its owner cost it votes in the young, liberal Californian market, where its fame had first spread.

It might be argued that the so-called malt liquor is an indigenous American beer, but this is nothing more than an undistingushed strong lager, low on hops, usually high on enzymes. A more truly original American style is represented by the curious hybrid which the Californians produced in trying to brew a beer with the characteristics of lager but without the use of ice from the Great Lakes.

This beer, fermented at ale temperatures but with a lager yeast, in uniquely shallow vessels, and then *krausened*, has a very lively head. Local lore has it that the pressure released when the casks were tapped led it to be called "Steam" beer. The name stuck, and this style is kept alive in the unique, distinctive, and delicious product of Fritz Maytag's Anchor Brewery, in San Francisco.

Until the late 1970s, the only other truly individualistic beer in the West was the excellent Rainier ale, from Seattle. Then, sixty miles north of San Francisco, at Sonoma, the tiny New Albion brewery was established to produce an outstanding, bitter, bottle-conditioned ale. This brewery, staffed only by its two partners, became the inspiration for several would-be revivalists in parts of the country, including its neighbour Tom DeBakker.

The other great influence in restoring the variety lost during Prohibition has been the growing number of imported beers, including those from other parts of the American continent. These include the very crisp lagers of the West Indies, like Red Stripe and Carib, lightly hopped and very thoroughly attenuated. They also include a number of beers from various Latin countries, among which the Mexican products are particularly interesting. Apart from conventional pale lagers, the Mexicans produce Münchener-style (*oscura*) brews, Vienna-style beers like Dos Equis, and strong, dark Christmas specials.

As ever, the ethnicity of its immigrants has influenced the tastes of the United States.

ASIA AND AFRICA

The exotic East gives suitably evocative names to its famous beers, though they are perfectly ordinary lagers. Just as the veterans of Vietnam remember the French-born "33" beer still to be found in the odd corners of Asia, so an earlier generation of servicemen recall Tiger Beer as a symbol of Singapore.

The Tiger was established in Singapore and Kuala Lumpur as a joint venture between a local soft-drinks firm and Heineken, after the Dutch company had run into set-backs with a plan to open a brewery in Java in 1929. In 1946, the famous slogan "Time for a Tiger" was introduced.

Anchor is a less hoppy beer brewed by the same company. Carlsberg produces a regular lager and its much more potent Special Brew locally in Malaysia, and the latter has a competitor in Gold Harp, a high-quality strong lager from a Guinness associate.

The strong, tropical-style version of Guinness is brewed in Malaysia, and in several countries of Asia and Africa (it was originally produced for the Nigerian market). It is also imported into some territories from Dublin. Stouts are held to have aphrodisiac properties by the Chinese.

China has bottom-fermenting "porters", as well as a good many conventional lagers. The best known in the West is Tsingtao, produced at a brewery originally set up by the Germans when they controlled Shantung.

Animal symbols, often beautifully designed, are widely used as trademarks by brewers and shippers in Asia. The most colourful of all is surely the dragon-horse, said by legend to have presaged the birth of Confucius. This potent symbol, the Kirin, was adopted in 1888 by a Japanese concern, which had acquired a small American-owned brewery in Yokohama.

Today, Kirin is the biggest brewer outside the United States, and its exports continue to grow. It dominates its competitors in the brewing industry, Sapporo, Asahi and Suntory, the last named a pioneer of micro-filtered unpasteurized beer. In addition to its everyday brews, and the odd stronger lager like Kirin's Mein Bräu, Japan has medium stouts and a category described as "black" beers. These are similar to the traditional Münchener.

Another giant is San Miguel, the name testifying to the Spanish colonial history of the Philippines, where the company is headquartered and owned.

Colonial history and early trading links have left their tangled marks on the brewing map of Asia and Africa. In some instances, the colonial firms survive; in others, independent local companies have been set up. In Africa, there are many joint ventures, sometimes with big banks, trading companies and governments as additional partners.

Most countries in Asia and Africa have at least one brewery, and Nigeria and Zaire have sizable brewing industries. Many Moslem countries have breweries "for the expatriate community and the tourists", though some have been threatened by Islamic fundamentalism.

In South Africa, the tobacco-based Rupert group failed to establish itself as a brewer locally, but has a major international stake through Carling in Canada and United Breweries (Carlsberg and Tuborg) in Denmark.

AUSTRALASIA

When Australia began to step out from the shadow of its mother country in the late 1960s, the rest of the world quickly learned of its formidable national thirst for beer. Not only are Australians noisily chauvinistic about their beers, they are also extremely partisan in lauding the products of their home state.

This, and a predilection for ice-cold lagers, has obscured the fact that Australia is the habitat of two unique classics, produced not in Sydney or Melbourne but in the less assertive southern state capital of Adelaide.

While today's classic pale ale in Britain has a truly sparkling clarity, it is easy to imagine that the celebrated original ale of the 1750s might have been much more like the magnificently robust product of Cooper's brewery in Adelaide. Cooper's Ale, described on the label as "sparkling", doesn't sparkle; it is cloudy, yeasty, full of hop character, superbly bitter, conditioned in wooden casks, bottled without filtration or pasteurization, at an alcohol content of around 5.75 per cent by volume.

As if that were not enough, Cooper's also produces a highly distinctive stout, at just under seven per cent by volume, with a woody, roasted-barley palate that is surely also a taste of history. This uniquely old-fashioned brewery, founded by a Yorkshireman in 1862 and still managed by his family, is the sole true guardian of the vanishing colonial tradition of brewing. Adelaide also has the South Australian Brewing Company, producing conventional lager beers. In Western Australia, the well-known Swan Brewery Company produces lagers and stouts under its own name and the Emu and Hannan's brands. It has breweries in Perth and Kalgoorlie, and has been a partner in several other ventures, including the only brewery in Darwin. Although the Northern Territory is the thirstiest part of Australia, it is known less for the quality or character of its beer than for the "Darwin Stubby" . . . a two-gallon bottle. Queensland's local brewer, Castlemaine

Perkins, produces Carbine Stout, named after a famous Australian racehorse, and a "Bitter Ale" which turns out merely to be an agreeably hoppy lager of just under five per cent by volume. Terms like "ale" and "draught" are used with some imprecision in Australia. In 1979, Castlemaine Perkins merged with the Sydney firm of Toohey's, well known for its dark ale, a style known as "old" in Australia. The epithet indicates that ale is an old style of beer, not that it has been fermented for a long time. Toohey's Old, and the Hunter Ale produced by its sister brewery in Newcastle, New South Wales, have an alcohol content by volume of around 4.25 per cent.

Toohey's, with its Irish name, was traditionally the favourite brewery of Sydney's Catholics. The Protestant population favoured Tooth's, founded in the 1830s by an Englishman from the hop-growing county of Kent. Both breweries produce old ales, stouts, and lagers under a variety of brand-names. Tooth's also owns the Resch's brand, under which label it produces the popular "KB" (Kent Brewery) lager, at about 4.7 per cent by volume.

Also in 1979, Tooth's took over a brewery established near Melbourne ten years earlier by the British firm of Courage. Although it had produced one or two interesting beers, the Australian Courage label had not been able to make a great deal of headway against the might of Carlton and United Breweries (C.U.B.), the national giant, which is also based in the state of Victoria.

Carlton has a number of breweries, and several different brand-names. Carlton Draught, very popular in Australia, is a relatively dry lager; the company also owns Foster's Lager, a rather sweet beer greatly yearned for by Australians in exile. Both of these brands have an alcohol content of just under five per cent.

Hops are grown in Victoria and Tasmania, and the island state has two breweries, Cascade and Boag's, both under the same ownership.

New Zealand has only three brewing companies, though they own a dozen breweries and at least as many brand-names. Although some of their beers are copper-coloured, and look rather like English ales, they are all lagers. Most of them have an alcohol content in the range of 3.5-4.5 per cent by volume. One of the three, Dominion breweries, is said to have invented continuous fermentation, which hardly makes it a favourite with the connoisseur. Dominion has a substantial market share, as does New Zealand Breweries, which also owns a stake in the much smaller Leopard company, of Hastings. Leopard is jointly owned with Heineken and Malayan Breweries.

NORTHERN EUROPE

Though the nations of the Nordic world have long and intertwining traditions of brewing, reaching back to Viking times and beyond, it is specifically Denmark which has played a significant part in the recent history of the art. Likewise, while Iceland, Norway, Sweden and Finland all place considerable restrictions on the production, sale and public consumption of alcoholic drink, Denmark has a more relaxed attitude. But all four countries have a lively and colourful home-brewing culture which is deeply rooted in their agricultural life.

It was from a farm in Jutland that Christian Jacobsen set out in the 1700s to seek his fortune in Copenhagen, subsequently set up as a brewer, and became the forebear of Carlsberg. For reasons not due to commercial success but to its visionary role in the 1800s, Carlsberg remains one of the most enduring names in modern brewing history.

Even this early Jacobsen was an innovator, being one of the first Danish brewers to use a thermometer instead of testing the heat by dipping his elbow in the brew; such advances may seem laughable today, but in the major brewing countries they were significant steps towards the creation of a consistent and dependable product.

Jacobsen's son, Jacob Christian, was responsible for much more important advances. When Jacob Christian Jacobsen became a brewer, Denmark's beers were top-fermented, usually made from wheat, and still of less-than-consistent quality; at the same time, there was a fashion among prosperous Danes, as there was throughout fashionable Europe, for the new lagers produced in Munich.

His remarkable response to this challenge has become a romantic legend. Jacob Christian went to work as a pupil in Munich at the Sedlmayr brewery, and on his return had learned enough to produce a drinkable lager in his mother's wash-copper. With a greater grasp of the situation than was common among most brewers at the time, Jacob Christian realized that the key to real success in lager-brewing was the yeast culture used. Quite how he did it is in some doubt, but he obtained two pots of yeast from the Sedlmayr brewery, and took them home to Copenhagen on what must have seemed an interminable journey by stagecoach. The legend has it that he protected the pots of yeast in his stove-pipe hat, and that at every single stop he had to get out of the coach and pump water on them to keep the culture alive.

With this magical agent of fermentation, Christian successfully brewed Denmark's first commercially produced bottom-fermenting beers, and he subsequently established a lager brewery in a Copenhagen suburb. The new brewery was on a hill, for which the Danish word is *berg*, and Christian named it after his young son Carl.

Towards the end of his life, Jacob Christian employed a young scientist called Emil Hansen, who made history while working at Carlsberg by isolating the first single-cell yeast culture. The single-cell yeast used by lager-brewers the world over is still known as *Saccharomyces Carlsbergenis*.

In one of the world's greatest gestures of philanthropy, Jacob Christian left his entire brewing business to the

Carlsberg foundation for the advancement of science. Carl Jacobsen built churches, public squares and gardens, donated the Little Mermaid statue to his native city, and bequeathed his part of the business to the New Carlsberg Foundation for the support of the arts. Donations and bequests from the two Jacobsens are evident in almost every major museum or institution for the arts or sciences in Denmark, and in many other parts of the world, and the profits from Carlsberg are still used wholly for philanthropic purposes.

In order to ensure that this would continue, a contract was drawn up requiring that the Carlsberg Foundation always hold at least fifty-one per cent of the joint stock company formed by the merger with Tuborg in 1970. The two companies had been friendly rivals since the earliest days, and long-time collaborators, but this provision made possible the merger, which was intended to strengthen the national brewing industry in readiness for Denmark's entry into the European Economic Community. It also probably helped muffle concern among Danish liberals that Carlsberg should, through the South Africans' holding in Tuborg, become a link in the Rupert group's international brewing chain.

The merged company is known as United Breweries of Copenhagen. It also owns Neptun and Wiibroe, two of the twenty or so small breweries in Denmark. Among the minnows, Faxe has a particular reputation among drinkers for its independent stance and unpasteurized Fad beer.

Having helped popularize lager brewing far from its original homelands, the Danes also developed their own style, which is a milder approximation of the classic Pilsener. They do, however, continue to brew in other modes.

These include two types of low-strength beer which are exempt from tax. One is known, perhaps in memory of the old wheat beers, as white ale (*hvidtøl*). Confusingly, a white ale is available in two hues: light (*lys*) or dark (*mørkt*). The other low-strength style is a roasty-tasting malt beer called ship's ale (*skibsøl*), which in days gone by would have fermented out to a much higher strength during long sea journeys. These low-strength brews have an alcohol content by weight of between one and two per cent.

Beers are customarily graded according to their alcohol content by weight in Denmark; the figure for volume would be higher by a proportion of one-quarter. Although most of the taxable beers are a conventional golden lager colour, there is the odd Vienna-style lager and one or two Müncheners. Those beers labelled *let* (this means light, but in weight rather than colour) have an alcohol content of less than 2.5 per cent, and are classified as grade II; everyday lagers in Denmark usually have a modest 3.75 per cent, and are classified as grade I; and premium grade "A" brands like Carlsberg Gold have 4.0-4.5 per cent. Beers stronger than that are classified as grade "B", among them seasonal brews for Easter (*Paske*), Whit (*Pinse*) and Christmas (*Jule*), at around 5.25-6.25. Year-round strong beers include Carlsberg's 1847 Vienna-style brew (5.5), Elephant (5.7, and known in some markets as Carlsberg '68), Tuborg Fine Festival (6.2) and the famous export brand Special Brew (6.8), along with one or two porters and stouts (around 6.0).

A much more restricted range of beers is available in the other Nordic countries. Iceland's Polar Beer is officially for export only, and the precise detail of restrictions on the strength of beer is a matter of constant political thrust and parry in Norway, Sweden and Finland.

THE BENELUX COUNTRIES

Hidden delights await the beer-drinker in Belgium. Belgian beers are unrivalled anywhere in the world in diversity and idiosyncrasy. They range from antique "Scotch" ales of great strength, and the specialities of Trappist monks, to "wild" wheat beers and sharp summer brews fermented with black cherries.

In seeking them out at the ubiquitous Belgian café, which is encouraged to provide strong and interesting beers by a law forbidding it from serving spirits, the drinker must first disregard the obvious. The fascia of the café will boldly announce a brand of beer which is an everyday lager: Stella Artois, Lamot, Jupiler, or one of several others. If this is the type of beer the drinker wants, he had best seek out the excellent Cristal Alken. The characteristic taste of Belgium is more likely to be offered on the menu card, or just identified as the speciality of the house.

Some of these specialities are so individualistic as to defy classification. An outstanding example in this respect is Duvel, one of the world's great beers. Duvel is an unusually pale top-fermenting brew with a soft taste which altogether belies its considerable strength of about 7.5 per cent alcohol by volume. It is conditioned for two or three months in the brewery, and in the 33-centilitre size is bottled with a yeast sediment, which imparts a great zest to the beer. Duvel is customarily served chilled, which is unusual for a top-fermenting beer, but refrigeration should be sufficiently gentle to preserve its delicate hop character.

While the qualities of Duvel are accepted by all Belgian connoisseurs, the yet more unusual Rodenbach, perhaps the most individualistic of all, is a taste which has to be acquired. The effort is worthwhile. Rodenbach has a sharp, fruity, lactic-acid palate, and a distinctive reddish colour. It is made by the blending of two top-fermented brews, one of which has been matured for eighteen months in oak. The regular version of Rodenbach is of medium strength, but the tissue-wrapped *Grand Cru* is, after having been blended, matured for anything from eighteen months to eight years, and has an alcohol content of 6.5 per cent.

Belgium has a truly astonishing range of top-fermenting specialities. These include potent brews like Gouden Carolus (8.0 per cent) and Bush Beer (10.0); locally brewed and imported Christmas and Scotch ales of 8.0, 9.0 and 10.0 per cent, such as have long ceased to be available in Caledonia; extra-strong versions of English-style pale ales at 5.5-6.0 per cent; the characteristic brown ales of Oudenaarde, as best exemplified by Liefman's Gouden Band "Provisie" (around 0.5), which is conditioned for eighteen months; at a more conventional strength, the superb, yeasty De Koninck beer of Antwerp, which should be sampled on draught; and a great many more. Every province has its own favourites.

The country also has five monasteries which produce

their own top-fermenting specialities, and a great many commercial breweries affect "abbey" styles. The genuine monastery breweries are all Trappist: Westmalle, in the north of Flanders, is especially famous for its unusually pale Triple, with an alcohol content of 8.0-9.0 per cent and a beautifully balanced palate. The other Flemish monastery, St Sixtus, at Westvleteren, brews only on a small scale, and contracts out most of its production to a nearby commercial company. In French-speaking Belgium, the monastery of Chimay is renowned for its aromatic Capsule Bleue (9.0 per cent). The nearby monastery of Orval produces only one beer, an extremely distinguished and bitter ale. A third monastery in the French-speaking region, Rochefort, produces a full range of typically Trappist beers but in smaller quantity.

Like Germany, Belgium has a tradition of "white" wheat beers, low in alcohol, brewed to refresh in the summer. This tradition is especially associated with Leuven (Louvain) and the Flemish areas to the east of that city. Today, it is kept alive by a single, tiny revivalist brewery in Hoegaarden.

While the "white" wheat beers are unusual, they are produced by a fairly conventional brewing process. This is not true of Belgium's unique, spontaneously fermenting *lambic* wheat beers, which are local to Brussels and are produced in the area to the immediate west of the city. *Lambic* beer is fermented very slowly, for periods of from one to two years or more, without the addition of yeast. Fermentation is brought about by the natural micro-organisms in the atmosphere, and it is said that the conditions are right only in the valley of the river Senne. A weak *lambic* primed with sugar to induce further fermentation is known as *faro*. A blend of several *lambic* beers is known as *gueuze*, and it is in that form that the beer is most commonly found. While a single *lambic* is still and cider-like, *gueuze* is livelier and fruitier. A further dimension is added when black cherries are fermented in *lambic* to make *kriek*, an age-old summer beer of this district.

In stark contrast, while Belgium represents variety, its culturally linked neighbours to the north are in the business of volume. The Netherlands is the home of Heineken, which took European beer to the United States in a big way, by exporting and not by licensing or producing locally. Heineken is, nevertheless, regarded very much as a mass producer at home and also owns Amstel. Skol is a largely Anglo–Dutch operation, owning the Oranjeboom and Breda/Drie Hoefijzers breweries in The Netherlands. Grolsch, a substantial independent, produces really excellent beers. So do many of the tiny breweries in Dutch Brabant and Limburg.

The third Benelux country, tiny Luxembourg, has half a dozen breweries, among which the family firm of Simon, in Wiltz, has the most interesting range of products.

Chimay is one of the best-known abbey breweries in Belgium, and the country has made a speciality of its monastic beers, which are usually strong, top-fermenting ales of a highly distinctive style. The Chimay brewery, especially noted for its capsule bleue, is on the borders of Hainaut and Namur, close to the French frontier

SOUTHERN EUROPE

Although it is broadly true that the warm southern countries of Europe cultivate grapes and make wine, while the cold north grows barley and drinks beer, the frontier between the two takes all sorts of twists and turns. Rhine wines flourish north of Bavarian beers, and there are many such wrinkles where Germanic and Romantic worlds meet.

In particular, the breweries in the north of France conspire to make that country, perhaps surprisingly, one of the world's major beer-producing nations. About half of France's breweries are in the northwest, and it is this area which accommodates most of those family firms that have so far escaped a tidal wave of takeovers and closures. The countryside around the city of Lille, and stretching to the coast, is culturally very Flemish, with English echoes, and so are its beers, in both name and nature.

Several of the beers are top-fermenting, and the typical style of this area is a rich, full-bodied ale which has been matured slowly to provide a surprising smoothness and lightness of palate. These are known as Bières de Garde, and are often presented in large, litre bottles, corked and wired in the manner of champagne.

Near Lille, the sizeable firm of Pelforth produces a well-known brown beer and an agreeable "Irish Red Ale". The latter is made under licence from the brewery of George Killian Lett, of Enniscorthy, County Wexford. It happens that Mr Lett hasn't brewed for twenty years, but wisely kept his licence up to date, and therefore has the right to franchise it. To the east of Lille, in Maubeuge, a porter called "39" was made popular by a local brewery. The brand now belongs to the large national grouping Union de Brasseries, which owns "33", Slavia and other labels.

The biggest national grouping of all – enveloped, ironically, by the BSN bottle-making company – owns some of the most famous names on the opposite side of the country, the northeast. These include La Meuse and Kronenbourg, though the latter is still managed by its founding family. In the northeast, where the industry is centred on the region of Alsace and the city of Strasbourg, the cultural influence is German, the beers bottom-fermenting, and the breweries very few but extremely large. Some excellent beers are produced by a sizeable local group under the Fischer/Pêcheur and Adelshoffen brands.

Across the Pyrenees, Spain has about twenty breweries, among which three are owned by the Filipino giant San Miguel. Spain has some agreeable Pilsener-type lagers, the odd Münchener and the occasional *Märzenbier*.

The northern parts of Italy and Yugoslavia both have brewing industries, the latter country also being an important producer of hops. Where the two countries meet, the city of Trieste had in Austro-Hungarian days a brewery owned by the great Viennese innovator Dreher. His name lives on in a present-day Italian brewery company which is headquartered in Milan and jointly owned by Heineken, of The Netherlands, and the British firm of Whitbread.

Across the water in Malta, the firm of Farson's produces the only English-style beers in the Mediterranean, a draught mild and bitter, the latter surprisingly pale but of excellent quality and substantial strength.

THE BRITISH ISLES

The beer-drinkers of Britain and Ireland are unique in their tastes. Although the 1960s and 1970s saw a great growth in the popularity of "international" lager beers, most of them brewed locally despite their Danish, German, Dutch and Canadian brand names, the trend in Britain towards these products began to falter before they had gained a third of the market. Although the big brewers had placed most of their capital investment, and almost all of their advertising, in support of these international brands, more than two-thirds of drinkers in Britain steadfastly preferred ales and stouts.

This insular independence does not end there. Because the brewers own more than eighty per cent of the pubs, they are in a position to determine what types of beer are available. In the 1960s and 1970s, many brewers tried to restrict supply to beers which had been filtered and pasteurized. This rendered the beers stable, which meant that they could be distributed over large distances from centralized breweries, and handled by unskilled bar staff who had not learned the craft of keeping and serving natural ale. These beers were packaged in sealed, carbonated kegs. Some were marketed under brand names such as Red Barrel, Double Diamond, Tavern and Tartan; others were simply known by the brewer's name, with nothing to distinguish them from their unfiltered, unpasteurized counterparts.

Although "keg" beers gained a substantial sale, in many cases at the free will of the consumer, but often because the customer for a time had little choice, they also provoked an organized campaign among drinkers who preferred what they called "real" ale. So successful was the Campaign for Real Ale that every major brewer executed considerable reversals in policy.

Not only does the serious beer-drinker in Britain stick out for ale, he or she also requires that the brew should be kept and served in the traditional manner. This means that it is delivered to the pub pasteurized, unfiltered, and not quite mature, so that it can be brought to the peak of condition on the premises, as it would have been if it were brewed there, in times past.

British beers should be served at cellar temperature, but not refrigerated, since they have the full flavour and character brought about by top-fermentation.

A cask-conditioned British beer, however reticent its natural carbonation, has a "live" palate rather like that of a cheese or yoghurt, and a hop bitterness unblunted by pasteurization. The hops used are usually English, from the southeastern county of Kent or neighbouring Sussex or Hampshire, or from the West Midland counties of Hereford and Worcester. Whichever the brewer, and almost all of them have a range of different products, the basic British beer is a cask-conditioned ordinary draught "bitter". Such a beer will have a very modest alcohol content; although

the British do not average
out as big drinkers, the committed pub-goer takes his beer
by the pint, and has a good few in
the course of the evening.

Although most native drinkers would
recognize a draught bitter instantly, it is
also true that the basic British style of ale
varies much more from brewery to brewery
than does any other category of beer elsewhere in the world. Just as there is a case to
be made for consistency, so there is a lot to be
said for variety and idiosyncrasy. Once the
taste has been acquired, a beer-drinker can
find the same surprises and pleasures in a
tour of British brews as a wine buff might
on a ramble round Bordeaux or Burgundy.

As in other countries, the number of
breweries declined drastically in the post-war
period, but the tide of rationalization and
centralization was slowed and then turned by
the activities of the Campaign for Real Ale. By
the middle of the 1970s, Britain was down to
about 150 breweries, owned by around 100
companies, and dominated by the Big Six and
their subsidiaries: Bass-Charrington, Allied
Breweries (Ind Coope, Ansell, Tetley), Watney,
Whitbread, Courage, Scottish and Newcastle.
Although one or two small mergers took place
in the late 1970s, there was also a remarkable
trend in the opposite direction. Small independent breweries which had been candidates for
closure suddenly began to show profits which
had doubled, tripled or quadrupled. The four
surviving one-pub breweries became magnets for
enthusiastic samplers. These home-brew houses

were joined by a new generation of pubs which decided to produce their own beer. Then tiny, one-man breweries, each serving only six or seven pubs, began to spring up all over Britain. By the end of the 1970s, there were about fifty of these new breweries. Although some of the very small breweries produce only a draught bitter, it is conventional to offer a much wider range. A brewery of small to medium size is likely to offer three or four draught beers, and a similar number in the bottle. Each bottled beer is more or less the pasteurized counterpart of a draught brew.

A style known simply as "mild" was once the beer of the industrial worker. The mildness is of hop character rather than alcohol content, though it is a fact that this style of beer is usually rather weak, at 3.0-3.5 per cent by volume. Though mild is difficult to find today in London, it remains popular in other parts of the country. Near London, the McMullen brewery of Hertford produces an excellent pale mild. In Britain, pale means copper-coloured, rather than golden. The more common type of mild is dark brown, coloured and sweetened with caramel. Good dark milds are produced in the Birmingham area (at Mitchells and Butlers' Highgate brewery, in Walsall, and Hanson's Dudley brewery, among others) and the Manchester area (where Thwaites, of Blackburn, is an excellent example). The bottled counterpart of dark mild is the conventional brown ale, opaque in colour,

BELHAVEN STRONG ALE

BELHAVEN BREWERY CO. LTD.
DUNBAR, SCOTLAND
Minimum Contents 9⅔ fl. oz. 275 mls.

Because no British brewery produces a comparable dry stout, Guinness enjoys a unique position. It is the only proprietary brand of beer to be available at every pub in Britain. Although the south of England gets its Guinness from a huge and long-established brewery in London, the home of the product is, beyond dispute, Dublin, Ireland

very sweet in palate, and low in alcohol content. This style of beer is different from the brown ale of the northeast, as typified by Newcastle Brown, Vaux Double Maxim and Sam Smith's Strong Brown. Those beers are a translucent copper colour, not quite so sweet, and considerably stronger, at around 4.5 per cent.

Most ordinary bitters are in the range of 3.5-4.0 per cent alcohol by volume, and the same is true of most "keg" beers. The bottled counterpart of these brews is a light ale. The description light refers to alcohol content rather than colour. Many breweries also produce a stronger, fuller-bodied and maltier bitter. Although this is not necessarily of a higher quality, it may be known as "best bitter" (sometimes abbreviated to BB), "special" or pale ale, the latter description sometimes prefaced by the word "India", in remembrance of the days when the Burton brewers had a big trade with the Empire. India Pale Ale is often abbreviated to IPA. By whatever name, these beers usually have an alcohol content of 4.0-4.5 per cent. Although pale ales were first brewed in London, the style was made popular by the brewers in Burton, who had the benefit of a chalkier and more suitable water. The classic Burton pale ales are Draught Bass, at just over four per cent, and the bottle-conditioned, sedimented Worthington "White Shield", at nearly five per cent; both are atypically well attenuated.

A draught strong ale is usually known as an "old" or "winter" brew. These beers usually range in strength from five to six per cent. Good examples are Young's Winter Warmer, in London, and Theakston's Old Peculier, in Yorkshire. Bottled strong ales, which are often sweeter, and sometimes stronger, are usually known as "barley wine". Most strong ales are dark brown in colour, though the nationally marketed and very strong Whitbread Gold Label (10.6 per cent) is pale.

In addition to all of these ales, some brewers produce a sweet or "milk" stout. The most widely available example is the Mackeson brand, made by Whitbread. Stout is a top-fermenting beer made with a very highly roasted barley. In some cases, the mash includes some roasted, unmalted barley. A sweet stout traditionally has a lactic-acid palate and a low alcohol content. England also has a single brand of strong stout, which was originally brewed for Catherine the Great. Imperial Russian Stout, brewed by Courage and matured for more than a year, has an alcohol content of more than 10.5 per cent.

Scottish beers are notably more full-bodied than their English counterparts and therefore, contrary to mythology,

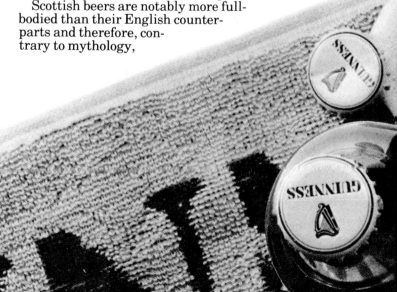

usually less strong. In place of mild, bitter, best and old, these rather different beers are known as 60, 70 and 80 shilling (long ago, the price per barrel), and "wee heavy". Maclay's and Belhaven are excellent breweries, and Traquair House, at more than 7.5 per cent, is the nearest thing to the strong "Scotch" ales of Belgium.

Throughout the British Isles, the term "porter" was once used to describe a medium-strength dry beer similar in character to stout. One or two brewers have now revived the term, though it is unlikely that any will match the character of the porter produced by Guinness in Ireland up until 1973. The famous Irish brewer has since experimented with a "light" Guinness, but that is hardly the same thing. Regular Draught Guinness, pasteurized in Britain but not in Ireland, has an alcohol content of around 3.75. Regular bottled Guinness (labelled as "Extra Stout") is never pasteurized and has an alcohol content of around four per cent. There are a variety of export strengths, all excellent beers, but the most interesting is the Tropical style, at 7.0-7.5 per cent. This is first soured slightly with old beer, and then pasteurized, so that a sharp and quenching taste is locked into a stout which combines strength with body and a high-roast palate. This superb and unique export brew is marketed in Britain as Triple X. All forms of Guinness are dry stouts, and Ireland's justifiably famous national brewer has two tiny local rivals producing the same type of beer. Both in the city of Cork, these are Murphy's, and Beamish and Crawford, each producing a dry stout of around 3.75 per cent. Guinness also has a controlling interest in a number of ale breweries, all producing the characteristic Irish version of the style, malty, full-bodied, reddish in colour and pasteurized.

CIDER

When the ancient Hebrews gave birth to the name *shekar* for a strong drink, they begat a great deal of confusion. Somewhere along the line from the Greek *sikera*, Latin *sicera* and Old French *sidre*, the name came specifically to mean a drink made from apples, but there remains beyond that little agreement as to its nature, or even its spelling.

In the United States, *cider* means a non-alcoholic apple-juice which has not been clarified or pasteurized; the term *hard cider* is used there to describe the fermented, and therefore alcoholic, version of this drink. In Australia, the non-alcoholic drink is usually spelled *cyder*, and the fermented version *cider*. In Britain, both spellings are used interchangeably to mean a drink which is always alcoholic, though the strength of most nationally marketed brands, filtered, pasteurized and artificially carbonated, is far less than that of the traditional and often potent *rough cider* served from the cask in rural counties.

In each of the major producing nations, cider is made in only a very limited area, usually comprising several districts which hang together in a strip or arc. In Britain, which is the biggest cider-making country, the main area of production describes an arc from the Welsh border county of Hereford and Worcester through the Avon district and into the deep West Country of Somerset and Devon. In France, where production is only slightly less, the adjoining northern coastal regions of Brittany and Normandy are famous for their *cidre*. In Spain, which comes some considerable distance behind as the third major producer, the cider-making area is in Asturias, on the northwest coast, though the drink is enjoyed right through the north. In Catalonia, notably in Barcelona, *sidra* is served with some ceremony. The barman holds a full *porrón* behind his shoulder, and pours it behind his back into a glass some distance away, thus causing a temporary effervescence. If there are two drinkers, both gulp the cider in turn from the same glass before it goes "flat". Spanish cider is usually primed with sugar to create a secondary fermentation, and the same practice is followed in Latin America, where considerable but unmeasured quantities are made as a cheap and agreeable substitute for sparkling wine. The only other major producing region is in the German-speaking world, which together makes a substantial amount, in an area curving through parts of Switzerland into Baden-Württemberg and Hesse. The dry, still, cloudy *Apfelwein* of Hesse is the local drink of the city of Frankfurt, where it is served from stoneware jugs, notably at bars in the Old Town area known as *Sachsenhausen*.

Although Hesse is surrounded by forests and hills, it is relatively accessible in comparison with other main cider areas. All are hidden among hill country, or thrust out on remote coasts and peninsulae, and their geography encourages the theory that cider was the drink of the Western Europeans who fled from the Romans. However, not all the evidence supports this explanation. Another thesis argues that the strips and curves of today's cider country were once part of a belt which was wrapped right round the waistline of Europe, from Ireland and the Channel Islands in the west to Austria and Hungary in the east. This belt seems to fit between the beery north and the vinous south.

Though this theory is a matter of conjecture, it is true that, while grapes are cultivated on arable land in warm

Cider is often served like wine, as an accompaniment to meals, in Normandy and Brittany. This occasionally happens in Britain, too. Not only is it versatile, manifesting itself in palates from the bone-dry to the sugar-sweet, it is also truly a wine made from apples. In its strong, farmhouse form, only the hardened rustic can take it by the pint or litre for a whole evening

climes, and barley on arable land in colder places, apples are grown in pasture country. Nor will all apples suit for the production of cider. The drink is made not from sweet "eating" apples but from bitter fruit high in tannins, and these grow well only in certain soils.

As with the grain and the grape, so with the apple – the maker of strong drink is faced with the delightful choice of simply fermenting or of also distilling, or of doing both. Applejack has been distilled in the United States since the time of the earliest settlers, and the French have long made *eaux-de-vie de cidre*, among which the Calvados of Normandy is the aristocrat. The Germans make apple *Branntwein*, and all orchard countries have some history of distillation, but either tradition or taxation have counted against such half-forgotten specialities as England's distillate, called *Cider Royal.*

In its native countries, cider commonly ranges in strength from one or two per cent by volume to around 7.5, but there are rare examples which almost double that figure. In North America and Britain, the more widely available table ciders are consumed as soft drinks, the rougher versions, especially in the West Country and in France, are deemed to be the poison of the alcohol-soaked yokel.

The major British cider brands are Coates, Gaymers and Whiteways, all controlled by Allied Breweries; Taunton Cider, owned by a consortium of four different brewers; and Bulmers, an independent company, the world's

biggest producer. Because of a shortage of cider apples, these big companies also blend in the pressings of dessert fruit in smaller quantities and use concentrate. Each has several products: sweet and dry, sparkling and still.

Bulmers pioneered the isolation of a cider-apple yeast, which makes for a controlled and predictable fermentation. The traditional method is simply to wait for fermentation to be brought about by the wild yeasts on the apples. In this respect, and because it undergoes no process of brewing, cider is technically an apple wine. The process used by Britain's farmhouse cider-makers is remarkably simple. The apples are pressed, and the pulp and juice is allowed to ferment. In some cases, nothing further is done, but usually the cider is "racked" – decanted into casks to mature. The sooner the racking, the sweeter the cider will be. The longer the process of fermentation, the drier and stronger it will be. Fermentation times vary wildly from weeks to months and very occasionally to years.

Among the best known of the small firms is Weston's, of Much Marcle, Hereford, and the same county has the excellent Symonds, at Stoke Lacey. The Avon area is particularly rich in small cider-makers, and Somerset has the superb firm of Perry's, sometimes fermenting for more than two years, at Dowlish Wake, near Ilminster. Further west, at Milton Abbot, near Tavistock, Devon, the firm of Countryman makes "vintage" ciders of up to eleven per cent, maturing them in brandy casks. In Stowmarket, Suffolk, Chevalier-Guild produces high-quality ciders as a reminder that the east of England was famous for this drink long before the west.

While the English farmhouse cider-makers often produce a rough, extremely cloudy still cider for serving on draught the French favour a complicated and ancient method of pressing with straw or reeds to achieve a natural clarification, and a secondary fermentation in the bottle (without any addition of yeast or sugar) to produce a natural carbonation. The French describe naturally carbonated cider as being *mousseux*. Best cider is described as being *pur*, run-of-the-mill examples as *marchand*, something made from second or third pressings as *boisson*.

Wherever apples are made into cider, it is always possible that pears may be made into perry, though this is a much less common drink. Britain is by far the biggest producer, and the best-known perry is served in tiny bottles as a cheap short drink which is intended to be reminiscent of a glass of champagne.

(left) True cider tavern glass with a thick stem and a large foot. (1700)
(right) Elegant cider glass in English lead crystal, decorated with the fruiting branch of an apple tree. (1760)
(far right) Goblet for cider or perry, decorated with a fruiting pear tree. (18th century)

APERITIFS COCKTAILS & MIXES

Cocktails and aperitifs are usually considered to be drinks for the pre-dinner hour – drinks to whet the appetite. In practice, almost any drink can be an aperitif. Cocktails, now experiencing a renewed popularity, can be enjoyed at any time of day and include everything from simple classic recipes to powerful concoctions with names as exotic as their ingredients. Punches and mulls have always been popular ways of combining alcohol with the freshness of fruit juice and aromatic herbs. Cocktails are based on the same principle, but are ingeniously varied in style and content.

APERITIFS

Campari is considerably stronger than vermouth. It is a unique, cryptically sharp aperitif of world renown, often taken just with ice, sparkling water and a slice of orange

The word "aperitif" derives from the Latin *aperire* – to open. It is as an "opener" to the appetite that aperitifs are usually taken; a liquid prelude to eating.

An aperitif can be anything to which one cares to give the title. You may take champagne as an aperitif, or enjoy an aperitif wine. Plenty of people enjoy nothing more exotic than whisky or a very simple gin drink. Sherry (dry or medium sweet) is a long-established aperitif (although it has justly been considered elsewhere in its own right, see Fortified Wines). It is increasingly realized that sherry is best served chilled. Fine sherry is usually too delicate to endure ice, but the heavier types may be served on-the-rocks, and often are in the USA. Chilled white port is finding renewed favour, and a glass of dry white wine has become a stylish item to call for.

Gourmets tend to despise aperitifs, claiming that they dull the appetite and weaken appreciation of fine food and wine. A flood of cocktails before a rich repast is obviously not to be recommended, but those who have a preferred aperitif should not be swayed by the pundits. The aperitif habit is an excellent one, providing a pre-prandial intermission, a period of *détente*, sociably dividing the aspects of the day.

Of the generic products classed as aperitifs, none is more universally made and consumed than vermouth.

It is customary to link vermouth with the old Roman medicinal *absinthianum vinum*, which was said to have descended from the legendary *vinum Hippocraticum*, the wine of Hippocrates, the Father of Medicine. Be that as it may, the ancients certainly knew the merits of the wormwood plant (*artemesia absinthium*) as a vermifuge: for centuries, intestinal worms were, owing to inadequate preparation of food, a curse at all levels of society.

Martini & Rossi are successors to the firm which was granted the first royal charter as producers of "Turin" vermouth, an early example of quality control

During the Dark Ages much medical knowledge was lost, yet in Bavaria at least, they continued to prepare a beneficial wormwood-infused wine (*vermutwein*). Towards the end of the sixteenth century a Piedmontese gentleman, Signor d'Alessio, uncovered the secrets of the Bavarian product and, believing it had commercial prospects, took it to France. Though he had some success in court circles, at a less rarefied level, his *vermutwein* found few takers. Where his medicine – for that it what it was – continued to be taken in France it became known as *vermout*.

Whether d'Alessio had more success in his native Piedmont is hypothetical. However, *vermout* became known there and in 1678 Leonardo Fiorranti wrote that it "is an aid to digestion; it purifies the blood, induces sound slumber, and rejoices the heart".

Prior to that, on 26 January 1663, Samuel Pepys recorded in his diary: "up and by water with Sir W. Batten to White Hall, drinking a glass of wormwood wine". The celebrated diarist makes no comment: obviously there was nothing unusual in taking this potion. The fact that vermout of a sort was being drunk in England proves that it was being traded. In fact, the spelling "vermouth" was a result of patronage by the English, whose historical influence on drinks had been very strong.

Today, vermouth comes in two established forms, plus two modern mutations adapted to new or regional tastes. It can be drunk on its own, mixed with syrups, iced, diluted or have spirits added. It is the supreme aperitif wine.

ITALIAN VERMOUTH

Vermouth was originally sold as a type of concentrate, and customers in a tavern would call for one or more measures, which they would then add to white wine in whatever proportion suited them. This practice is said to have given rise to the first brand of pre-blended vermouth.

Towards the end of the eighteenth century, Antonio Carpano, a maker of vermouth, ran a bar in Turin. The local way of indicating how many measures of vermouth were required was by "points" (*punti*). Legend has it that, one day, fluctuations on the Turin Stock Exchange were running at around one and a half points, and a customer in the bar, concentrating on business, when asked how many "points" he wanted, answered "*punt e mes*" ("one and a half" in local dialect). When Signor Carpano started putting out pre-blended vermouth in 1786, he used an equivalent formula and named it Punt e Mes.

Today, the Italian vermouth trade is dominated by its two giants, Martini & Rossi, and Cinzano. Perhaps the internationally most famous is Martini & Rossi. This company is comparatively young; the concern from which it stems received the No. 1 certificate from King Carlo Alberto in 1840, when he issued licences to protect Turin vermouth from makers elsewhere who were not entitled to assume the prestige of the true Piedmontese wine. Originally noted for their Martini Rosso, in recent years, Martini Extra Dry has come to lead the market in many countries. They also produce much *bianco* and the newer *rosé*.

The Cinzano family were wine producers in Pecetto, an ancient village in the Turin region, centuries before their name appeared on the records of the Guild of Confectioners and Distillers in 1757. Cinzano was clearly the senior vermouth concern, and established the first commercial vermouth-manufacturing house. At the beginning of the nineteenth century they moved to Turin, and expanded globally with manufacturing plants, bottling concessionaires and agents spread very widely. Cinzano were the initiators of vermouth *bianco* and *rosé*. Their dry vermouth is peculiarly delicate – perhaps not quite robust enough for dry martinis.

There are about eighty vermouth producers in Italy. Gancia – probably the biggest seller in Italy – and Stock are very big names in vermouth, though outside Italy the former is probably better known for Asti Spumante and the latter for brandy.

Newest of all in the top vermouth league is the firm started in 1921 by Ottavio Riccadonna; it now rivals Gancia within Italy. In 1932 he built his headquarters at Canelli near Asti, and put up another factory only three years later. Under his son, Angelo, Riccadonna vermouth has made giant strides, becoming extremely strong in Italy and enjoying increasing exports.

Piedmont's pre-eminence in vermouth owed much to the suitability of the local white wine, the profusion of herbs, and the ease of contact with Venice, Livorno and Genoa, which all traded to exotic places. Two hundred botanical ingredients are listed in recipes in the Martini Museum near Turin; between thirty and fifty is the average today. Wormwood flower is the one ingredient vital to all vermouth

recipes (which remain the secret of the makers) and there are distinct taste differences between brands. This makes for firm brand loyalties among knowledgeable drinkers.

There are only basic similarities in the production of vermouth by the big Italian brands. The principles are as follows: an infusion of the herbal ingredients is prepared and, in the appropriate fluid (some botanicals render their essential oils and aromas better when mixed with alcohol than with water), constantly agitated and mixed for a week or more. The resultant highly flavoured liquid is separated from the residual solids and stored. With some botanicals, simple macerating in vats may suffice, while others may only give up their integral flavour through a form of distillation. The result of these processes is combined to form the basic flavouring according to the house style. After blending for standardization, it is thoroughly clarified – that is important – and the flavouring carefully introduced. At the same time, grape spirit is added to raise the strength to an average eighteen per cent volume. Further resting takes place before the vermouth is subjected to intense refrigeration: this inhibits precipitation of deposits to which white wines may be liable. The vermouth is then pasteurized, filtered yet again and is then ready for shipping and bottling.

FRENCH VERMOUTH

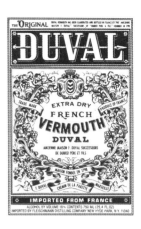

Until comparatively recent times it was customary to speak of "Italian" vermouth (sweet) and "French" vermouth (dry), not just to differentiate between two distinct styles but to mean an actual geographic origin. Then Italian "sweet" vermouth started to be made in France and, later, French "dry" vermouth in Italy. Thus, as descriptions, the purely nationalistic adjectives disappeared. Nowadays, the most important dry vermouth is that of Martini & Rossi, made in several countries, while France produces huge quantities of *rosso* (sweet) vermouth.

Yet the Dry Martini cocktail would never have existed if France had not invented a dry version of vermouth. It started in the Midi, in around 1800, when experiments were made to produce a particular vermouth, in competition to the burgeoning Italian variety. The first success, and a lasting one, was that of Louis Noilly. The firm of Noilly Prat was founded in Marseilles in 1813. The tart wines of that region – the Hérault department – are high in alcohol, low on character. For the best dry French vermouth, a blend of Hérault and less dry wine is used and this is matured by long exposure to the elements in large casks. *Mistelle* – a mixture of grape spirit and grape juice – is added, and the herbal ingredients are then long macerated in some of this matured wine, producing a strong infusion. This is blended with more of the wine and fortified up to nineteen per cent alcohol. Further treatment

is not very different to that for Italian vermouth, though, because of its special qualities, it takes rather longer to make French vermouth. Of course, for lesser French vermouths there are various short-cuts, as indeed there are for the smaller domestic Italian houses and the numerous vermouths of all styles made around the world.

Noilly Prat suffered a setback after the Second World War when they continued to produce a traditional French vermouth, whilst Martini & Rossi in particular introduced a lighter, extra-dry style which was better attuned to the accelerating move towards paler, lighter drinks. But Noilly Prat have staged a considerable comeback and never lost their reputation for quality.

A splendid style of vermouth owing something to both Italy and France – yet retaining its own special character – is French Chambéry, from the Savoy department. A generous glass of chilled dry Chambéry is the ideal prelude to a full-scale Gallic repast.

There are four producers of Chambéry, the senior being Dolin, established in 1821. There are also four types of Chambéry. The refreshingly clean-tasting dry is the most popular. There is a red, which can seem disappointing beside Italian *rosso*, and a bitter-sweet "Americano". Unique to the district is Chambéryzette, dry and flavoured with the juice of wild strawberries. Chilled – without ice in the drink – this is a memorable aperitif wine.

Serving vermouth

The uses to which vermouth is put are many and both sweet and dry varieties feature in numerous tried and tested recipes. Already containing some spirit, it goes well with gin, vodka, whisky, brandy or rum, though it is with white spirits that it is most frequently mixed. Yet on its own, it is an admirable aperitif and dry vermouth is widely drunk as such, particularly in France with the addition of cassis (though this mix is not as popular as it once was).

Punt e Mes is the distinctive, bitter-sweet Italian vermouth, which is probably closest to what was drunk two centuries ago in Turin: it stands up robustly to on-the-rocks treatment and a slice of lemon or orange.

Rosso vermouth lends itself admirably to drinking on-the-rocks; a slice of lemon gives it extra zest. Dry vermouth is probably best chilled in the bottle or by pouring through ice, as excessive dilution will take away the flavour in a way that does not happen with the more robust red. A twist of lemon peel, rather than a slice, is usual with dry. Or try mixing sweet and dry in equal proportions.

Bianco (white) vermouth being, despite its light colour, fairly strong in flavour may be well iced, and it is often served as a long drink with soda or sparkling spa water, 7-Up or fizzy lemonade, and a slice of lemon will cut the sweetness. This is an excellent summer cooler.

In the wake of the vogue for *rosé* wines, a vermouth *rosé* was inevitable. The intention was not to divert existing vermouth drinkers but to attract new ones. In short order, this new *rosé* gained six to seven per cent of the market in Germany and Austria, and is doing remarkably well in Great Britain.

The new vermouth lends itself to chilling rather than on-the-rocks treatment, and since it has a peculiarly delicate bouquet, one might think twice before adding a slice of lemon. It is a pleasing compromise between the traditional rosso and dry vermouths – less luscious than the former, less anhydrous than the latter. Vermouth rosé can look forward to a successful future.

CAMPARI

Of all the great aperitifs, one that is hard to classify is internationally celebrated Campari. It is variously called a vermouth, which it is not; a bitters, which is what is on the label – but it is certainly not bitters as understood in bar practice; a fortified wine, to which it is only vaguely related; and a spirit (in Britain) because of its strength of twenty-five per cent alcohol. It has the virtues of all these.

The company is an industrial giant with worldwide trade and a magnificently modern plant, yet it manages to retain the aura and undivided loyalties of a family company. This aperitifal empire started with the budding genius of Gaspare Campari, who left home at the age of fourteen to find his fortune in Turin. There he was apprenticed to a well-known liqueur-maker, Bass, where he mastered his craft. It is probable that he took a look at the vermouth trade and found that expanding business too crowded: he left Turin and, after starting his own business in a smaller town, moved to the metropolis of Milan, where he established the recipe for Campari bitters. His son Davide was to make Campari world famous.

OTHER APERITIFS

Among the other important proprietary brands of aperitif is Dubonnet, perhaps best described as a fortified and sweetened wine, sharpened with quinine: it epitomizes French aperitifs. The traditional, and extremely popular, darkish Dubonnet, based on red wine, has been joined by Dubonnet Pale Dry in deference to current demand for lack of colour in drinking.

Ambassadeur, a French fruit- and gentian-flavoured wine by Cusenier, with a smooth, yet faintly acidulous taste, is a comparative newcomer in the field. There is also Amer Picon, a bitter French aperitif, excellent when given a touch of crème de cassis, and Byrrh, the fortified, herb- and quinine-flavoured red wine. The latter presents a linguistic trap for foreign visitors, who are as likely to get a *bière* when ordering (add the word "aperitif" unless your accent is perfect!).

Lillet, better known in its white wine version than in the red, was launched by two brothers of that name in 1872. The wines, from family estates up the Garonne from Bordeaux, are unusually long-matured before delicate herbal flavouring is added, plus a little quinine. St Raphael is another typical popular quinine-flavoured fortified red wine, and Suze, flavoured with gentian.

Other aperitifs from Italy include Fernet and Cora. Fernet is a generic, very aromatic bitters of which by far the most celebrated is Fernet Branca. This is often employed as a *digestif* or morning-after cure abroad, but in Italy is relished as an aperitif. Cora, in the form of Amaro Cora, is a mildly bitter aperitif; there is also Cora Americano, a bottled version of the Americano cocktail.

Most of these aperitif products lend themselves to serving chilled, with ice, lemon or orange (always orange with Campari); diluted with sparkling waters; with gin or vodka added; served with cassis; or mixed in a variety of ways.

COCKTAILS AND MIXES

Drinking a mint julep aboard a steamboat; an American illustration from 1855. A straw would not usually be employed today– but perhaps served a purpose on a rough trip

The show "Wonder Bar" of German origin, when produced in London was considered very novel, as it incorporated the front stalls of the auditorium into the stage set: drinks were served to these ticketholders. Cocktails (below) were very much part of the scene in the fashionable world of Berlin of the 1920s

A mixed drink of three or more ingredients that needs special preparation – that is to say, it is shaken or stirred, as opposed to simply poured like a gin and tonic – is, of course, a "cocktail". The word itself is universally familiar, yet its original meaning has never been satisfactorily defined, and its source remains something of a mystery. Of the many theories that have been put forward, however, perhaps the most probable is that it originated in England, from a term applied to certain types of horses.

In the eighteenth and early nineteenth centuries, it was customary to dock the tails of good horses of mixed breeding – not thoroughbreds – and to refer to such animals as "cocktails". At that time, mixed drinks such as Negus (hot, sweetened wine and water) and the like, were popular and consumed in quantity in horsey circles, and to have given them an appropriate, equine name has a certain logic. Nevertheless, there is no firm evidence to support this or, indeed, any other theory, and some of them are manifestly sheer myth.

The first known positive link between the word "cocktail" and something that would be recognized by that name today was in an American journal, *The Balance*, in 1806, where it was described as a "stimulating liquor, composed of spirits of any sort, sugar, water and bitters". It is appropriate that it was in the USA that the cocktail obtained its first recorded explanation. The Americans have been drinking cocktails, in the modern sense, for longer than any other people. They have shown much ingenuity in concocting them (an ingenuity sometimes verging on the bizarre) and, with very few exceptions, the great, internationally known "classic" cocktail mixes were evolved in the USA or by Americans elsewhere in the world.

A cocktail can be all things to all men. There is no hard and fast rule governing the number or type of ingredients, or the proportions in which they are mixed. A recent newspaper report of the theft of a glass from a bar stated that the accused had committed the crime while being under the influence of a single drink. The drink was a "cocktail" named Jelly Beans – consisting of whisky, gin, vodka, Pernod, cherry brandy, Babycham and lemonade!

Powerful concoctions are, of course, nothing new: at the turn of the century in the Australian mining fields at Coolgardie, a Brain Buster was a popular cocktail. It consisted of one-third gin, one-third rum and one-third a mixture of cayenne pepper and powdered opium. Inventiveness can thrive in the most unlikely locations.

Inevitably the first book on cocktails was by an American, Jerry Thomas, who in 1862 published *The Bon Vivant's Guide or How to Mix Drinks*. The author, from California, invented the Martinez cocktail – later confused with the Martini. He gained fame in the old Metropolitan Hotel in New York City, where he invented the Blue Blazer: more spectacular than ambrosial, it involved igniting whisky. The recipe is not reproduced here, for fear it should cause harm to amateur bartenders!

Jerry Thomas toured Europe. He had sterling-silver bar equipment worth, even then, £1000, and he certainly had enormous influence in spreading the cocktail habit.

Twenty years after the pioneering *Bon Vivant's Guide*, another Californian, Harry Johnson, published his *New and Improved Illustrated Bartenders' Manual or How to Mix Drinks of the Present Style* – not exactly a snappy title, but a surprisingly modern book: it includes the Manhattan and Old-Fashioned cocktails. The author won the American championship at the first-ever Cocktail Competition, held in New Orleans in 1869.

Though acceptable in the USA in all but the most straightlaced of high society circles, at the turn of the century the drinking of cocktails was not considered good form in other countries and the custom was confined to sporting or "fast" persons. (In John Galsworthy's *The Forsyte Saga*, for example, to emphasize that one of the characters, Monty Dartie, is a cad he is portrayed drinking a cocktail during the passing of Queen Victoria's funeral cortège.)

Having shown that cocktails are not, in fact, particularly modern, it is fair to say that, at least under that name, they were not really very widely drunk, and a great many ordinary people remained totally unaware of their existence, until Prohibition blanketed the USA. This gave an incentive to the natural, bibulous inventiveness of Americans, for not everyone could obtain good (legal) liquor. It became imperative to devise concoctions to disguise the evil flavour of hooch, and so cocktails proliferated. No longer were they confined to the smart set in top bars, or to the rich in their mansions; in humbler homes and speakeasies, cocktails found increasing favour. The art of mixing drinks spread abroad, and American (that is, "cocktail") bars sprang up everywhere. The Cocktail Age had arrived. To give a cocktail party became the height of fashionable entertainment.

Without this shift in social attitude, that ultra-fashionable playwright, Frederick Lonsdale, would not have introduced the serving of cocktails on the stage (in *Spring Cleaning*, 1925). He just beat the rising Noel Coward who, in the following year, used the cocktail as a sign of sophistication in *The Vortex*. He followed this up with no fewer than four cocktails (and other drinks) in *Fallen Angels*. The Bright Young Things, epitomized in these brittle, new type of plays, soaked up cocktails.

In the thirties, as the Cocktail Age burgeoned amongst the social trend-setters of the world's great cities, though there were many enthusiastic amateur mixers, outside the USA there was a lack of trained bartenders, and many an American professional found a lucrative niche in Europe and elsewhere. The progenitor of the Dry Martini, Signor Martini di Arma di Taggia, returned to Italy, as did his acolyte, Luigi. To London, came Harry Craddock, and made the bar at the Savoy a mecca for cocktail drinkers. He was the author of *The Savoy Cocktail Book* which ap-

That mixed drinks are nothing new is clearly illustrated in this rumbustious scene in an American tavern in 1810. "Tom and Jerry" and "Mint Julep" advertised in these premises have survived to our times

An illustration from an early Vogue *magazine indicates that cocktails have always been considered an adjunct to good living*

peared in 1930. The most enduring of such publications outside the USA, it is still in print.

In the more serious world of the late 1930s, in a natural reaction to the furious pleasure-seeking of the previous decade, cocktails went into a decline. The advent of the sober (and economical) sherry party, a pale shadow of its spirit-inspired precursor, was deplorable enough, but it was followed by something worse: the aridity of war.

Whilst the Americans never seriously faltered in their love affair with the cocktail, after the repeal of Prohibition, their drinking habits became more conservative. In other countries, cocktails were enjoyed by only a small upper-crust of society and, even then, not very adventurously. The man in the street had only heard about cocktails.

In recent years, this has greatly changed. Standards of living have risen and people are roving farther afield, spending holidays abroad and becoming much more cosmopolitan in their ways, including their drinking habits. The subsequent demand for new, more exotic drinks has resulted in a cocktail revival. Cocktails are now being sold in fashionable, American-style bars. Books on cocktails are selling well. Renewed interest has extended not only to drinking but to making cocktails. A revival of the Cocktail Age is taking place, in its way just as exciting as the first – and one not just confined to the privileged few.

It is an odd thing indeed, the cocktail – faintly wicked, slightly mysterious, pleasantly nostalgic, decidedly enticing – and remarkably enduring.

The Greatest Cocktail

The most international of all cocktails is the Dry Martini. It precedes business luncheons from Buenos Aires to Bangkok; it is a feature of diplomatic cocktail parties; it is the most requested mix in many bars; and it sets a smart tone before dinner in homes great and small. It is the most discussed of cocktails – even by people who do not drink it. It has survived where thousands of other cocktails have enjoyed their day and vanished. The Collins (in its many

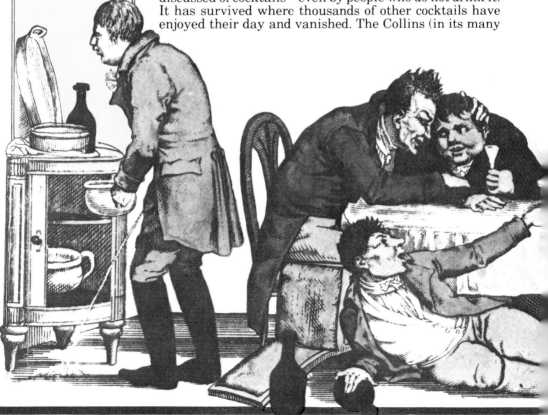

forms), the Bloody Mary, the newer Harvey Wallbanger and Tequila Sunrise have eroded its dominance of the mixed drink scene – yet they cannot usurp its position as the king of cocktails and the universal first choice of serious cocktail drinkers. It is also an extremely potent, even dangerous, mix: it presents a challenge along with its delights. More has been written about the Dry Martini than about any single mix. The true origins of the Dry Martini are briefly outlined in the recipe section. One notion is that it is named for the famous vermouth. In fact, the first recorded use of Martini & Rossi dry vermouth was in the mid-twenties in San Remo: the company was not making *dry* vermouth when the Dry Martini first saw glass.

A fine Dry Martini is to dedicated cocktail drinkers what a great vintage Bordeaux is to wine lovers.

Mixing Cocktails

The equipment for making cocktails is extraordinarily simple; in fact, there is nothing that will not be found in a reasonably well-equipped kitchen. If you have no shaker, a liquidizer (blender) will stand in very adequately. However, a certain mystique is inseparable from making a good cocktail. You can probably cook an admirable boeuf bourguignonne in a bucket, and prepare a more than adequate Manhattan in an old teacup, but who would expect them to have the same effect as they would prepared and presented in the traditional manner? The visual effect is as important in mixology as it is in gastronomy. To watch a really expert bartender at work is to appreciate that art has very wide boundaries.

The home bartender needs no more than a shaker, a bar (mixing) glass and strainer. As to the shaker, if you do decide to invest in one, the three-piece type is the best to go for. One can move on to the more professional and difficult-

The drinking habits of English 18th-century gentlemen portrayed – accurately – by a French artist

At the height of the "Cocktail Age", some of the smartest "American bars" were to be found in Paris

to-use Boston shaker when more experienced.

Ice is an essential ingredient, yet it is too easily forgotten that it can only be as good as the water it is made from. Ice from a domestic refrigerator is slow-frozen and somewhat porous. Commercial ice is "harder" – colder and less quick-melting. A satisfactory equivalent is ice made in a plastic container (to allow for expansion) in a home freezer switched to "fast freeze". To break the block up to the required size, fold a cloth round it and bash it with what the police homicide squads call a "blunt instrument". Or you can use another favourite murder weapon, an ice pick.

Citrus fruit which is not home grown is best washed, as the skin may have been sprayed with preservative – not harmful but capable of faintly tainting a delicate mix. Use fruits with discretion: there is a common tendency to over-decorate mixed drinks with fruit and other embellishments to the point of making the liquid irrelevant.

In the USA cocktail "mixes" and pre-prepared cocktails have been around for a long time and become very popular in recent years. Their success has not been repeated overseas, but there are one or two which can be strongly recommended, including the excellent Bullshot mix and an interesting variation on the Bloody Mary made with the Clamato (clam juice) mix.

BITTERS AND SYRUPS

The most famous of bitters is the proprietary brand Angostura, the aromatic and strongly alcoholic compound originally evolved by J. G. B. Siegert, founder of the firm that bears his name. Angostura was the Venezuelan town where the company was established in 1823. Not long afterwards, production was moved to Port-of-Spain, Trinidad. Angostura is essential to Pink Gin and several other mixes.

Of native American bitters, the aromatic Abbott's Aged, made in Baltimore for over a century, and Peychaud's, from New Orleans, are the most celebrated. Other bitters are made by Campari and Fernet Branca, both usually taken as aperitifs. The German Underberg brand, however, is more a *digestif*, and a first-rate pick-me-up for the morning after. Underberg comes in tiny, one-dose bottles, for tipping straight down in one go.

Syrups are a non-alcoholic relative of *crèmes*. Virtually essential in bar practice is Gomme *sirop*, a commercial mixture of water and pure unrefined cane sugar. A satisfactory sweetener may be made by boiling 1 lb (500 g) sugar in 1 pint (55 cl) water; this can be stored indefinitely in a domestic refrigerator. It is far better to use a sugar syrup than dry sugar, and recipe quantities are the same for both.

Of all syrups, grenadine is the most attractive; its flavour and colour derive from pomegranates. Almond-flavoured Orgeat is found in the USA. The Germans like a rowanberry syrup, and blackcurrant is popular, particularly in Britain.

Lime juice cordial is useful in a similar capacity to that of syrups in mixed drinks, though it must not be used when "lime juice", meaning unsweetened fresh lime juice, is stipulated. Roses, the best-known lime juice cordial, is a blend of fresh lime juice and pure sugar.

RECIPES

Every day, new cocktails – fresh mutations of established ones, strange mixtures – make their appearance. They are created to mark a new decade, a coronation, an important world event – or at the whim of the bartender. Their popularity is generally ephemeral, sometimes of no more than a single evening's duration: yet it is not the prize-winners that occasionally conquer but the accidental ones that, almost by a freak of fortune, find a permanent place in the fickle affections of drinkers.

The following recipes are personal selections from the vast world repertoire of alcoholic mixed drinks: individual cocktails, including the great "classics" and the generic drinks such as slings, sours and fizzes; party mixes, such as punches and mulls; and to rectify any damage that may be caused by the foregoing, pick-me-ups for the morning after. Simple, everyday mixes such as vermouth-cassis and vodka-and-lime are not included.

When making mixed drinks, remember that a recipe is basically a guide, not immutable law. Personal taste will inevitably influence the proportions and quantities suggested in recipes – which, in the case of drinks, encompass even more variations on the original theme than those found in the culinary domain.

Methods are presented as concisely as possible. Please note the full implications of the instructions *shake* (prepare in a cocktail-shaker and strain into a suitable glass) and *mix* (stir in a bar [mixing] glass before straining).

All drinks listed should be made with ice unless otherwise specified. *On-the-rocks* means that the liquid is added to a glass containing ice.

Cocktail glasses should be used except where another type is specified or it is obvious that a larger glass is needed: common sense is the rule. A "cocktail" glass means any stemmed glass, but it should not be too small. When fresh limes are hard to obtain, rather more lemon juice may be substituted. It is not the same, but it will suffice.

A "dash" of bitters, etc., is equivalent to the amount that would fill the tip of a tilted teaspoon (1-2ml).

Finally, headings marked with an asterisk (*) indicate celebrated cocktails: "classic" or modern, or ones that are particularly interesting.

WOLFSCHMIDT
68°Proof KUMMEL 57cl

CRÈME DE CACAO liqueur
70cl 25%
GIFFARD

Polmos
Extra
ZYTNIA
Vodka
100 PER CENT NEUTRAL
SPIRITS DISTILLED FROM RYE
0,5 L. 40°
·PRODUCE OF POLAND

INDIVIDUAL COCKTAILS AND MIXED DRINKS

All measurements in this section are based on a unit of 3 cl (about 1 fl oz), and thus 1 = 3 cl (1 fl oz), ½ = 1½ cl (½ fl oz)

A.1
½ Grand Marnier
1 gin
1 dash lemon juice
1 dash grenadine
Shake. Add a twist of lemon

ADDINGTON
1 red vermouth
1 dry vermouth
Mix. Top with soda water and a slice of orange

ADONIS
1 dry sherry
½ red vermouth
1 dash orange bitters
Mix. Top with orange peel

AFFINITY
1 Scotch whisky
½ sweet vermouth
2 dashes Angostura bitters
Mix

ALASKA
1½ gin
½ yellow Chartreuse
Shake

ALEXANDER*
1 brandy
1 crème de cacao
1 fresh cream
Shake

ALLIES
1 gin
1 dry vermouth
2 dashes kümmel
Shake

AMERICAN BEAUTY
½ brandy
½ grenadine
½ dry vermouth
½ orange juice
1 liqueur glass port
1 dash crème de menthe
Shake

AMERICANO*
1 Campari
1 red vermouth
Pour over ice in a wine glass, stir, top with soda water and add a slice of orange

ANTONIO
1 gin
1 brandy
½ maraschino
½ crème de menthe
Shake

APPARENT
1 gin
1 Dubonnet (red)
1 dash Pernod
Mix

APPLE
½ gin
½ brandy
½ calvados
½ sweet cider
Shake

APPLEJACK RABBIT
½ lemon juice
½ orange juice
½ maple syrup
1 calvados
Shake

ATHOLL BROSE
There are at least two versions of this well-known Scottish potion, and they are as follows:

A SCOTCH COCKTAIL
2 Scotch whisky
1 fresh cream
1 honey
Mix in a warmed glass and allow to cool. Stir with a spoon. (No ice)

An alternative version is made by omitting the cream and topping with hot milk, making, in effect, a hot toddy

TRADITIONAL ATHOLL BROSE
Based on the Duke of Atholl's original recipe

Scotch whisky
finely ground oatmeal
honey
cream (optional)
Mix proportions of the above to personal taste. Shake well and leave to mature for a few days

ATOM BOMB
1 brandy
1 Pernod
Mix

AURUM
1 Aurum
1 gin
2 sweet vermouth
Mix

BACARDI*
1½ Bacardi carta blanca
½ fresh lime juice
1 teaspoon (5 ml) grenadine
Shake

This is very similar to Daiquiri, but must preferably be made with Ron Bacardi

BALALAIKA
1 vodka
1 Cointreau
1 lemon juice
Shake

BAMBOO
1 dry sherry
1 dry vermouth
1 dash orange bitters
Mix. Add a twist of lemon

BANANA BLISS
1 brandy
1 banana liqueur
Mix

BARBICAN
1 Scotch whisky
¼ Drambuie
¼ passion fruit juice
Shake

BARONIAL
1 Lillet
½ lemon gin
2 dashes Angostura bitters
2 dashes Cointreau
Mix

BARTENDER
¼ gin
¼ medium sherry
¼ Dubonnet
¼ dry vermouth
1 dash Grand Marnier
Mix

BENTLEY
1 Dubonnet
1 calvados
Mix

BERMUDIANA ROSE
1 gin
¼ apricot brandy
¼ grenadine
¼ lemon juice
Shake

BETSY ROSS
1 brandy
1 port
½ Cointreau
1 dash Angostura bitters
Shake

BETWEEN-THE-SHEETS
1 Bacardi
1 brandy
1 Cointreau
1 dash lemon juice
Shake

BILLY HAMILTON
1 brandy
1 orange curaçao
1 crème de cacao
1 egg white
Shake

BLACK RUSSIAN*
1 Kahlua
1 vodka
On-the-rocks

BLACK THORN
1 Irish whiskey
½ dry vermouth
2 dashes Angostura bitters
2 dashes Pernod
Shake

BLACK VELVET*
In a tankard:
half-and-half Guinness (pref-
erably draught) and chilled
champagne

BLOOD AND SAND
1 Scotch whisky
1 cherry brandy
1 red vermouth
1 orange juice
Shake

BLOODY MARY*
Almost certainly, this was invented
by a Frenchman, Fernand Petiot,
working in Harry's New York Bar,
Paris, in the 1920s. As well as one
of the most famous classic cocktails,
it is especially recommended as a
morning-after cure for the effects of
over-indulgence

2 vodka
5 tomato juice
1 dash Worcestershire sauce
1 dash Tabasco sauce
cayenne pepper
celery salt
½ lemon juice
Shake, mix or serve on-the-
rocks

Made with tequila, this becomes a
Sangre

BLUE DEVIL
1 gin
½ lemon juice
½ Bols blue curaçao
Shake

BLUE JACKET
1 gin
1 blue curaçao
1 dash orange bitters
Mix

BLUE RIBAND
1 gin
½ white curaçao
¼ blue curaçao
Mix

BLUE STAR
1 Lillet
1 orange juice
½ gin
½ blue curaçao
Shake

BOBBY BURNS
1 Scotch whisky
½ red vermouth
1 teaspoon (5 ml) Bénédictine
Mix. Add a twist of lemon

BOMBAY
½ brandy
¼ dry vermouth
¼ sweet vermouth
1 dash Pernod
2 dashes orange curaçao
Mix

BOSOM CARESSER
1 brandy
½ Cointreau
1 teaspoon (5 ml) grenadine
1 egg yolk
Shake well

BOURBONELLA
½ dry Bourbon
¼ dry vermouth
¼ orange curaçao
1 dash grenadine
Mix

BRAINSTORM
2 Irish whiskey
1 teaspoon (5 ml) Bénédictine
1 teaspoon (5 ml) dry vermouth
Mix. Add a twist of lemon

BRANDY GUMP
½ brandy
½ lemon juice
2 dashes grenadine
Shake

BRAZIL
1 dry sherry
1 dry vermouth
1 dash Pernod
1 dash Angostura bitters
Mix. Add a twist of lemon

BRONX*
1½ gin
½ dry vermouth
½ red vermouth
½ orange juice
Shake

With the addition of a dash of
Pernod, this becomes a Minnehaha.
Though it is a famous gin cocktail
Bronx has also been listed as made
with whiskey

BROOKLYN
1 rye whiskey
1 red vermouth
1 dash Amer Picon
1 dash maraschino
Mix

BUCK'S FIZZ*
This is France's champagne à l'orange as adopted by Buck's Club in London

5 very cold champagne
3 freshly squeezed orange juice
(No ice)

BULLDOG
2 gin
1 juice of an orange
Serve on-the-rocks with ginger ale

BULLSHOT*
Make a Bloody Mary, but use condensed consommé in place of tomato juice and mix very thoroughly indeed. This makes an excellent substitute for breakfast

Made with a combination of tomato juice and consommé, it becomes a Bloody Bullshot

BYRRH
½ Byrrh
½ gin
Mix

CANADA
1½ Canadian whisky
½ Cointreau
2 dashes Angostura bitters
1 teaspoon (5ml) sugar
Shake

CANADIAN
2 Canadian whisky
2 teaspoons (10ml) grenadine
2 dashes Angostura bitters
Shake

CARUSO
½ gin
½ dry vermouth
½ crème de menthe
Mix

CHAMPAGNE COCKTAIL*
1 lump of sugar
2 dashes Angostura bitters
1 brandy
Top with chilled champagne. (No ice)

CHARLESTON
¼ each of
gin
dry vermouth
sweet vermouth
Cointreau
kirsch
maraschino
Shake well. Add a twist of lemon

CHICAGO
1 brandy
1 dash Cointreau
1 dash Angostura bitters
Shake. Strain into glass with rim frosted with sugar. Top with champagne

Bloody Mary (and its mutations – Bullshot, Bloody Bullshot and Sangre) offers considerable scope for individuality.

CLARIDGE
½ gin
½ dry vermouth
¼ Cointreau
¼ apricot brandy
Mix

CLASSIC
1 brandy
¼ lemon juice
¼ orange curaçao
¼ maraschino
Shake. Frost rim of glass with sugar. Add a twist of lemon

CLOVER CLUB*
1½ gin
½ grenadine
½ lemon juice
1 egg white
Shake. Serve in a wine glass

COBBLER
An old mix of American renown, this was the most popular drink of all at the time of Harry Johnson (see Bloody Mary)

2 teaspoons (10 ml) sugar syrup or sweet liqueur such as Cointreau
2 whisky or other spirit, as preferred
Add the sugar syrup or liqueur to a fairly large goblet almost filled with ice, then the spirit. Stir until well blended, decorate with fruit or mint and serve with straws

Fruit juices are not used in a true Cobbler. At least twice the amount of wine may be substituted for the spirits. There are many variants

COLLINS*
For all practical purposes, the distinction between a Tom Collins (made with Old Tom gin) and a John Collins (made with Dry gin) has gone. Dry gin is the favoured spirit. Variants are numerous, and tend to reflect the spirit used: e.g. Bourbon for Colonel Collins, for Mike Collins, Irish whiskey, Scotch whisky for Sandy Collins and rum for Pedro Collins. It was named after a London head waiter in the nineteenth century, John Collins

1 gin
½ tablespoon (10 ml) sugar
2 lemon juice
Add ice and top with soda water

COLONIAL
1 gin
½ grapefruit juice
1 teaspoon (5 ml) maraschino
Shake

COMMODORE
1 rye whiskey
¼ fresh lime juice
2 dashes orange bitters
Sugar to taste
Shake

CORPSE REVIVER
See section on Pick-me-ups

COWBOY
1 rye whiskey
½ cream
Shake with crushed ice

CROW
1 Bourbon
½ lemon juice
1 dash grenadine
Shake

CRUSTAS
This old-fashioned description is little used today. A crusta is distinguished by the rim of the glass being moistened and dipped in fine sugar (or salt, for a Margarita). A proper crusta, however, has the whole of the glass lined with a continuous piece of citrus rind. In a shaker, a cocktail of spirit (traditionally brandy), lemon juice, sugar and (optionally) peach or orange bitters, is made and strained into the prepared glass

CUBA LIBRE*
1 white rum
½ lime juice
Pour over ice cubes in a tall glass. Top up with Coca-Cola

CUPID
3 dry sherry
1 egg
1 teaspoon (5 ml) fine sugar
1 dash cayenne pepper
Shake

CZARINE
½ vodka
¼ dry vermouth
¼ apricot brandy
1 dash Angostura bitters
Mix

DAIQUIRI*
This famous mix is said to take its name from the Daiquiri nickel mine in Oriente province, Cuba, where it was invented for American engineers during a shortage of imported liquor

2 white rum
1 lime juice
1 grenadine
Shake. Serve very cold

For Frozen Daiquiri, blend the ingredients thoroughly with crushed ice. Do not strain

DAIQUIRI BLOSSOM
1 fresh orange juice
1 white rum
1 dash maraschino
Shake

DANDY
½ rye whiskey
½ Dubonnet
1 dash Angostura bitters
3 dashes Cointreau
Twist of orange and lemon
Mix

DAWN
1 chilled champagne
1 lime juice
1 dry sherry
Shake lightly

DEAUVILLE
½ each of
Cointreau
calvados
brandy
lemon juice
Shake

DEMPSEY
1 gin
1 calvados
2 dashes Angostura bitters
2 dashes grenadine
Shake

DEPTH-CHARGE
1 gin
1 Lillet
2 dashes Pernod
Shake

DEVIL
1 portwine
1 dry vermouth
1 teaspoon (5ml) lemon juice
Shake

DIKI-DIKI
1 calvados
½ Swedish punsch
½ grapefruit juice
Shake

DIXIE
1 gin
½ dry vermouth
½ Pernod
Shake

Variations on one basic design – a selection of cocktail shakers. Each is a different shape; two have handles; three have spouts through which the liquid is strained. They are made from silver-plate, chrome and glass; lavishly embellished or functionally plain

To "frost" a glass turns the drink it contains into a Crusta– to use a pleasing old-fashioned term. Dip the rim in iced water or, preferably, in lime or lemon juice, and touch this gently into fine sugar spread out on a plate–or into salt for the very popular Margarita cocktail

DRY MARTINI*

Almost certainly this was invented at the Knickerbocker Hotel, New York City, in about 1910, and is named after that establishment's bartender – and not from the Martinez cocktail associated with the aforementioned Jerry Thomas

2 gin
1 dash dry vermouth
Mix thoroughly to chill. Add a twist of lemon: immerse peel if liked. (It was formerly the practice to add an olive)

Traditionally, Dry Martinis are served without ice ("straight-up"), but they are of course extremely popular on-the-rocks. Variants are many. They include the Naked Martini (simply iced gin), the Vodkatini and the Gibson. Older recipes for the basic Dry Martini include orange bitters

DUBONNET
½ Dubonnet
½ gin
Mix. Add a twist of lemon

EAST INDIA
1 brandy
¼ orange curaçao
½ pineapple juice
1 dash Angostura bitters
Shake. Add a twist of lemon and a cocktail cherry

EGG NOG
See Nogs

EMBASSY ROYAL
½ Bourbon
¼ Drambuie
¼ sweet Martini
2 dashes orange squash
Shake

FALLEN ANGEL
2 gin
1 lemon juice
2 dashes crème de menthe
1 dash Angostura bitters
Shake

FIBBER McGEE
2 gin
1 unsweetened grapefruit juice
1 red vermouth
2 dashes Angostura bitters
Mix. Add a twist of lemon

FIXES
Also known as "Daisies", these date from an era when a lot of fruit decoration was the order of the day. This is a basic recipe:

2 gin
1 teaspoon (5 ml) maraschino
1 tablespoon (15 ml) lemon juice
Pour into a goblet nearly filled with crushed ice, add fruit and serve with straws

FIZZES
See Gin Fizz, Merry Widow Fizz

FLIPS
These are a mixture of spirit, sugar and a whole egg, shaken and strained

FLYING HIGH
2 gin
1 fresh orange juice
1 cherry brandy
1 teaspoon (5 ml) lemon juice
1 dash Angostura bitters
1 egg white
Shake briskly

FOURTH DEGREE
½ gin
½ dry vermouth
½ sweet vermouth
2 dashes Pernod
Mix

FRAPPÉS
The best-known frappé (derived from the French verb "frapper" in the sense of "to ice" rather than "to hit") is Crème de Menthe. The liqueur is poured over finely crushed ice and served with straws

FUN AND GAMES
1 gin
½ crème de cassis
½ lemon juice
1 dash Angostura bitters
Shake. Serve with small slice of lemon

GIBSON*
The name derives from the celebrated American artist Charles Dana Gibson, for whom the drink was invented by Charley Connolly, bartender of the Players' Club in New York during Prohibition

To make it:
add a cocktail onion on a stick to a Dry Martini

GIMLET*
1 gin
1 lime juice cordial
Shake

GIN FIZZ*
1 gin
2 lemon juice
2 teaspoons (10 ml) sugar
Shake. Top with soda water

See also Buck's Fizz and Merry Widow Fizz

GIN-GIN
1 gin
1 ginger wine
1 orange juice
Shake

GIN SLING
A sling, as a simple mix, used to be made with any spirit. The Gin Sling is the only survivor, and is very similar to a Collins

2 gin
2 lemon juice
1 heaped teaspoon (7.5 ml) of sugar
1 dash Angostura bitters
Mix. Top with water

See also Singapore Gin Sling and Pimm's

GLAD EYE
1 Pernod
½ crème de menthe
Mix

GLOOM CHASER
½ Grand Marnier
½ Cointreau
½ grenadine

½ lemon juice
Shake

GOLDEN CADILLAC
1 Galliano
1 crème de cacao
1 fresh cream
Mix in a liquidizer (blender) with a little crushed ice and strain into a wine glass

GRASSHOPPER
½ white crème de cacao
½ green crème de menthe
½ cream
Shake

GREEN ROOM
1 brandy
2 dry vermouth
2 dashes orange curaçao
Mix

GROG
Originally, grog was simply spirit diluted with cold water, and was named after Admiral Vernon of the Royal Navy, who ordered the dilution of the rum issued to ordinary seamen. His nickname was "Old Grog", after the cloak of "grogram" he wore. Today the word implies a hot drink composed of spirit (a heavy dark rum), sugar, lemon juice and boiling water

HARRITY
1 Canadian whisky
1 dash gin
1 dash Angostura bitters
Mix

HARROVIAN
1 Canadian whisky
1 dash gin
1 dash Angostura bitters
Mix

HARVARD
½ brandy
½ sweet vermouth
2 dashes Angostura bitters
1 dash sugar syrup
Mix. Add a twist of lemon

HARVEY WALLBANGER*
Add 1 Galliano liqueur to a Screwdriver

HAWAIIAN
1 gin
½ orange juice
½ Cointreau
Shake

HELL
1 brandy
1 crème de menthe
Shake. Sprinkle with cayenne pepper

HIGHBALL*
This can be any spirit, though traditionally it is whiskey, with ice and soda water or other mixer. It is usually served in a tall glass. The term is said to have originated in St Louis in the late nineteenth century: on many American railroads, if a ball was hoisted on a pole at a depot, it was an indication to an approaching locomotive driver that he should speed up. The term subsequently came to mean a simple, speedily made drink such as whiskey and water

A Highball with cider is a Stone Fence

HONEYMOON
½ Bénédictine
½ calvados
½ lemon juice
3 dashes orange curaçao
Shake

HORSE'S NECK
A Highball made with a continuous spiral of lemon peel hanging from the rim of the glass. The mixer is ginger ale; any spirit may be used

ICEBERG
2 vodka
1 teaspoon (5 ml) Pernod
On-the-rocks

IDEAL
1 gin
½ dry vermouth
2 dashes maraschino
1 tablespoon (15 ml) grapefruit juice
Shake

IRISH COFFEE
This is said to have been invented by Joe Sheridan in the 1940s when he was head chef at Shannon Airport, Ireland. The official version is as follows:

2 Irish whiskey
1 teaspoon (5 ml) sugar or more to taste
Freshly made hot, strong black coffee
2 double (thick) cream
Put the whiskey into a warmed, large wine glass and sugar to taste. Pour in the coffee and stir. Add the cream, dribbling over the back of a spoon. Allow cream to settle on top and do not stir

JARANA
2 tequila
2 sugar
Pour over ice in a tall glass and top with pineapple juice

JEREZ
2 dry sherry
1 dash orange bitters
1 dash peach bitters
Shake

JULEP
See Mint Julep

KIR*
This is an aperitif rather than a cocktail

1 glass chilled Chablis or other dry white wine
1 teaspoon (5 ml) crème de cassis
Add the crème de cassis to the wine. (No ice)

For Kir Royale, use champagne instead of dry white wine, and raspberry cordial instead of crème de cassis

KISS-ME-QUICK
2 Pernod
1 teaspoon (5 ml) Cointreau
2 dashes Angostura bitters
On-the-rocks. Top with soda water

KITTY LOVE
1 Cointreau
1 kirsch
1 Punt e Mes
Shake. Add a twist of orange

KNOCK-OUT
½ gin
½ dry vermouth
½ Pernod
1 teaspoon (5 ml) crème de menthe
Shake

LIBERAL
½ Canadian whisky
½ red vermouth
3 dashes Amer Picon
1 dash orange bitters
Mix

LOCH LOMOND
2 Scotch whisky
1 teaspoon (5 ml) sugar syrup
2 dashes Angostura bitters
Shake

LONDONER
2 gin
½ rose-hip (or other flavoured syrup)
2 lemon juice
½ dry vermouth
On-the-rocks. Top with soda water, add a slice of lemon

MAIDEN'S PRAYER
1 gin
¼ Cointreau
½ orange juice
½ lemon juice
Shake

The secret of Irish Coffee is to start with a good-quality, and strong brew. Sweetness (brown sugar is recommended) is a matter of personal preference – and so is the proportion of whiskey. Pouring the cream is best done carefully over the back of a warmed teaspoon

MANHATTAN*

This is said to have been invented in Maryland – a quickly made mix of whiskey, syrup and bitters to revive a wounded duellist in 1846. In the 1890s in New York, sweet vermouth replaced sugar and the drink was named after the fashionable quarter. There are various versions

1 Bourbon
½ dry vermouth
½ red vermouth
1 dash Angostura bitters
Mix. Add a cocktail cherry

MAPLE LEAF

1 Canadian whisky
¼ lemon juice
1 teaspoon (5ml) maple syrup
Shake

MARGARITA*

1½ tequila
½ Cointreau
½ lime juice
Shake. Dip the rim of the glass in lime juice and touch in salt

MARTINI

See Dry Martini

MERRY WIDOW FIZZ

Make a Gin Fizz with a mixture of orange and lemon juice

The same name has been applied to a fizz made with Dubonnet and with the addition of egg white

MEXICAN

1 tequila
1 pineapple juice
1 dash grenadine
Shake

MINNEHAHA

See Bronx

MINT JULEP*

Redolent of the scent of magnolias, and the sight of Southern belles running Scarlett O'Hara-like across lawns surrounding gorgeous Colonial mansions, this is the drink once served by doting black manservants to white-bearded colonels of the Old South. The name "julep", however, is of Middle Eastern origin: medical men of ancient Persia employed that term to describe the additives they put into foul potions in order to make them palatable. This is from the Bourbon Institute recipe:

2 Bourbon
1 lump sugar
1 tablespoon (15ml) water
4 sprigs mint
Mix the mint, sugar and water

in a tall glass and fill with crushed ice. Add the Bourbon but do not stir. Garnish with the mint sprigs

MISSISSIPPI MULE

1 gin
1 teaspoon (5ml) lemon juice
1 teaspoon (5ml) crème de cassis
Shake

MONKEY GLAND

1 gin
½ orange juice
2 dashes Pernod
2 dashes grenadine
Shake

MOSCOW MULE*

1½ vodka
½ lime juice
ginger beer
Add the lime juice to the vodka and top with the iced ginger beer

MULLS

See next section

MUSCOVITAL

1 vodka
2 ginger wine
1 Campari
Mix. Serve with a cherry

MY FAIR LADY

1 gin
½ orange juice
½ lemon juice
1 teaspoon (5ml) strawberry liqueur
1 egg white
Shake well

NEGRONI*

Add 1 gin to an Americano

NEW YORK

2 Scotch whisky
1 teaspoon (5ml) fresh lime juice
1 teaspoon (5ml) sugar
Mix briskly. Add a twist of lemon

NOGS

Now an American festive tradition, these were once taken semi-medicinally by the British. A nog is basically a combination of hot, sugared spirit with an egg beaten into it. However, not all nogs are served hot. Rum, whisky and brandy are the most suitable spirits. A simple, cold Egg Nog – in total contrast to, say, a Tom and Jerry (see next sec-

tion), which might be described as a prototype nog – can be made as follows:

1 egg
1 teaspoon (5 ml) sugar
2 rum, whisky or other spirit, or more of wine
6 milk
Shake all the ingredients vigorously with crushed ice. Strain into a tall goblet and dust with powdered nutmeg

OLD ETONIAN
1 gin
1 Lillet
2 dashes orange bitters
2 dashes crème de noyau
Shake. Add a twist of orange

OLD-FASHIONED*
This drink was first evolved for racegoers at Louisville's Pendennis Club. It was popularized during Prohibition, with extra fruit to disguise the taste of hooch

1 teaspoon (5 ml) sugar
3 dashes Angostura bitters
2 American whiskey
Put the sugar and bitters in a tubby glass (such as the glass that takes its name from the drink), dampen with water and stir. Add the whiskey, top with ice, a slice of orange and a cocktail cherry

OPERA
1 gin
¼ Dubonnet
¼ maraschino
Mix. Add a twist of orange

ORANGE BLOSSOM
1 gin
1 orange juice
Shake

ORIENTAL
1 rye whiskey
¼ sweet vermouth
¼ Cointreau
½ fresh lime juice
Shake

PERFECT
1 gin
1 dry vermouth
1 red vermouth
Shake

This is a smarter version of a one-time British favourite – "gin and mixed". The same drink is also called Trinity, but so is a version of the Manhattan – which shows how confusing the names can be

PIMM'S*
This splendid British contribution to the drinking scene is a unique proprietary product, tasty, cold, long and refreshing. Formerly subtitled "the original gin sling", Pimm's "No 1 Cup" is gin-based, all other ingredients being a secret shared only among six top executives at Pimm's

1 Pimm's
2-3 lemonade, 7-Up or ginger ale
Add plenty of ice and a slice of lemon, orange or cucumber

The common practice of turning the drink into a glorified fruit salad is quite unwarranted

PINA COLADA
½ white rum
½ dark rum
1 each of orange, pineapple and lime juice
1 dash grenadine
Pour over crushed ice, stir, top with coconut milk, decorate with slices of lemon and orange. Serve with straws

PINK GIN*
This aperitif, associated historically with the Royal Navy, was probably invented in the West Indies in the latter part of the eighteenth century. It is usually made with Plymouth gin, though others are sometimes specified

2 gin
1 dash Angostura bitters
Add water or soda water to taste and ice if desired

POUSSE-CAFÉ
Costly, nauseous and pointless, this drink was allegedly invented in New Orleans, and must once have been popular, since it has a special glass named after it: a pousse-café is a narrower than usual, straight-sided liqueur glass. The drink is made by pouring (preferably over the back of a spoon) liqueurs of varying density, starting with the heaviest. The end-product, for those with very steady hands and reasonable powers of concentration, is a layered, many-coloured concoction. Traditionally, there should be an odd number of layers, from three to seven. The version that follows is called Rainbow

1 crème de cacao
1 crème de violette
1 yellow Chartreuse
1 maraschino
1 Bénédictine
1 green Chartreuse
1 cognac

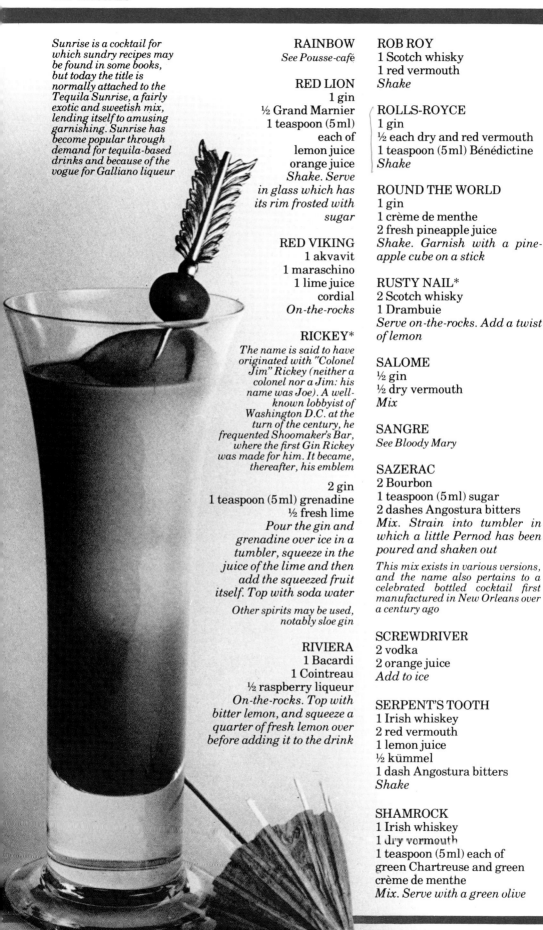

Sunrise is a cocktail for which sundry recipes may be found in some books, but today the title is normally attached to the Tequila Sunrise, a fairly exotic and sweetish mix, lending itself to amusing garnishing. Sunrise has become popular through demand for tequila-based drinks and because of the vogue for Galliano liqueur

RAINBOW
See Pousse-café

RED LION
1 gin
½ Grand Marnier
1 teaspoon (5 ml) each of
lemon juice
orange juice
Shake. Serve in glass which has its rim frosted with sugar

RED VIKING
1 akvavit
1 maraschino
1 lime juice cordial
On-the-rocks

RICKEY*
The name is said to have originated with "Colonel Jim" Rickey (neither a colonel nor a Jim: his name was Joe). A well-known lobbyist of Washington D.C. at the turn of the century, he frequented Shoomaker's Bar, where the first Gin Rickey was made for him. It became, thereafter, his emblem

2 gin
1 teaspoon (5 ml) grenadine
½ fresh lime
Pour the gin and grenadine over ice in a tumbler, squeeze in the juice of the lime and then add the squeezed fruit itself. Top with soda water

Other spirits may be used, notably sloe gin

RIVIERA
1 Bacardi
1 Cointreau
½ raspberry liqueur
On-the-rocks. Top with bitter lemon, and squeeze a quarter of fresh lemon over before adding it to the drink

ROB ROY
1 Scotch whisky
1 red vermouth
Shake

ROLLS-ROYCE
1 gin
½ each dry and red vermouth
1 teaspoon (5 ml) Bénédictine
Shake

ROUND THE WORLD
1 gin
1 crème de menthe
2 fresh pineapple juice
Shake. Garnish with a pineapple cube on a stick

RUSTY NAIL*
2 Scotch whisky
1 Drambuie
Serve on-the-rocks. Add a twist of lemon

SALOME
½ gin
½ dry vermouth
Mix

SANGRE
See Bloody Mary

SAZERAC
2 Bourbon
1 teaspoon (5 ml) sugar
2 dashes Angostura bitters
Mix. Strain into tumbler in which a little Pernod has been poured and shaken out

This mix exists in various versions, and the name also pertains to a celebrated bottled cocktail first manufactured in New Orleans over a century ago

SCREWDRIVER
2 vodka
2 orange juice
Add to ice

SERPENT'S TOOTH
1 Irish whiskey
2 red vermouth
1 lemon juice
½ kümmel
1 dash Angostura bitters
Shake

SHAMROCK
1 Irish whiskey
1 dry vermouth
1 teaspoon (5 ml) each of green Chartreuse and green crème de menthe
Mix. Serve with a green olive

SIDECAR*
This is one of the "classics" attributed to Harry's New York Bar, founded at 5 rue Danou, Paris in 1911

1 brandy
½ lemon juice
½ Cointreau
Shake

SILVER STREAK
1 gin
½ kümmel
½ lemon juice
Shake

SINGAPORE GIN SLING*
This was almost certainly evolved in the famous Raffles Hotel, Singapore, possibly in 1915, as an elaboration of simpler gin slings widely drunk in the East

2 gin
4 lemon juice
1 heaped teaspoon (7.5 ml) sugar
½ Cointreau
½ cherry brandy
Pour the gin, lemon juice and sugar over ice in a tall glass, almost topping with soda water, then add the Cointreau and cherry brandy. Decorate with a slice of lemon. Serve with a straw

SLINGS
See Gin Sling

SMASH
An almost archaic term, "smash" denotes a julep made in a shaker, strained and decorated with mint. A cherry may also be added

SNOWBALL
1½ advocaat
lemonade or 7-Up
Put the advocaat in a tumbler with cracked ice and top with the lemonade or 7-Up. Garnish with a slice of orange and a cherry. Serve with straws

SOURS
See Whisky Sour

STARBOARD LIGHT
1 sloe gin
½ green crème de menthe
½ lemon juice
Shake

STINGER
1 brandy
½ crème de menthe
Mix

SUISSESSE
1 Pernod
1 lemon juice
1 egg white
Shake. Strain into tumbler and add a little soda water

SUNRISE*
1½ tequila
½ Galliano
½ crème de banane
½ fresh cream
1 dash grenadine
1 dash lemon juice
Shake. Serve in a tall glass

Some sources list quite different references for a cocktail of this name, but the tequila version now rules

SWIZZLES
A description that has fallen into disuse, this used to denote any drink served on crushed ice in which a swizzle-stick had been inserted, so that the drinker could agitate the mix himself and frost it to his requirement

TAMAGOZAKE
Perhaps the only boiled cocktail, this recipe comes from the All Nippon Bartenders' Association

6 sake
1 egg
1 teaspoon (5 ml) sugar
Boil the sake and ignite it. Remove immediately from the fire and stir in the egg and sugar. Serve in a mug with a handle

TODDIES
These were originally humble drinks of sugared spirits. More elaborate versions, with extra spices and juices, make the toddy a form of punch. The best base for a true toddy – primarily a "night-cap" to encourage sound slumber – is whisky

1 heaped teaspoon (7.5 ml) sugar
2 whisky
Put the sugar in a warm glass, add the whisky, stir and pour

in boiling water. Top with more whisky

Atholl Brose I is a more aristocratic version of the toddy. A cold toddy is virtually identical with a sling (see Gin Sling) made with whisky, except that soda, not ordinary, water is used

TWISTER
2 vodka
½ fresh lime juice
On-the-rocks in a tall glass, topped with 7-Up

VODKATINI
This is a Dry Martini made with vodka, improved by increasing the amount of dry vermouth and adding grapefruit peel, instead of lemon

WASHINGTON
1 brandy
½ dry vermouth
3 dashes grenadine or sugar syrup
2 dashes Angostura bitters
Shake

WHIP
¼ brandy
¼ Pernod
¼ dry vermouth
¼ Cointreau
Shake

WHISKY MAC*
1 Scotch whisky
1 green ginger wine
Add the whisky to the chilled ginger wine. Do not add ice

WHISKY SOUR*
1 whisky
½ teaspoon (2.5ml) sugar
2 lemon juice
1 teaspoon (5ml) egg white (optional)
Shake. If omitting egg white, top with a splash of soda water

WHITE HEATHER
1 gin
¼ Cointreau
¼ pineapple juice
¼ dry vermouth
Shake

WHITE LADY*
This is another invention from Harry's Bar, Paris

1 gin
½ Cointreau
½ lemon juice
1 egg white (optional)
Shake

PARTY MIXES
The following can mostly be made in bulk and served from a punch bowl or similar vessel

BOURBON FOG
2 pints (1 litre) strong black coffee, ice cold
2 pints (1 litre) vanilla ice-cream
2 pints (1 litre) Bourbon whiskey
Blend slowly in a punch bowl. Serve in mugs. For about 20

GLÖGG
This is a Scandinavian winter mix, very popular in Sweden. There are several variations but the following is a simple version, which can be treated as a good basis for further experiment

8 dashes Angostura bitters
1 bottle medium-dry sherry
1 bottle brandy
½ bottle sound red wine
1 tablespoon (15ml) powdered cinnamon
Heat without boiling, stirring gently all the time. Pour into warmed mugs containing a few raisins and an unsalted almond. For about 16

MULLS
A mull consists of wine or dark beer slowly heated, traditionally by inserting a red-hot poker. In winters of old, this was a favourite means by which ageing rustics would bring warmth to their arthritic bones in the local tavern. Mulled wine is still an efficient reviver on a glacial evening. The following recipe may be varied

2 bottles red wine
½ bottle ordinary port
¼ bottle ordinary brandy (not cognac)
1 large lemon stuffed with cloves
peel of 2 lemons
1 teaspoon (5ml) powdered nutmeg
3 cinnamon sticks
Bring all the ingredients slowly to near boiling, stirring continuously, but do not allow to boil. Gradually stir in brown sugar, tasting at intervals until the degree of sweetness is acceptable. Serve in mugs. For about 16

It is important to remember that a mull should always be served really hot, but never boiled, otherwise the alcohol will evaporate

BURGUNDY MULL
1 bottle red burgundy
1 wine glass dry sherry
2 brandy
1 small bottle blackcurrant cordial
2 pints (1 litre) water
3 lemons
1 small cupful sugar
1 teaspoon (5 ml) ginger
few cloves
Slice the lemons up small and place them in a saucepan. Add the sugar and ginger. Mix well and add other ingredients. Heat but do not allow to boil. Add cloves, strain and serve hot in teacups. For about 8

MULLED CLARET
1 bottle claret
1 wine glass port
1 pint (½ litre) water
1 tablespoon (15 ml) sugar
rind of half a lemon
12 whole cloves
grated nutmeg
Put the spices into a saucepan with the water and simmer gently for 30 minutes, then strain. Pour the claret into a pan and add the spiced water. Add the port and sugar and bring to near boiling, but do not allow to boil. Serve hot, decorated with thin slices of lemon peel. For about 8

MULLED SPICED ALE
Dissolve 1 teaspoon (5 ml) sugar in a metal half-pint tankard and add a pinch of powdered cinnamon. Top with strong, dark beer, and heat by inserting a white-hot poker. For 1

In these days of all gas/electric homes, you will have to heat the beer by other means which is not half so much fun

NEGUS
An old-fashioned mixed drink, popular in the eighteenth century

1 bottle sherry
2 pints (1 litre) boiling water
1 lemon
1 miniature bottle brandy
grated nutmeg
Warm the sherry in a saucepan very slowly, slice the lemon and add to the sherry, then pour in the boiling water. Add a little grated nutmeg and sugar to taste then add the brandy. For about 16

PUNCHES
The word "punch" is an English corruption of the Hindi pantsch (five): the original mixtures concocted in India by British and other colonists in the seventeenth century had five ingredients by custom – tea, water, sugar, lemon juice and arrack. The following selection of punches, hot, cold, individual or bulk, represents a good basis for experimentation – important if not essential with punches. Degrees of sweetness, if only that, are very much a personal matter

APPLE RUM PUNCH
6 oranges
1 bottle mellow rum
½ bottle brandy
4 tablespoons (60 ml) sugar
3 bottles apple juice
cinnamon, nutmeg and cloves
Stick the oranges with 10 cloves apiece and bake them until browned. Put them into a warmed punch bowl and add the rum, brandy and sugar. Stir well. Set the mixture alight and then extinguish with apple juice. Sprinkle with ground cinnamon and nutmeg and serve warm in teacups or in glasses with handles. For about 30

BACCIO PUNCH
1 bottle gin
1 bottle pure grapefruit juice
1 bottle champagne
1 siphon soda water
½ bottle anisette
Except for the champagne (which should be chilled), mix all the ingredients together in a large bowl, with lumps of ice. Add sliced fruit in season and, at the last moment, the chilled champagne. For about 24

BISHOP (English version)
12 cloves
1 orange
1 bottle port
allspice, grated nutmeg
rum and brandy to taste
brown sugar
Stick the cloves into the orange and bake until well browned. Cut into quarters and place in a saucepan. Pour in the port and heat slowly, without boiling, stirring in the spices and spirits. Adjust the sweetness with brown sugar. Serve in mugs in which a little powdered cinnamon has been sprinkled. For about 8

BISHOP (American version)
2 orange juice
and 1 lemon juice
1 tablespoon (15 ml) sugar
red wine
*Dissolve the sugar in the fruit
juice in a tall glass, add a wine-
glass of soda water, plenty of ice
and top with red wine. For 1*

BOOTH'S PARTY PUNCH
6 wine glasses gin
1 wine glass Cointreau
½ wine glass brandy
6 lemon juice
1 heaped tablespoon (20 ml)
sugar
1 bottle fizzy lemonade
*Mix well in a glass bowl or jug.
Add fizzy lemonade and plenty
of ice. Decorate with slices of
cucumber. Serve in wine glasses.
For about 12*

CHAMPAGNE PUNCH
2 bottles non-vintage dry
champagne
4 brandy
3 Cointreau
3 maraschino
1 siphon soda water
*Mix ingredients (except cham-
pagne and soda) and chill. Add
the iced champagne and chilled
soda water just before serving
and decorate bowl with fruit.
Try to keep as cool as possible.
For about 24*

CLARET CUP
1 bottle light red wine
1 lemon
1 orange
6 slices fresh pineapple
1½ each
brandy
Cointreau
sugar syrup

1 tablespoon (15 ml) lemon juice
1 siphon soda water
*Slice orange and lemon and in
a very large glass jug, pour the
other ingredients over them
with large ice lumps. Add wine,
a siphon of soda water; stir,
decorate with fruit. For about 8*

FISH HOUSE PUNCH
*This recipe evolved in Philadelphia
in the eighteenth century*

2 bottles rich rum
1 bottle brandy
3 pints (1½ litres) water
1 tablespoon (15 ml) orange
bitters
*Blend the ingredients thor-
oughly and pour over a large
block of ice in a suitable bowl
(reduce the proportions if your
bowl will not take this amount
of liquid). For about 30*

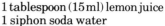

MARCO POLO

2 bottles medium madeira
½ lb (250 g) sugar
½ bottle cognac
10 sticks cinnamon
10 slices lemon
Stick each slice lemon liberally with cloves. Heat all ingredients slowly, stirring constantly, until near boiling. Serve very warm in teacups. For about 30

PENNSYLVANIA PUNCH
(modern version)

Juice of 12 lemons
2 pints (1 litre) water
1 small cup sugar
1 bottle Bourbon
1 bottle brandy
½ bottle Peach Brandy
Stir together with ice in a punch bowl. Garnish with slices of orange. For about 24

PLANTER'S PUNCH*

Though traditionally composed of one sour (lime juice), two sweet (sugar), three strong (rum) and four weak (water and ice), the following is probably a better option for taste

1 syrup
2 freshly squeezed lime juice
or 4 lemon juice
3-4 rum
1 dash grenadine
Put finely cracked ice, equivalent to five large cubes, in a shaker, then add the above ingredients and shake vigorously. Pour into a tall, pre-frosted glass, garnish with lime rind (or lemon rind) and sprinkle with grated nutmeg. For 1

RED WINE PUNCH

2 bottles red wine
1 bottle ordinary port
½ bottle cherry brandy
juice of 6 oranges and 4 lemons
¼ lb (125 g) sugar
Mix in a large bowl and add a block of ice. Add 1 pint (½ litre)

DOMECQ

RIO VIEJO

DRY OLOROSO SHERRY

PRODUCE OF SPAIN

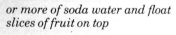

or more of soda water and float slices of fruit on top

WHITE WINE PUNCH

7oz (20 cl) sugar syrup
12 fresh lemon juice
1 bottle dry sherry
½ bottle brandy
3 bottles medium-dry white wine
2 cups strong tea
Mix in a large bowl and refrigerate. Before serving, add soda water and sliced cucumber. For about 30

SANGRIA

This is essentially a wine cooler, usually made with red wine – white looks less attractive. It is the modern version of a traditional, much simpler Spanish drink

1 bottle inexpensive red wine
slices of orange, lemon or any other fruit to hand
cinnamon and sugar to taste
Add to ice in a large jug, stir and leave under mild refrigeration until required. Just before serving add about 1 pint (½ litre) soda water. For about 8

This is a basic recipe. One particular, more potent, version includes Burgundy, champagne, brandy, Cointreau and fresh fruit

TEA PUNCH

½ bottle dark rum
½ bottle cognac
10 sugar syrup
2 pints (1 litre) strong, hot tea
1 large lemon
sugar lump
Rub the lump of sugar on the lemon. Heat a silvered punch-bowl. Put in the spirits, sugar-syrup, lemon-treated sugar and the juice of the lemon. Stir, set on fire and extinguish the conflagration with the hot tea. (The spirits will not ignite unless sufficiently warmed.) For about 12

A strong, black tea is recommended for this drink

TOM AND JERRY

Nothing to do with the well-loved cartoon characters, but a noble American mix of fair antiquity. There are several versions

12 eggs
½ lb (250 g) sugar
1 tablespoon (15 ml) each of powdered cinnamon, cloves and allspice
¼ bottle dark rum
2 whiskey
milk
grated nutmeg
Beat separately the yolks and whites of the eggs. Beat the sugar and spices, except the nutmeg, into the yolks. Stir in the rum and fold in the egg whites. Put a generous dollop in a big mug and add the whiskey. Top with boiling hot mixed milk and water. Dust with the nutmeg. For about 24

See also Nogs in previous section.

PICK-ME-UPS

The drinks in this section have been chosen primarily for their therapeutic, or shock, effect

CORPSE REVIVER (I)

½ brandy
½ orange juice
½ lemon juice
2 dashes grenadine
Shake. Serve in a wine glass, topped with champagne

CORPSE REVIVER (II)

1 brandy
1 crème de menthe
1 Fernet Branca
Shake

HAIR OF THE DOG

2 Scotch whisky
1½ double cream
1 honey
Add crushed ice and shake

HEART-STARTER

2 gin
Andrew's liver salts, Alka-Seltzer, or similar
Put in a tumbler and add iced water

PRAIRIE OYSTER*

The legend attaching to this renowned concoction concerns two US pioneers of the Old West. One fell very sick and in his delirium cried out for oysters. His friend broke some wild turkey's eggs into a mug and added some whiskey. The invalid, believing he was receiving the delicacy he so craved, devoured them and recovered

2 brandy
2 teaspoon (10 ml) each Worcestershire sauce and wine vinegar
1 dash cayenne pepper
salt
1 egg yolk
Blend all ingredients except the egg. Pour over the unbroken egg yolk in a glass and toss the potion down

YANKEE INVIGORATOR

1 egg
12 (36 cl) strong black coffee (cold)
2 brandy
1 port
sugar
Beat the egg in a cocktail shaker. Add the coffee, brandy and port, and sugar to taste. Shake and serve in a large goblet

SOFT DRINKS

The refreshing taste of sparkling mineral water;
the sharp tang of real lemonade; the rich
creaminess of a thick milkshake – soft drinks
provide delicious alternatives to their alcoholic
counterparts. There are many types to choose
from: carbonated proprietary drinks; fruit
juices, fresh, frozen, canned or concentrated; still
or sparkling spa waters; and flavoured or plain
milk drinks. Soft drinks play an increasing role
in the world of drinks, catering for children and
teetotallers, or mixing perfectly with wines and
spirits in cocktails, punches and long drinks.

SOFT DRINKS

World War I calendar advertisement for Coca-Cola. 1917

Though some people will agree that "A soft drink turneth away company" (Oliver Herford), the many different soft drinks play a large social and commercial role. There are many occasions when only a temperance tipple will do.

Even in the non-alcoholic category, the world of drinks is not straightforward; its once reasonably well-defined borders have become blurred in some cases. For example, a British brewery has successfully evolved a "beer" containing no alcohol for export to Moslem countries. There is also "near beer", invented in the USA and so weak as to be virtually non-alcoholic. Yet another company markets a temperance "cider". These types of paradoxical classification occur, outside of politics, mainly in vegetarian cuisine where carnivorous phraseology describes herbivorous food – e.g. "nut cutlets". Similarly, there are drinks which have been described as "non-alcoholic cocktails" – surely a contradiction in terms.

There are, of course, people who will imbibe only non-alcoholic drinks, refusing to touch alcohol on moral or religious grounds. The teachings of Islam include a firm injunction dating back to the early pronouncements of Mohammed prohibiting the use of wine, and the influence of this is apparent today throughout the Moslem world. From the earliest times too, efforts were made by concerned bodies to combat drunkenness, but it was in the early nineteenth century that the total abstinence movements became established and grew in number and strength. The influence of this movement was marked throughout the Western world, but particularly in the USA, where the effects of the various Temperance Societies, Bands of Hope and Women's Christian Movements culminated in the misery of Prohibition in the early twentieth century.

The commercial manufacture of non-alcoholic drinks is today a worldwide industry, dominated by the extraordinary success of such proprietary drinks as Coca-Cola. Current concern for natural, healthy living has meant an increase in the sale of bottled spa waters, and low-calorie drinks are big business too. Children, of course, are still, and always have been, insatiable consumers of soft drinks – and many adults have found that there is nothing quite like a large, cold glass of *aqua pura* after indulging in precisely the opposite. What is more, soft drinks go excellently with spirited companions and indeed many have been designed specifically for this purpose.

(bottom left) Taking the waters at a German spa

(bottom right) Bathing in the springs at Wiesbaden, Germany. Woodcut from Munster Cosmographia

WATER

Water is, of course, essential to both life and the production of *aqua vitae*.

To be enjoyed on its own, water must have certain qualities: it must be clear and colourless, with no smell and with an agreeable taste. Many people are fortunate in having tap water in their homes which has all these qualities, but for many more, the mains supply, though medically pure, has been treated so as to make it a less than perfect drink.

The provision of mains water goes back to the ancients: the Romans built aqueducts, conduits and fountains to supply their towns and cities. The poor often relied wholly on water for drinking. Yet in the Middle Ages, water was a drink to be avoided. This was not simply a precaution against contaminated sources, but because water was generally considered bad for the health ("Cold, slow and slack of digestion"). In 1542, Andrew Boorde's *A Compendyous Regyment or a Dyetary of Helth* stated, "Water is not wholesome, sole by itself" and recommended that those who diluted their wine should only use strained and boiled water, or preferably herb-flavoured distilled water.

Nowadays, the question of fluoridization of mains water is highly controversial in medical circles the world over. Fluoride's protagonists claim that it helps prevent tooth decay: other, equally expert opinion, condemns fluoride on medicinal grounds, and some critics simply disapprove of faceless bureaucrats forcing them to accept additives to their water supply.

Chlorination is also widely debated: a retired British army colonel recently gained ephemeral fame by publicly denouncing his local water authority for adding excessive amounts of chlorine to the water, thereby ruining his evening Scotch. The colonel would have been better off with bottled water; he would certainly have had a wide choice.

BOTTLED WATER

Quite apart from the question of taste, more Americans and Britons are now drinking bottled waters because they think they have true therapeutic value. The continental Europeans have done so for a long time, especially the French, who entertain now unjustifiable doubts about all tap water, and who set great store by the real or imagined benefits of certain springs.

There are some 1200 springs registered in France, and it is only water from fifty of them that is bottled for general consumption. In order of sales, the French favour Evian (which claims its origins to be mountain rain and melted snow), Vittel, Contrex, Perrier and Vichy. These and the other two leaders, Badoit and Volvic, have the distinction of being allowed to call themselves *eaux minerales naturelles* (natural mineral waters). This form of *Appellation Contrôlée* is gained through recommendation by the independent Academy of Medicine to the Health Ministry. The mineral waters to receive this special honour are guaranteed to maintain the highest standards.

The "father figure" of spring water, however, must surely be Spa in Belgium, which gives its name to the source of "spa" towns where, in the seventeenth and eighteenth centuries, the well-to-do, surfeited with good living, used to go to take the waters, both externally and internally. The habit of "taking the waters" may have begun

with good intentions, but as the spa towns expanded to cope with growing numbers of people, they simply became fashionable, and health a secondary – sometimes non-existent – reason for visiting them.

France is a very big exporter, especially of Vichy, Perrier and Evian (the best-selling brands in the British market). Perrier is the biggest imported spa water in the growing USA market, where the prestige of imported water seems to justify the considerable transport costs, and this despite the excellent domestic springs – Saratoga Springs in New York State, Caddo Valley and Mountain Valley in Arkansas, and Poland Springs in Maine. The German naturally sparkling water, Apollinaris from the Ahr valley, is the

second brand in the USA in this premium field.

Apollinaris was also the first imported water to gain any significant popularity in Britain (the Apollinaris company was in fact established there, not in Germany). So popular was Scotch (or brandy) and "Polly" that by 1913 forty million bottles were being sold yearly. Subsequent wars inhibited the brand's sales, but they are now soaring again. Perrier, too, was first exploited by a British company.

Germany has about two hundred companies producing "spa" waters, and sparkling varieties predominate. A natural spring water loses nothing of its purity or character by being carbonated – Apollinaris, like Perrier, is naturally effervescent. Highly carbonated Seltzer is the

other best-known water: the name has come to mean any carbonated, bottled mineral water. However, Germany is also a net importer of waters.

Italy's main contribution internationally is the slightly *pétillant* San Pellegrino. San Bernardo, a comparative newcomer (1926) from the maritime Alps, is also gaining ground both at home and abroad.

Britain's brand-leader in the bottled water business is Schweppes, whose own Malvern water has been sold since 1851. Coming from a spring in granite rock, it has a pleasing mild hardness and goes splendidly with Scotch. There are various other smaller UK firms – Prewetts in Hampshire, Ashbourne in Derbyshire and several in Scotland – which bottle spring waters, but without the national distribution achieved by Malvern.

Whether people drink spring waters, still or sparkling, because they think they are beneficial to their health or that they prefer the flavour to that of tap water, or use them as mixers with cordials, fruit juices, wines or spirits, there is no doubt that they are a growth industry.

SODA WATER

In the early days soda water was a medicinal product, the brainchild of a few enterprising chemists who decided to

try and reproduce spa waters artificially. The name
derives from the sodium carbonate from which the
essential ingredient, carbon dioxide, was originally produced.) By 1789, Nicholas Paul of
Geneva had perfected the method, and in
1792 one of his partners, Jacob
Schweppe, went to England and
commenced manufacture there.

By 1798 he was successful enough
to take on three partners and
in 1799 he returned to
Geneva, leaving behind
a business which
flourishes to
this day.

CARBONATED SOFT DRINKS

It is a pleasing irony that the manufacture of certain fermented liquors produces a by-product that is an essential ingredient in effervescent, non-alcoholic beverages. Carbon dioxide, the gas in question, can be lethal in concentration, yet when introduced into a liquid, enlivens it and also acts as a preservative.

Carbon dioxide is found in natural form in wines such as champagne and in spring waters such as Perrier, and it is forced into millions of bottles of carbonated drinks, some generic (e.g. fruit-based), some proprietary brands (e.g. Coca-Cola). All of these drinks contain purified water, carbon dioxide, sweeteners, fruit flavours (fresh or synthetic) and sometimes special herbs or chemicals. Citrus fruits are the most usual form of flavouring, yet it is a tribute to science that in many cases, better flavour – leaving aside any other considerations – may be obtained by the use of synthetics than from the natural juices. Sugar is the usual sweetener, however, since certain artificial substances are banned in some countries.

Most countries produce their own makes of soft drinks, but their real home is the USA. It is estimated that the top ten brands alone sell about 14,000 million litres a year there, and of all the soft drinks manufactured it is computed that something approaching 600 bottles are drunk annually by every US citizen.

The soda fountain, too, from which a huge range of non-alcoholic drinks is dispensed has its home in America. Soda fountains have been emulated in cities in other countries, yet have never achieved the effulgent glory of the native establishment.

Not all popular American drinks have caught on overseas: readers who are old enough, may remember a hit song with the line "Would you like a sars'parilla?" which would mostly have mystified non-Americans. The root of the sarsaparilla plant, a tough, climbing shrub indigenous to Central America, provides a syrup which was once lauded in the USA as a medicine – for no sound reason. Sarsaparilla is also one of the ingredients, along with other roots – principally dandelion and sassafras – from which a particularly American speciality, root beer, is brewed.

COCA-COLA
Coca-Cola's extraordinary dominance of the proprietary soft drinks market is widely recognized, as is its sensational worldwide distribution.

The product was created in Atlanta, Georgia, in 1886 by pharmacist Dr John S. Pemberton, who, according to legend, first made the syrup in a three-legged pot in his back yard. It went on sale at five cents a glass as a soda fountain drink in Jacobs Pharmacy ("Everything Retailed At Wholesale Prices") a few doors down from Dr Pemberton's establishment. The famous name was suggested by Frank M Robinson, Dr Pemberton's partner, who also scripted it in the flowing style of the day.

Although the drink was popular, its success was confined mostly to Atlanta and Dr Pemberton remained unaware of its potential. In 1887, in poor health and in need of money, he sold the manufacturing rights and two-thirds interest

to two acquaintances. Four months before he died in 1888 he sold the remaining shares to an Atlanta pharmacist, Asa G. Candler, who then proceeded to acquire the additional rights and complete control of Coca-Cola.

By 1892 sales had increased ten times and in the same year Candler formed the Coca-Cola Company. Eight years later sales reached a million gallons a year.

Coca-Cola's increasing success owed a great deal to Candler's belief in imaginative advertising and promotion. He gave away coupons entitling the bearer to a free glass of the drink, souvenir fans, calendars, clocks and more, all embellished with the famous name.

Coca-Cola was, however, still a soda fountain drink; it was first bottled in Mississippi by an enterprising pharmacist who installed bottling machinery in his soda-fountain and sold bottled Coca-Cola to the lumber camps and plantations along the river. By 1895, Asa G. Candler could announce "Coca-Cola is now drunk in every state and territory in the United States".

In 1919 the Candler family sold out to an Atlanta banker, Ernest Woodruff, for $25 million. The following year, the word "Coke" was established (in a legal battle with the "Koke Company of America") as the sole property of the company: it was a name chosen by the American people as Coca-Cola became part of the country's way of life.

In 1923 Robert W. Woodruff (Ernest's son) became President of the company and commenced fifty years of a leadership which had every intention of taking Coca-Cola to every part of the globe. Like Candler he was a firm believer in advertising, and the packaging of the product became all-important. The distinctive bottle (which first appeared in 1916) was pushed to the forefront of campaigns; later came a six-bottle carton, and then a special Coca-Cola cooler from which the bottles were served. A distinctive glass appeared in 1929, and memorable slogans were a big feature, from the "Delicious and Refreshing" of 1886 to "The Pause that Refreshes" in 1928, on to "Things Go Better With Coke" in 1963 and, the most recent, "Have A Coke And A Smile."

For a considerable time in the company's period of expansion, the basic syrup – the secret of the whole gigantic operation – was made only in Atlanta and distributed to a few franchised bottlers. It is now produced in various centres abroad as well. In the 1960s it was estimated that a new (franchised) Coca-Cola plant was being opened every two weeks somewhere in the world.

This impetus resulted from a wartime act of policy by the company, which established no less than sixty-four overseas bottling plants. The declaration of war prompted Robert Woodruff to make the announcement that every man in uniform would be able to obtain Coca-Cola for five cents a bottle, no matter where he was and regardless of how much it cost to get it to him. The first plant was opened in Algiers in 1943, and others followed, shipped out and set up in Europe and the Pacific close to combat areas.

Today, the growth rate of plants has eased as those being built are bigger and can serve wider areas. In fact, Coke is sold in over 135 countries, and is a familiar word in more than eighty languages. A very early result of the Sino-American detente in the late 1970s was the reintroduction of Coca-Cola to mainland China, where a whole generation had grown up unaware of it.

The public's faith in Coca-Cola has never faltered; its success perhaps best summed up by the neon sign in Times Square which greeted the Apollo astronauts returning

from their moon flight and which read: "Welcome Back to Earth, Home of Coca-Cola."

PEPSI-COLA

Coke's most famous rival is Pepsi-Cola and that, too, has worldwide distribution. It was invented in the 1890s by Caleb Bradham, a self-styled doctor, who served a bracing concoction of his own making in his minute pharmacy in New Bern, North Carolina. It was known locally as "Brad's Drink". "Doc" Bradham was, however, a man of wider vision and he dreamed up the name Pepsi-Cola, registering the trademark in 1903. By 1916 he had over a hundred franchised bottlers.

In the early 1930s, Pepsi brought out a larger-than-usual bottle at the higher-than-usual price of ten cents, which did not go down too well in the Depression-wracked USA. So the company boldly halved the price. This, coupled with the slogan, "A Nickel Drink, Worth a Dime", was an enormously successful move. At the same time Pepsi recorded the first sung radio commercial. After the war, the dynamic Alfred Steele took control and vastly improved Pepsi's fortunes. To the general public, he became better known as the last husband of the actress Joan Crawford, who, on his death, became an active ambassador for Pepsi.

Also in the big-time league is the American soft drink 7-Up, the nearest product the USA has to British fizzy lemonade. Other popular drinks include Dr Peppers (unique to the USA), which is similar to Coke, but sweeter and fruitier. Britain has a trio of proprietary drinks, Tizer, Vimto and Dandelion & Burdock, all different and with flavours that belie accurate description. Fizzy fruit drinks are popular everywhere and there are numerous brands, and for figure-conscious drinkers, low-calorie soft beverages such as Diet-Pepsi are increasingly in demand.

MIXERS

Fluctuations in the popularity of various spirits have been the spur to the invention of new carbonated soft drinks as mixers: for example, Schweppes Russchian, and Canada Dry's Vostok, aimed at vodka drinkers.

Among international mixers, tonic water is probably the best known. Though in most countries it is drunk mainly with gin, in France it is a very smart beverage (usually simply ordered as "une Schweppes") and treated as a drink in its own right, a custom which the company has highlighted in its advertising in other countries. In fashionable places, however, it is often absurdly expensive. It is gener-

ally recognized everywhere that Schweppes produces the best "tonic" (and has been doing so since 1858) though facing growing competition, particularly from brewery-controlled brands in Britain, the home country.

At one time, it looked as if bitter lemon, also pioneered by Schweppes, would seriously erode the market for tonic. However, whilst bitter lemon is tremendously popular, tonic remains supreme as the gin mixer.

Ginger ale is another favourite mixer, especially with Scotch. Canada Dry were largely responsible for popularizing "American" ginger ale, the sweeter variety which is now dominant, as against the tarter "Original" (the best of which is made by Schweppes). Canada Dry did market a brand called Canada Dry Extra, really gingery and close to the original, sharp ginger beer of yore.

PACKAGING

Efficient packaging is essential for the distribution and marketing of all beverages on a large scale. At the beginning of the nineteenth century, when bottled carbonated drinks began to come on to the market, no better closure could be found than a cork wired in place, like the closure used for champagne bottles. Most of the closures invented later proved too cumbersome or expensive. In 1870 H. Codd invented a system whereby a glass ball enclosed in the bottle neck was forced by gas pressure against a rubber washer. To release the liquid, the ball was pushed free. It was simple and effective, but unhygienic. The first practical screw top was introduced in 1879; in 1888 W. J. King invented a lever closure.

Finally, in 1891, William Painter of Baltimore invented the Crown Cork, as we know it today, except that plastic liners have now largely superseded cork. This cheap, disposable bottle-stopper preserved the contents and protected the pouring edge from contamination. It is still the standard closure for bottled carbonated drinks.

Nowadays, bottles have been overtaken by cans, and these are also facing increasing competition from plastic containers. Plastic is suitable for any drink except those with a high alcohol content, since in these cases the material will contaminate the contents if stored for an extended period. Few, if any, reputable distillers will package their products in anything but glass, but plastic is still popular for spa waters, inexpensive fruit drinks and economy-size mixers. Concern for bio-degradable packaging and the rise in the price of petroleum products may eventually see these too, return to their original glass bottles.

FRUIT DRINKS

Fresh fruit juice is probably the simplest and most popular kind of non-alcoholic drink. The manufacture of fruit drinks of all kinds is big business; juices are canned, bottled, frozen and powdered, as well as marketed in the form of fruit concentrates, for dilution with water. Pure, fresh juice – orange is the most popular – must be kept under refrigeration; otherwise it must contain permitted preservatives and sweeteners, and even so it will not keep satisfactorily outside the refrigerator once opened, unless it has been pasteurized.

The powdered fruit drinks are useful "convenience" drinks and surprisingly tasty. Although they contain ingredients other than dehydrated juice concentrate, they also customarily include additional vitamins.

Although regulations inevitably vary from country to country, there are basically two forms of bottled fruit concentrates, particularly in the case of citrus fruit drinks, the most popular of all. One form contains a high percentage of pure juice together with comminuted fruit (comminuation involves liquefying the whole fruit, including the peel, and producing a clarified beverage). The other is a drink containing only comminuted fruit plus, possibly, other constituents which are preservatives or synthetic flavourings. The latter are normally cheaper in price and less "fruity" in flavour.

Sadly, with all the styles and flavours of fruit drinks that are available commercially, the art of making drinks at home from basic ingredients has all but disappeared. How many people now bother to make true lemonade? It is a delicious drink and simple to make. Easiest of all is France's *citron pressé*, which is made by adding the juice of a lemon to a glass of crushed ice, and topping up with water or soda water. It is then sugared to taste and served with a stirring spoon and straws.

In the recipes that follow, *shake* means shake in a cocktail shaker and strain into suitable glasses, and servings are individual unless otherwise stated. All drinks should be served with ice.

RECIPES

Measurements are based on a unit of 3 cl (about 1 fl oz), thus 1 = 3 cl (1 fl oz), ½ = 1½ cl (½ fl oz)

TRADITIONAL DRINKS

LEMONADE
3 lemons
3 tablespoons (45 ml) citric acid
8 oz (225 g) sugar, preferably brown
3 pints (1.75 litres) boiling water

Pare the rind from the lemons. Squeeze the juice and put into a big jug with the citric acid, peel and sugar. Pour on the boiling water and stir. Allow to cool. Strain and refrigerate. Quantities sufficient for about 8 servings

To make a concentrated lemonade double all the quantities except water

MRS BEETON'S RECIPE FOR GINGER BEER
Ginger beer is a traditional English beverage and a marvellous summer time drink. It is available commercially but started as a home brew made in some quantity. According to Mrs Beeton, this recipe makes enough to fill 48 ginger-beer bottles, which hold about ½ pint (25 cl) each

2½ lb (1 kg) loaf sugar
1½ oz (43 g) bruised ginger
1 oz (28 g) cream of tartar
rind and juice of 2 lemons
3 gallons (13.5 litres) boiling water
2 large tablespoons (40 ml) fresh brewer's yeast

Peel the lemons, squeeze the juice, strain it and put the peel and juice into a large heavy pan, with the bruised ginger, cream of tartar and loaf sugar. Pour over these ingredients 3 gallons of boiling water; let it stand until just warm, then add the yeast. Stir the contents of the pan well and stand it in a warm place all night, covered with a cloth. Next day, skim off the yeast and pour the liquor carefully into another vessel, leaving the sediment; then bottle immediately, and tie the corks down; in 3 days the ginger beer will be fit for use

For some, the above proportion of sugar may be too much, and it can be reduced according to taste

NON-ALCOHOLIC COCKTAILS

CINDERELLA
½ each of
lemon juice
orange juice
pineapple juice
Shake

KEELPLATE
2 tomato juice
1 clam juice (or Clamato)
2 dashes Worcestershire sauce
2 dashes celery salt
Shake

PARSON'S PARTICULAR
2 fresh orange juice
1 lemon juice
1 egg yolk
4 dashes grenadine
Shake

PUSSYFOOT
½ each of
lemon juice
orange juice
unsweetened lime juice
½ teaspoon (2.5 ml) sugar
1 egg yolk
Shake. Add soda water. Top with a cocktail cherry

SLIM JIM
2 each of
tomato juice
fresh grapefruit juice
½ teaspoon (2.5ml)
Worcestershire sauce
Shake

APPLE TANKARD
Three-quarters fill a silver or glass tankard with chilled pure apple juice. Add the juice of an orange and slices of any suitable fruit to hand, plus a few ice cubes

NICOLAS
2 each of
orange juice
lemon juice
Rose's lime juice cordial
1 teaspoon (5 ml) egg white
1 dash grenadine
Shake vigorously and strain into a tall glass a quarter-filled with crushed ice. Serve with straws

MILK

Milk and its by-products have been used as food by mankind throughout the time of recorded history. Milk has always been valued as a sustainer of life and revered as a symbol of plenty – Canaan was "flowing with milk and honey" – and at its most exotic has even been used for bathing.

It is the first liquid tasted by the majority of people, who continue to drink much of it throughout their lives, and to eat it in the form of butter, cheese and so on. Though milk from mares, asses, goats, ewes, camels, buffaloes and even reindeer is drunk in various parts of the world, the prime source is the cow.

After water, milk is the commonest of beverages and, like water, today's availability of safe, fresh milk is taken very much for granted. Before the mid-nineteenth century, however, clean milk was virtually unknown and the consumption of liquid milk was low, especially by the inhabitants of towns and cities. The cows themselves were often diseased, their cowsheds dirty and the milk soured by the time it reached the consumer. In the 1860s, Louis Pasteur succeeded in preventing wine and beer from souring by exposure to high temperatures. The same process was applied to milk and, by the end of the nineteenth century, milk was being commercially "pasteurized".

Most milk sold now is pasteurized; it may also be homogenized (the fat blended into the liquid), sterilized (for long life), skimmed (the fat removed for butter), evaporated, condensed and powdered.

Milk is the basis for a number of drinks which are fundamentally of dietary merit and are usually taken at bedtime. They are mostly sold in the form of powders, soluble in water, milk or a mixture of the two. Generically, the most important is malted milk, in which concentrated essence of malted cereals is combined with dehydrated milk. As a hot drink, malted milk is generally considered a nutritious beverage, free from any ingredients that might discourage sleep. However, served chilled it makes an attractive refresher at any time, and malted milk added to milk shakes and similar concoctions gives them extra character.

Cultured milk drinks include buttermilk, a pleasant, refreshing drink made from pasteurized, skimmed milk incubated with butter culture, and variations on yogurt-types (which can be taken as beverages as well as a solid food). These include Kefir, Kumiss, Airan, Southern Sweet Milk (all from Central Asia), Whey Champagne and Felisokwa (Polish), and Kraeldermalk (Scandinavia), none of which are particularly commonplace outside their own countries. "Traditional" yogurt is made from raw, whole milk and the cultured product is manufactured on a commercial scale in the USA and Europe.

Two other developments concerning milk by-products deserve mention.

It may come as a surprise to many that good alcohol can be made from milk. An excellent example of how a national surplus may be turned into something else comes from Ireland, where in October 1978 a creamery was reported to be producing daily 3000 gallons of alcohol at a strength of 96.5 degrees.

The theory of producing alcohol from milk is nothing new, but it had never before been made into a practical commercial proposition: this plant, Carbery Milk Products, was the first of its kind in the world. The alcohol

comes from the whey left after the production of cheese. The protein is extracted and the lactose is fermented and distilled. The resultant spirit is suitable for gin or vodka, being similar to alcohol derived from molasses, or for pharmaceutical purposes.

The capacity of the plant is eight million litres produced annually from 108 million litres of milk. Distilling from whey instead of processing it in the conventional way saved in capital cost. However, the Carberry operation is valid only because it is Europe's largest cheese factory, and it does not herald the final solution to the EEC's surplus milk problem: we may not, unfortunately, look forward to a gin lake in place of milk lakes and butter mountains.

Quite a different association of milk and alcohol was the introduction into the US market in 1976 of milk-based pre-mixed cocktails. These bottled drinks, known as Cows, are quite weak; in effect, they are alcoholic milk shakes, and the flavourings available include chocolate, banana, walnut, strawberry and coconut.

In the recipes that follow, ordinary, everyday milk as used in the home is implied. Of the recipes, Country Milk Shake, Rosanna Milk, Rose Milk and Blackcurrant Velvet are especially enjoyed by children. Yogurt, surprisingly, can form the basis for refreshing beverages. Tiger's Milk and Milk Punch are alcoholic (one cannot ignore the fact that milk blends excellently with some spirits). All servings are individual unless otherwise stated.

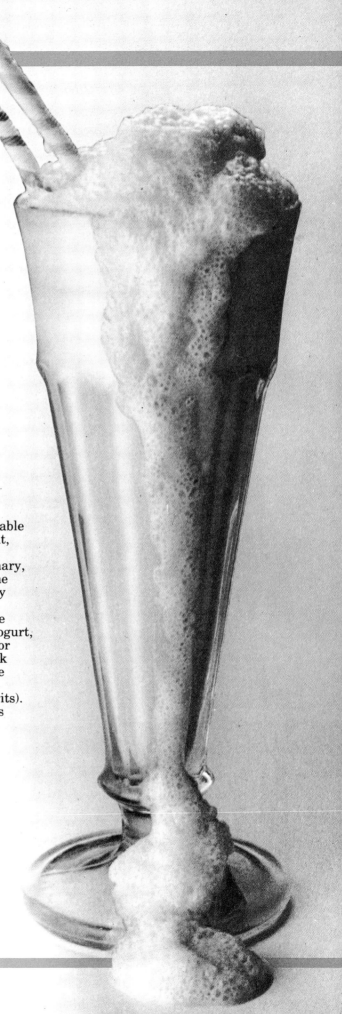

Milk shakes can be made quite simply with milk and whisked egg; more elaborate affairs consist of milk, ice cream, soda water or lemonade, topped with whipped cream, cherries and candied decorations. They are very popular in the United States and can be made in almost any flavour

RECIPES

Measurements are based on a unit of 3 cl (about 1 fl oz), thus 1 = 3 cl (1 fl oz), ½ = 1½ cl (½ fl oz)

BLACKCURRANT VELVET
3 blackcurrant syrup
1 pint (50 cl) milk
Stir the syrup into the milk and serve with a slice of orange in the glass for decoration. For 3

COUNTRY MILK SHAKE
1 pint (50 cl) milk
1 tablespoon (15 ml) fruit syrup
8oz (250g) soft vanilla ice cream
Whisk together and serve with a little granulated brown or coloured sugar sprinkled on top. For 4

MILK SHAKE
1 egg
½ pint (25 cl) milk
sugar to taste
Shake vigorously (or liquidize). Dust with powdered nutmeg if desired

ROSANNA MILK
3 fairly ripe bananas
3 rose-hip or other fruit syrup
1 pint (50 cl) milk
few drops vanilla essence
Mash the bananas and stir in the syrup. Whisk in the milk. For 3

ROSE MILK
3 orange juice and rose-hip or other syrup
1 pint (50 cl) milk
8 oz (250 g) vanilla ice cream
Stir the juice and syrup into the melting ice cream and whisk thoroughly into the milk. For 3

CHOCOLATE MILK
3 chocolate syrup
1 pint (50cl) milk
Stir the syrup with the milk and serve with a little grated chocolate for decoration. For 3

YELLOW DWARF
1 each cream and almond syrup
1 egg yolk
Shake. Top with a splash of soda water

YOGURT DRINKS

AIRAN
4 natural yogurt
salt to taste
grated nutmeg
Beat the yogurt with the salt until runny enough to drink. Add a little water if the yogurt is still thick. Top with grated nutmeg

YOGURT AND TOMATO COCKTAIL
½ pint (25 cl) chilled tomato juice
¾ pint (40 cl) chilled natural yogurt
1 teaspoon (5 ml) Worcestershire sauce
salt and pepper to taste
Mix all ingredients together. Pour into glasses and top with sprigs of mint. For 4

LEMON FIZZ
4 natural or lemon-flavoured yogurt
1 small bottle bitter lemon
Mix ingredients together. Pour into glasses, top with orange or lemon slices. For 2

ALCOHOLIC MILK DRINKS

MILK PUNCH
½ pint (25 cl) milk
1 egg
3 teaspoons (15 ml) sugar syrup
2 Scotch whisky, dark rum or cognac
Shake. Strain and top with powdered nutmeg.

A Prohibition edition of this omits the spirit

TIGER'S MILK
1 teaspoon (5 ml) sugar syrup
1 teaspoon (5 ml) egg white
1 drop vanilla essence
1 pinch powdered cinnamon
2 brandy
Milk
Sweet cider
Shake all but the milk and cider vigorously with ice cubes. Strain into a tall glass and top with equal amounts of sweet cider and milk. Sprinkle with powdered cinnamon

BEVERAGES

Tea, coffee and cocoa are the everyday drinks,
consumed in vast quantities all over the world.
Everyone can appreciate the aroma of freshly
ground coffee, savour the fragrance of hot tea,
enjoy a comforting cup of cocoa, or benefit from a
herbal infusion. There are as many ways of
preparation as there are blends to choose from,
and most people seem to have a favourite method
to go with their own particular brand. But, as
with other types of drink, experimenting with
different varieties adds pleasure to what is part
of the daily ritual.

BEVERAGES

"...absolutely pure" 1888 advertisement for Cadbury's cocoa

It probably says something about the nature of mankind that the recorded use of alcoholic beverages goes back much further into antiquity than non-alcoholic drinks. The only obvious exception is milk, although there are still societies in which milk is not only not part of the daily diet, but is even considered indigestible.

Certainly of the three main non-alcoholic beverages, tea, coffee and cocoa, tea seems to have the longest history, even though its use did not become widespread in the Western world until comparatively recent times. What is rather more certain is that it is now the most commonly used non-alcoholic drink of all, excluding all the carbonated cold drinks, which fall into so many categories that there is no useful comparison. For millions upon millions of Chinese, Japanese and other Far Eastern peoples, life would be almost insupportable without all those daily infusions, and even those tea-drinking champions of the Western World, Great Britain, Australia and Ireland, would slip into a miserable torpor without an assured supply of hot, sweet tea.

There are also plenty of nations in which coffee plays a similar role. The people of northern Europe and the Scandinavian and the Nordic states are the world's most dedicated coffee drinkers, with Sweden in the lead. To be deprived of coffee would be an almost unbearable hardship

The Japanese tea ceremony or chanoyu *is a ritual influenced by the teachings of Zen Buddhism*

Taking afternoon tea. From La Vie Parisienne, *1923*

for them. Equally, the people of the Mediterranean coast and of the United States have come to regard coffee as an indispensable ingredient of civilized living.

Of the three, cocoa – or chocolate – has suffered the most severe eclipse, although it still has its devotees. This is a pity, because well-made chocolate is an excellent drink, fragrant, soothing, and with many of the restorative qualities of the other two. In a weight-conscious world the fact that cocoa is fattening may count against it.

But in any event, tea, coffee and cocoa all provide a living for literally millions of growers in some of the poorest parts of the world. If these drinks were to fall from favour the results would be catastrophic. However, although the carbonated drinks are certainly taking an increasing share of the market for non-alcoholic beverages, tea and coffee still hold their own, and even chocolate drinks maintain a respectable place on the shelves of the world's food stores.

TEA

According to some historians, tea was introduced to China from southern Korea as early as 800 BC, but it only became really known in the post-Han Dynasty period of AD 25 to 250. It took even longer to cross the sea to Japan and according to Japanese records it arrived on the islands some time between AD 700 and 800.

Early botanists called the plant *thea*, but to the Chinese it was *tcha* and to the Indians *cha*. In Eastern Europe Russia, Romania and Turkey, it is still known as *tcheai* and spelt *çeai*. The fragrant leaf first became known to Europe at the end of the sixteenth century, and the first written reference appears on the correspondence of the East India Company in 1615, where it is mentioned as *chaw*. The Portuguese, who came upon it at around the same time, called it *chia*.

It appears that *thea* was originally regarded mainly as a medicinal herb in China, and for a time after its introduction to Japan tea-drinking was practised exclusively among Zen Buddhist priests, who used it to stave off drowsiness during their long periods of meditation. When it first reached Europe in the seventeenth century, it usually came in small consignments, often as a gift to some notable; London certainly regarded it at first as nothing more than an outlandish curiosity which, because of its rarity, fetched around £15 a pound.

It was half a century after that first mention by the East India Company, in 1657, before the first commercial consignment reached London and three years later it had become dutiable – which made it an interesting and profitable proposition for smugglers.

Like coffee and cocoa, the use of tea was originally confined to the rich and the fashionable. But by 1773 – when the citizens of Boston had demonstrated their dislike of excessive British taxes by dumping a consignment of tea into the harbour in the Boston Tea Party – tea's importance as a commercial product had obviously become well established.

When the East India Company's China trade

A samovar is a type of metal urn common in Russia where it originated, which is used for boiling water to make tea. Samovars are usually nickel- or silver-plated bronze or copper; more elaborate versions exist made entirely of silver or even platinum

monopoly was broken in 1833, competition opened up and the price of tea began to fall rapidly and it soon became the favourite non-alcoholic beverage of the British. And because the British had taken so readily to the drink, the planting of tea was strongly encouraged throughout the British Empire and especially in India and Ceylon. Even now, India, Pakistan and Ceylon remain the world's major producers with Britain the major consumer.

Tea was first grown on a commercial scale in the Assam area of India and by the 1830s the Assamese plantations were among the most important commercial enterprises in the business and their prolific output helped substantially to confirm the British in their tea-drinking habits. Ceylon – or Sri Lanka – came to tea-growing some forty years later, after the dreaded leaf rust disease had wiped out the coffee plantations there.

Tea usually flourishes at high altitudes and it needs a good deal of rain during the hot season, so it is mostly grown in the tropics or the sub-tropical areas of the world's temperate zones. Tea-planting started moving westwards at the beginning of this century, but it was not until after the two world wars – and especially the second – that new and important tea plantations began to be established in Africa and South America, to add to the established production of India, China, Japan and the other Southeast Asian countries, and Asiatic Russia.

Plantations were established in East Africa, South Africa, the Zimbabwe-Rhodesia Highlands, Brazil and Argentina. Later still, Tanzania, Kenya and Zimbabwe-Rhodesia began to grow Assam-type teas.

The tea plant is of the Camellia family and it can grow to a considerable height if it is not pruned back; wild tea plants, 15 metres high, have been found, but the cultivated variety is not allowed to grow more than 1.5 metres high, which not only makes it easier to treat but also makes it possible for the pickers to reach the younger, tender shoots and leaves at the top, which yield the best taste and aroma.

The two main types of tea that reach the world's markets are green tea, where the leaves are dried immediately after picking so that they retain much of their original colour, and black tea which is allowed to ferment in its own moisture for a short while before being lightly roasted and dried again. This black tea is the one which the Western world most favours and it is sold in dozens of blends, all carefully put together to suit not only local tastes but often the type of water available in different districts.

The green teas, known as "China" teas, have a smaller market and they are usually drunk after meals and without milk or sugar. It is the green tea known as *matcha* which is always used in the famous Japanese tea ceremony. This ceremony had its origins in the fourteenth century, when a game called *tocha* – that is, a tea contest – was introduced from China. This was a diversion in which guests were served several cups of tea grown in various regions and asked to select which cup contained the tea grown in the best region.

At this time tea plantations were beginning to flourish and the Uji district near Kyoto was producing the very best quality (it still does). This changed the nature of the game and instead of competing for prizes the aim became the enjoyment of the solemn and profound atmosphere in which the tea was being drunk. The lives of the ruling Samurai warriors were also increasingly being governed by a strict formality and this was soon reflected in the tea ceremony.

Murato Shuko (1423-1502) evolved the fundamental

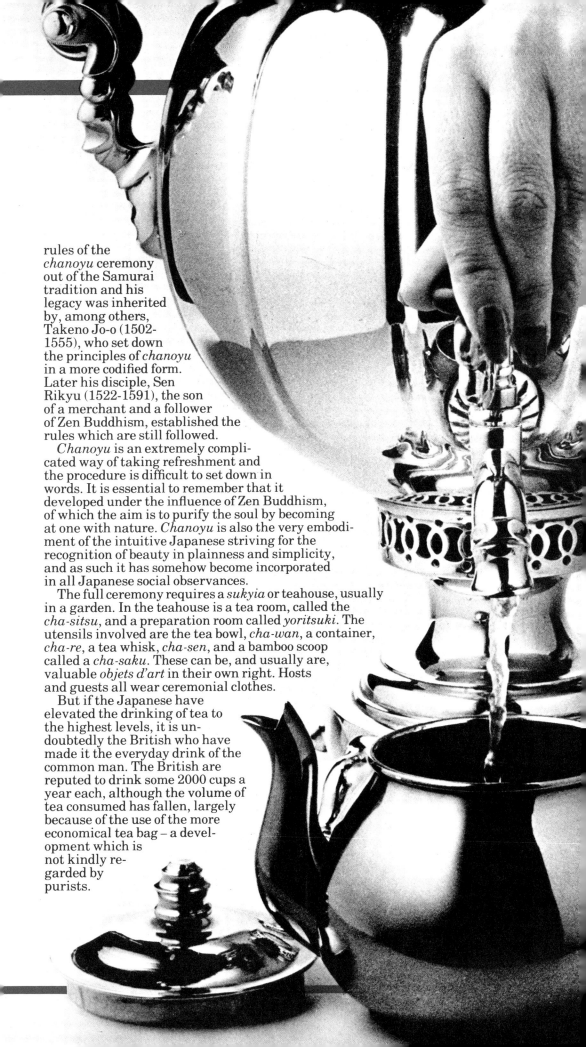

rules of the
chanoyu ceremony
out of the Samurai
tradition and his
legacy was inherited
by, among others,
Takeno Jo-o (1502-
1555), who set down
the principles of *chanoyu*
in a more codified form.
Later his disciple, Sen
Rikyu (1522-1591), the son
of a merchant and a follower
of Zen Buddhism, established the
rules which are still followed.

Chanoyu is an extremely complicated way of taking refreshment and
the procedure is difficult to set down in
words. It is essential to remember that it
developed under the influence of Zen Buddhism,
of which the aim is to purify the soul by becoming
at one with nature. *Chanoyu* is also the very embodi-
ment of the intuitive Japanese striving for the
recognition of beauty in plainness and simplicity,
and as such it has somehow become incorporated
in all Japanese social observances.

The full ceremony requires a *sukyia* or teahouse, usually
in a garden. In the teahouse is a tea room, called the
cha-sitsu, and a preparation room called *yoritsuki*. The
utensils involved are the tea bowl, *cha-wan*, a container,
cha-re, a tea whisk, *cha-sen*, and a bamboo scoop
called a *cha-saku*. These can be, and usually are,
valuable *objets d'art* in their own right. Hosts
and guests all wear ceremonial clothes.

But if the Japanese have
elevated the drinking of tea to
the highest levels, it is undoubtedly the British who have
made it the everyday drink of the
common man. The British are
reputed to drink some 2000 cups a
year each, although the volume of
tea consumed has fallen, largely
because of the use of the more
economical tea bag – a development which is
not kindly re-
garded by
purists.

Because tea drinking came to Britain from the Far East, tea cups and saucers and tea pots are still often made of porcelain although, in Georgian times, exquisitely elaborate silver tea-making sets were used. Nowadays, tea pots tend to be made of more common materials, including glass, but the only type of tea-making equipment that really needs to be avoided at all costs is the aluminium teapot, which will destroy even unremarkable blends.

The rules of correct tea-making vary from household to household, but tea professionals are generally agreed on one foolproof procedure.

First of all, heat the teapot before putting in one teaspoon of tea for each cupful and "one for the pot". *Freshly* boiled water is then poured over the leaves, bringing the kettle to the pot so that the water is not still actually bubbling; never use water which has been boiling for more than a minute or so. The brew is then left to infuse for up to five minutes. If milk is used it should be put in the cup before the tea is poured, because there is a belief that if the tea is poured in first and the milk added later the tea-leaves – or dust if a strainer is used – will not settle at the bottom of the cup as they should. Sugar, if used, is added to taste, but many people still believe that unsweetened tea is best.

But that is tea as drunk by the British, their Australian and New Zealand cousins and the Irish, who are also tea-drinking champions. The tea habit in continental Europe and the United States has evolved rather differently and, in any case, coffee remains mostly the best favoured non-alcoholic beverage, except in Eastern Europe.

True, the wealthier classes in France did adopt the English habit of "afternoon tea" at the turn of the century, although they did not, as the English do, take it at three o'clock in the afternoon; in France it was "le five o'clock", which later merged imperceptibly with "le cocktail hour". The French also preferred the lighter green "China" teas, while the British like the dark leaves.

In Eastern Europe, and especially in Russia, tea also took a great hold. The Russians especially can be credited with the invention of the samovar, a sort of metal vase which can stand anything up to three feet high and which has a funnel through the middle and a charcoal burner at the base. The samovar was kept full of boiling water, which issued through a tap at the bottom. In Tsarist times, Tula in Central Russia, famous for its cannon foundries, was the centre of the samovar-manufacturing industry.

The devices were made, variously, of nickel or silver-plated bronze or copper, but some of the grander dukes had theirs fabricated in silver or, in a few really ostentatious cases, of platinum. Every carriage in the Trans-Siberian Railway still has its own samovar.

Teapots are used in Russia, with the tea immersed in a perforated egg-shaped container on a chain. The Russian style is to place a little sugar – or blackberry conserve – on the tongue, and then sup the tea from a glass. Noisily.

In ports along the Danube, tea-drinking was an unavoidable component of concluding grain sales. The tea was poured into wide, willow-patterned cups, but most people preferred to tip it into the saucers and allow it to cool before drinking it. Again, sugar was taken separately. The tea-houses were known as *thscheainarias* and they were frequented by itinerant fortune-tellers who read the future from the patterns of the tea-leaves at the bottom of the cup.

The Chinese themselves, although they have an almost reverent respect for the finest and rarest teas, take a far less awed view of their everyday drink. Green tea is served

in glasses, without milk or sugar, and on long train journeys the glasses are topped up from time to time with hot water from vacuum flasks so that the brew becomes progressively weaker – although still essentially refreshing.

A universal thirst-quencher and refresher is tea without milk or sugar but with a slice of lemon, served in a glass. And in the United States delicious iced tea, often made from instant tea and sometimes with other flavours added, is a firm summertime favourite.

Worldwide, the greatest demand is for the dark or Indian-type teas. Darjeelings and Ceylon teas are both considered more aromatic, although France and Belgium both particularly appreciate the Assam teas.

Even so, the China teas are by far the most interesting and exotic, and more and more shops in the West – especially in those countries where the longing for a return to life's simpler excellencies is strongest – are beginning to stock a fuller range of these elegant varieties. Of all the China teas, Lapsang Souchong is probably the most familiar, although it is usually possible to find others like Orange Pekoe, Oolong, Pan Yong and Peking. It is also hard to beat the delicate Pekoe Blossom and Jasmine teas as an after-dinner *digestif*, and no self-respecting Chinese restaurant would be without them.

As with coffee, there is no infallible guide to what will suit an individual palate best. The only answer is to try as many blends as possible – Earl Grey, a China tea with subtly aromatic Indian undertones is a classic – and then settle for what you like best.

JACKSONS

EARL GREY'S TEA

INGREDIENTS: TEA. NATURAL OIL OF BERGAMOT

125 g net 4.41 oz

METRIC PACK

Jacksons of Piccadilly

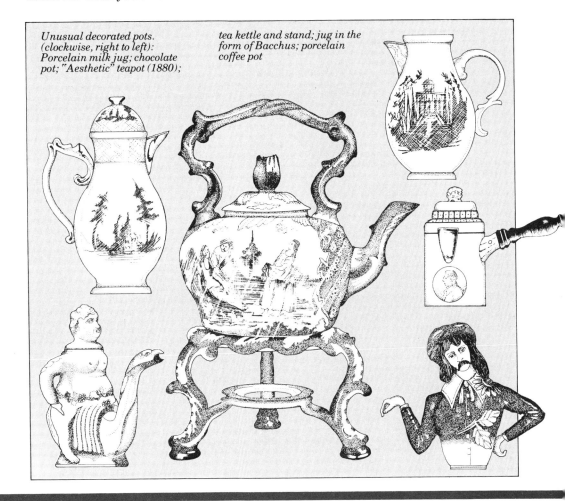

Unusual decorated pots. (clockwise, right to left): Porcelain milk jug; chocolate pot; "Aesthetic" teapot (1880); tea kettle and stand; jug in the form of Bacchus; porcelain coffee pot

COFFEE

Coffee is cultivated in some forty countries lying largely between the Tropics of Capricorn and Cancer, and the coffee bushes come to maturity between three and four years after planting. The cherry-red, ripe berries, which appear at the same time as the fragrant blossom, have to be carefully hand picked before the outer pulp and the husk are removed, either by fermentation or by sun drying.

To flourish, the trees need an equable climate, good soil, plenty of moisture and not too much sun, and the very best coffees, the delicate *coffea arabicas*, are grown at altitudes of between 600 and 1800 metres. The more hardy *coffea robusta* flourishes in far less congenial conditions and at lower altitudes, especially in Africa, but it is much harsher in taste and less fragrant. On the whole, the *robustas* are mostly used for processing into instant coffees or in the cheaper blends of roast coffee.

But by far the most important fact about coffee – and the one that most people find hardest to grasp – is the huge size of the international coffee industry; coffee is the second most valuable commodity traded worldwide, and only petroleum oil is bigger. This startling truth is reflected in the sheer scale of production. Although there are huge plantations in places like Brazil and Angola, most coffee is grown on family smallholdings and it provides the main source of cash income for literally millions of people who, between them, can pick up to seventy million 60-kilogram bags of coffee a year, although it has been many years since there has been a world crop of that size. The devastating Brazilian frost of 1975 and civil disturbances in Angola and other coffee-producing countries make it unlikely that production will ever return to that level. World coffee consumption has been upwards of fifty million bags – coffee is traditionally shipped in jute bags – in recent years, and production is just a little ahead of that.

But after the facts, the legends. The most attractive of these is that, at some time in the remote past, an Ethiopian goat-herd called Kaldi noticed that his flock became markedly more lively after eating the bright red berries from some nearby trees. He tried chewing a few himself and found that they immediately produced a feeling of profound well-being. He reported his discovery to some monks in a nearby monastery and, after some earnest debate about the propriety of using a stimulant, they hesitantly tried a few. What clinched their conversion to coffee was that it helped them to stay awake during the long nights of prayer and meditation. Centuries later they learned to roast, grind and infuse the beans.

Certainly it is true that coffee was not originally regarded as a beverage. The beans were pounded with animal fat and shaped into balls which marauding bands of warriors carried as an essential part of their rations on long-distance raids. In fact, coffee is still used in this way in some parts of Africa, by people undertaking long and arduous journeys.

It is also true that *coffea arabica* is native to Ethiopia and that some wild coffee trees still grow there, although most Ethiopian coffees are now properly cultivated. But it was first seriously cultivated in what is now the Yemen, possibly at some time in the sixth century, and was eaten in the African manner rather than brewed. Some centuries later the Arabs were producing a type of fermented coffee "wine", but by the thirteenth century the practice of removing the outer pulp and husk and roasting and pounding the beans to make what we would regard as coffee was firmly established.

Of course, given the Prophet Mohammed's ban on the use of alcohol by Muslims, it is not surprising that coffee first flourished as a drink throughout the Islamic Empire and produced rituals of preparing, offering and drinking coffee which still survive in some forms. Not that it was instantly accepted when it first arrived in Mecca towards the beginning of the sixteenth century, and many Mullahs remained convinced that it fell within the Prophet's prohibition of stimulants, so that the early coffee houses in Mecca and Cairo were frequently criticized and sometimes suppressed altogether. This attitude persisted among Christian theologians and rulers when the drink spread to the West, and coffee also provoked heated controversies among Western medical men. Later in the sixteenth century Pope Clement VIII was obliged to baptize coffee for Christian use, after his cardinals had condemned it as a Devil's brew.

In the event, coffee houses were flourishing in Italy in the mid-seventeenth century and the coffee habit soon spread to Venice, the Austro-Hungarian Empire, Paris and, later, to London. Paris, in particular, took to coffee with enthusiasm after it had been introduced to the Court by the Turkish ambassador. The city's intellectuals in particular flocked to the coffee houses, and the Café Procope, now a restaurant in the Boulevard Saint Germain, numbered Voltaire, Diderot, Rousseau and Beaumarchais among its clientele.

Surprisingly, the tea-addicted English were originally great devotees of coffee in the seventeenth and eighteenth centuries until the establishment of links with India and China, plus the devastation of the Ceylonese coffee plantations by leaf disease, made tea more attractive. Indeed, the world's biggest insurance organization, Lloyds of London, had its origins in a coffee house.

But coffee had its enemies. Charles II of England tried to suppress coffee houses as hotbeds of sedition, physicians in France declared that it made men sterile, and Frederick the Great of Prussia considered the drink debilitating and employed "coffee-sniffers" to track down illicit coffee roasters. In Constantinople, the Grand Vizier Koprili instituted a scale of punishments for coffee drinkers which ranged from being beaten-up to being flung into the Bosphorus sewn up in a skin bag.

But once coffee ceased to be an Arabian monopoly, its advance was unstoppable. Coffee was planted in Java and brought back to Amsterdam as a medical curiosity, but the real foundations were laid by the Frenchman Gabriel Mathieu de Clieu, who managed to acquire – through the good offices of a lady friend at the French Court whose physician had cultivated a tree presented by the Dutch – three coffee seeds, which he took to Martinique, where they flourished. Later, cultivation spread to other French and Dutch Caribbean islands.

Then, in 1727, Lieutenant-Colonel Francisco de Melo Palheta from Brazil charmed the wife of the Governor of French Guiana into giving him coffee cuttings, concealed in a bouquet of flowers. They were the foundation of Brazil's coffee fortunes, and of the coffee industry today. Brazil is now still the world's biggest producer of *arabica* coffees, with Colombia a close second.

The *robusta* coffees, which were originally developed in

what was the Belgian Congo, tend to be concentrated in Africa, although Indonesia is now probably the world's leading *robusta* grower.

Angola and the Ivory Coast used to be the leading growers, but Angolan production has been drastically curtailed by political unrest and the Ivory Coast is turning to other cash crops; Uganda, another major *robusta* producer, has still not recovered from the years of General Amin and the subsequent war. But for most people, the important thing about coffee is drinking it, and this is where the troubles arise. If all national tastes were similar there would be no problem, but preferences can vary from district to district, let alone from country to country. In general, the northern Europeans and North Americans tend to prefer the lighter, more "acid" coffees, whereas the Mediterranean coffee drinkers like a stronger, darker brew, more heavily roasted and containing a higher proportion of *robustas* in the blends. In fact, most commercial coffees are blends of many origins and coffee professionals generally agree that very few individual coffees are satisfactory on their own. Most proprietary brands of coffee contain a percentage of Brazils, a selection of "Milds" from a variety of sources and, according to the price, a proportion of *robustas*.

In the old days, almost every neighbourhood had its own local coffee roaster, using a small rotating drum to roast the beans a pound or so at a time, and this is still largely the case in Italy, France, Spain and Portugal. But ever since the Second World War the small roasters have increasingly ceased to be economic, and the business is now dominated by the major concerns, which roast coffee by the ton and either pack it into cans or in plastic vacuum packs to preserve the flavour. In fact, this system is rather kinder to the coffee than the old method. The modern, electronically controlled and automated roaster can roast the pale green beans to precisely the correct shade of brown and, since coffee begins to lose flavour within hours of roasting and grinding, the vacuum packs are a decided advantage.

As far as the proprietary coffees are concerned, the price usually dictates the quality, but increasingly these days people – especially the young – are beginning to hanker after something more individualistic and more and more speciality coffee shops are springing up to cater to them. Ideally, these shops should stock a reasonable range of good-quality coffees which are freshly roasted in a modern, small-scale version of the bulk roasters. Look for a shop with a high turnover; that way you can be sure that beans have been freshly roasted. Buy whole beans in small quantities and grind them in a hand mill or an electric grinder just before use. Both ready-ground coffees and beans should be stored in an airtight container, preferably in the refrigerator; properly packed beans can also be stored in a deep-freeze for a month or so.

The simplest way of making good coffee is to put a tablespoonful (15 ml) of coffee for each cup into a heated stoneware jug and then add freshly boiled, but not *boiling*, water. Leave to brew for a few minutes and then pour carefully into heated coffee cups. Add sugar, cream or milk, but not boiling milk, if you like. The drip filter method, including the automatic machines, also makes a good brew, but no method which involves boiling the coffee should ever be used.

You *can* roast coffee at home, but it is seldom worth the trouble. One method is to put the green beans in a pan and start them on a medium to slow heat until they begin to turn brown, when the heat should be raised rapidly and the beans stirred constantly with a wooden spatula until they are an acceptable colour; in general, the darker the roast the stronger the flavour. Beans can also be roasted in a roasting tin in an oven set at 475°F (240°C, gas mark 9) for twenty minutes, shaking occasionally, or, for a high roast, reduce the heat to 400°F (200°C, gas mark 6) for a further twenty minutes. All methods tend to produce clouds of pungent smoke.

The choice of blend is, ultimately, a matter of taste and the only way of discovering what suits your palate best is to experiment. A good standard blend, for everyday use, is ½ lb (250 g) Brazil Bourbon Santos, plus ¼ lb (125 g) each of Costa Rica and Mysore Mocca, but the choice is up to the individual and possibilities are infinite. Try blends combining Brazils with the always reliable Colombian, Guatemalas, Kenyas and Hawaiian Konas. You could also experiment with Javas, Mexicans, Tanzanians or Indian coffees. Unhappily, genuine Ethiopian and Yemeni Mocca coffees can be hard to come by, and always beware of anything described as "Blue Mountain". The original Jamaican Blue Mountain is in very short supply and is generally only available in a few highly specialist shops in the United States; Japan

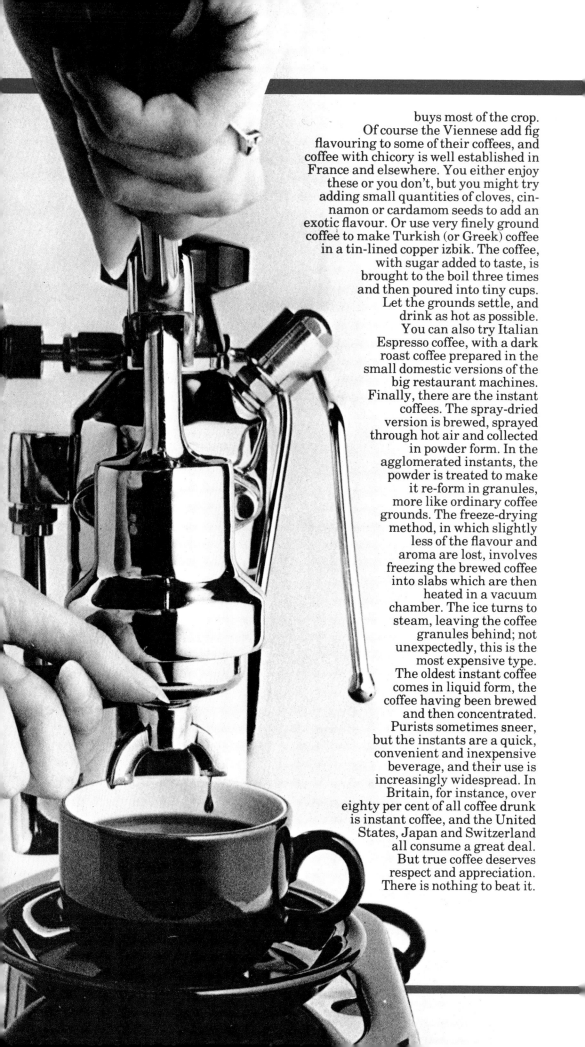

buys most of the crop.
Of course the Viennese add fig flavouring to some of their coffees, and coffee with chicory is well established in France and elsewhere. You either enjoy these or you don't, but you might try adding small quantities of cloves, cinnamon or cardamom seeds to add an exotic flavour. Or use very finely ground coffee to make Turkish (or Greek) coffee in a tin-lined copper izbik. The coffee, with sugar added to taste, is brought to the boil three times and then poured into tiny cups. Let the grounds settle, and drink as hot as possible.

You can also try Italian Espresso coffee, with a dark roast coffee prepared in the small domestic versions of the big restaurant machines. Finally, there are the instant coffees. The spray-dried version is brewed, sprayed through hot air and collected in powder form. In the agglomerated instants, the powder is treated to make it re-form in granules, more like ordinary coffee grounds. The freeze-drying method, in which slightly less of the flavour and aroma are lost, involves freezing the brewed coffee into slabs which are then heated in a vacuum chamber. The ice turns to steam, leaving the coffee granules behind; not unexpectedly, this is the most expensive type. The oldest instant coffee comes in liquid form, the coffee having been brewed and then concentrated. Purists sometimes sneer, but the instants are a quick, convenient and inexpensive beverage, and their use is increasingly widespread. In Britain, for instance, over eighty per cent of all coffee drunk is instant coffee, and the United States, Japan and Switzerland all consume a great deal. But true coffee deserves respect and appreciation. There is nothing to beat it.

COCOA

Cocoa is the New World's first major contribution to the list of non-alcoholic beverages, but of course most people know it as chocolate. In fact, most cocoa-based products are consumed as chocolate bars or confectionary these days, but it was first used in the West as a beverage and one often credited with medical or aphrodisiac powers.

As far as is known, the Old World's acquaintanceship with the bean began with the discovery of the Americas by Christopher Columbus in 1492. He brought back with him to the Court of King Ferdinand of Spain a treasure-trove of strange and wonderful objects and plants, and among these were a few dark brown beans which somewhat resembled almonds, but which had no apparent use.

It remained for Hernando Cortez and his Conquistadores to grasp the true potential of this remarkable vegetable treasure. During his conquest of Mexico, Cortez found that the Aztec Indians used cacao beans in the preparation of a beverage which was reserved for the use of Aztec royalty. It was called *chcolatl*, which means "cacao and water" and Cortez first tasted it when the Emperor Montezuma had it served at a banquet for the Conquistadores in 1519. It was a cold drink, made from powdered cacao beans and served in golden goblets.

But the *chcolatl* did not appeal to the Spaniards. It was too bitter for their taste, so they sweetened it surreptitiously with cane sugar. It was in this sweet form that they took the drink back to Spain, where it immediately found favour with the grandees and their ladies, who, in turn, made refinements of their own, adding cinnamon or vanilla. Others found that it tasted better served hot.

It did not take Spain's rulers long to spot the commercial possibilities in the fashionable new drink, and cacao trees were soon being cultivated in all Spain's colonies. This, then, is how the foundations were laid for today's vast cocoa and chocolate industry. The Spanish were not inclined to pass on their secrets, and the formula for preparing chocolate was closely guarded until some talkative monks let slip the information. All Europe was soon hailing this delicious and nourishing beverage. (Unlike tea and coffee, cocoa does have nutritive properties).

France was, naturally, the first country to adopt the drink, but it soon crossed the Channel and the first chocolate houses opened in England in 1657. In those days the beans had to be ground by hand, a laborious and expensive process, but the advent of the steam engine led to the development of mechanical grinding, and mass manufacturing led, inevitably, to a wider market. The price of cocoa, which had been around £1.50 a pound, fell sharply so that those besides the very wealthy could afford it. The invention of the cocoa press in 1828 cut prices even further and helped to improve the flavour by removing part of the cocoa butter, which gave the drink a new smoothness.

The first American chocolate was produced in pre-revolutionary New England in 1765, and chocolate production in the United States progressed faster than anywhere else in the world. Eating chocolate is now the basis of a multi-billion dollar international industry, far outstripping drinking chocolate in terms of production.

Scientists are still debating the origins of the cacao tree, a delicate and beautiful plant that thrives only in tropical climates, within 20 degrees north and south of the Equator,

where the balance of temperature, rainfall and soil are exactly right. Some believe that it first grew in the Amazon basin of Brazil, but others say that it probably came from the Orinoco valley in Venezuela. A third group suggests that it was a native of Central America.

Given the conditions required to grow cocoa successfully it is not surprising that the Ivory Coast – which processes most of them – is the world's largest producer. Brazil, Ghana and Nigeria – in that order – come next, but cocoa is also grown in Cameroun, the Dominican Republic, Ecuador, Venezuela, Mexico, Trinidad and Tobago, Costa Rica, Jamaica, Haiti, New Guinea, Samoa and Java.

Being a sensitive plant, the cocoa tree needs constant protection from both wind and sun, especially in the first two or three years of growth. Newly planted seedlings are often sheltered by banana or rubber trees. The seedlings themselves are usually grown in nurseries, where seeds from high-yield trees are planted in fibre baskets. They are ready for transplanting in a few months, and the plantations are usually in valleys or on coastal plains, where the soil and drainage are good and the rainfall balanced. The trees grow to a height of between 6 and 7.5 metres and begin to yield good crops in the third or fourth years.

Beneath the large and profuse leaves of the tree are small, odourless pink or white flowers which blossom in clusters directly attached to the trunk and its main branches. There can be as many as 6000 of these flowers, but only a small percentage are fertilized.

The fruit ripens into pods and, as is so often the case in the tropics, the growth cycle is continuous and the trees may bear leaves, blossoms and pods of varying sizes all at the same time. Within the pods, which vary in length between 15 and 20 cm at maturity, are the seeds, the cocoa beans from which chocolate is made. Each pod can yield between twenty and fifty beans and the average tree yields between twenty and forty pods a year.

Because the trees are so delicate, the pickers – called *tumbadores* – use hooked knives in long handles to cut down the pods without injuring the bark. The pods are split with machetes and the beans begin to turn brown as the oxidizing process sets in. The fermentation which follows lasts six days or more and the beans have to be turned over in their plantain baskets at regular intervals before, finally, being spread out to dry in the sun or, in humid conditions, in heated sheds.

The manufacturing process varies from one chocolate manufacturer to another, and each keeps his own technique a closely guarded secret. But, in general, it begins with the careful sorting and cataloguing of each consignment according to type and origin before the beans are stored in hoppers well away from the main plant to avoid contamination by other odours.

The beans are then cleaned and blended to a specific formula before being roasted at temperatures of 250°F (120°C) for up to two hours. The moisture content evaporates and the beans darken and begin to give off the distinctive chocolate aroma. The beans are cooled immediately after roasting and the now brittle shells are removed in a winnowing machine known as a "cracker and fanner".

The kernels, or "nibs", contain about fifty-four per cent cocoa butter and they are crushed in mills; the process of grinding generates enough heat to liquefy the cocoa butter and form a chocolate liquor. Some chocolate liquor is pumped into giant hydraulic presses (weighing 25 tons each) and these remove a proportion of cocoa butter which is then squeezed through metallic screens and later used in the making of eating chocolate. The pressed cake which remains is then cooled and pulverized to make cocoa powder.

This, then is turned into a drink simply by adding hot water or milk. The least common types are known as "breakfast" cocoas and must contain at least twenty-two per cent cocoa butter (the mass market types must, however, also contain at least ten per cent cocoa butter). The Dutch also use an alkali process, which develops a slightly different flavour and a darker powder.

You don't need any special skills or special equipment to make good cocoa. French schoolchildren still start the day with a buttered roll and a cup of the rich "breakfast" cocoa, which is generally known as drinking chocolate.

Mixed with malt, cocoa is also transformed into a late-night drink to induce sound sleep – which seems to conflict with its former reputation as an aphrodisiac! Cocoa is not a drink for slimmers. Apart from the milk and sugar which are added, cocoa itself has a high calorie content.

Although making a cup of cocoa or chocolate is essentially a simple business, involving nothing more than spooning the powder into a saucepan containing the appropriate measure of hot water or milk and adding sugar to taste, the manufacturers have now simplified the procedure even further. They have produced bottled, liquid chocolate drinks which can also be added to cold milk, and instant chocolate powders which dissolve in a flash.

Cocoa also forms the basis of a number of alcoholic liqueurs, but it is always added as a flavouring agent, and, as far as is known, no alcoholic beverages are made from the beans themselves. However, hot cocoa or chocolate with a dash of dark rum makes one of the most warming revivers known to man.

OTHER BEVERAGES

Although many people in Europe had to drink coffee substitutes made out of roast barley, acorns and a whole host of other substances during the Second World War, even before the war there were a certain number of people who actually preferred the cereal-based beverages. In parts of Scandinavian countries these enjoyed a lively sale until comparatively recent times, and they were regarded as drinks in their own right and not as *kaffee ersatz*.

These were roasted and ground in much the same way as coffee, and brewed. Their one virtue was that they contained no caffeine and they were also cheaper.

The Church of the Latter Day Saints, the Mormons, also produced a non-stimulant drink, known as Instant Postum which was often given to children as a night-time drink. It certainly did have a high nausea potential, but it is no longer widely available, if at all.

There are many more tea-type infusions, though. In many cases, these probably had their origins in witches' brews and old wives' remedies, and were usually taken for medicinal purposes. Of these, two in particular are still widely used and enjoyed.

Maté is especially popular in Argentina, where it has become the hot drink of the gauchos. It gets its name from the traditional serving bowl. This can sometimes be no more elaborate than a simple gourd, but there are also finely carved wooden bowls chased with ornate silverware which are collectors' pieces. The leaf is called *yerba*, which really means grass. The plant is the wild holly, *Ilex Paraguayensis*, and the drink, sometimes called Paraguay tea, is drunk through a silver tube with a filter at one end: unfiltered maté can stain the teeth black.

The other most widely used infusion is camomile, made from the dried flower. It is particularly popular in France because it is considered to have medicinal properties. In Eastern Europe, it is often a cheap substitute for tea.

The French in particular are generally fond of *tisanes* or herb teas, as are most Eastern European nations. Almost any herb can be used to make tea. All that is needed is one teaspoonful (5 ml) per person of the finely ground leaf, which should be allowed to infuse for a minute. Elderflower, balm, jasmine and rose-hip are most commonly used.

The medicinal properties of plants and herbs are also exploited. One of the most infamous plants used in this way is Korean ginseng. It is often referred to as a tea, which it is not: it is ground root. Originally imported in some quantity into China, where it was attributed almost universal healing qualities, it is now considered one of the world's superior aphrodisiacs. Its medicinal reputation goes back 2000 years, yet has only recently been recognized in the West, where it is available from specialist stores.

In Eastern Europe, cherry stalks and the "hair" from corn cobs are dried and made into a drink believed to have diuretic qualities. Exotic plants from South America such as *Don Diego de la noce*, a wild shrub that grows in Chile, is said to cure stomach ulcers. Senna leaves are well-known emetics and mint makes a pleasant *tisane*, especially after a heavy meal. All over the world herbs are used for medicinal infusions or refreshing drinks.

INDEX

COMPILED BY RICHARD BIRD

BIBLIOGRAPHY

Bellinger, Cyril Ray (Peter Davies)
Booth's Handbook of Cocktails and Mixed Drinks, John Doxat (Pan Books)
Cognac, Cyril Ray (Peter Davies)
Decanter magazine
Dictionary of Drinks and Drinking, Oscar A. Mendlesohn (Macmillan)
Encyclopaedia of Wines and Spirits, Alexis Lichine (Cassell)
Grossman's Guide to Wines, Spirits and Beers, Harold J. Grossman (Scribner)
Harper's Wine and Spirit Trade Gazette (London)
International Beverage News (London)
International Guide to Drinks, United Kingdom Bartender's Guild (Hutchinson)
Jones' Complete Bar Guide, Stanley M. Jones (Barguide Enterprises)
Liqueurs, Peter Hallgarten (Wine and Spirit Publications)
Off-licence News (London)
Stirred, Not Shaken: the Dry Martini, John Doxat (Hutchinson Benham)
Tea and Coffee, Edward Bramah (Hutchinson)
The Book of Waters, Steven Schwartz (A & W Publishers Inc.)
The Fine Art of Mixing Drinks, David A. Embury (Faber)
The Penguin Book of Spirits and Liqueurs, Pamela Vandyke Price
The Savoy Cocktail Book (Constable)
The Whiskies of Scotland, R.J.S. McDowall (John Murray)
The World Atlas of Wine, Hugh Johnson (Mitchell Beazley)
The World Guide to Beer, Michael Jackson (Mitchell Beazley)
Wine, Hugh Johnson (Mitchell Beazley)
Wine and Spirit magazine

ACKNOWLEDGEMENTS

The publishers would like to acknowledge the help received from the enormous number of organizations all over the world who assisted in the research and compilation of this book.
Studio photography by Duncan McNichol
Assistants Fran Harper and Chantal Mattar; Stylists Jan Davis and Pippa Muirhead; Models Howard Kingsnorth and Rod Morgan; Prints by Adrian Ensor
Illustrations by Gary Marsh on pages 42, 51, 101, 152, 171, 207

PICTURE CREDITS
A: above   B: below   C: centre   L: left   R: right
10: Ronald Sheridan's Photo Library   11: Michael Holford/British Museum   12(AR): Lords Gallery   12(CL): Mary Evans Picture Library   13(A): Mary Evans Picture Library   13(B): BBC Hulton Picture Library   14(AL,CL): Moro/Rome   15: Bulloz/Musée d'Art Moderne, Paris   16(A,B): Welsh Folk Museum   17(A,B): Mary Evans Picture Library   18(AL): Bulloz/Musée de Cluny   18(AR): Mary Evans Picture Library   19: Mary Evans Picture Library   34(A): Bavaria Verlag   34(B): Lords Gallery   35(A,B): Mary Evans Picture Library   38(A,B): Moro/Rome   64(A,B): Mansell Collection   74(A,B): Mary Evans Picture Library   75(A,BR): Mansell Collection   75(BL): Mary Evans Picture Library   76(AL,BL): Mansell Collection   76(CL): Mary Evans Picture Library   77(A): Mary Evans Picture Library   77(B): Peter Newark's Historical Pictures   78: Moro/Rome   79: Moro/Rome   80(B): Mansell Collection   81(AL): Peter Newark's Western Americana   81(AR): Mansell Collection   81(B): Mary Evans Picture Library   82(A): Ann Ronan Agency   82(B): Mary Evans Picture Library   94(A): BBC Hulton Picture Library   94(B): Mary Evans Picture Library   102(AL,CL): Mary Evans Picture Library   102(CR): Peter Newark's Historical Pictures   122(A,B): Mary Evans Picture Library   123(A,B): Mary Evans Picture Library   124(AL): The Bettmann Archive Inc.   124(AR): Mansell Collection   124(B): The Brewers' Society   125(A): National Gallery, London   125(C): Ullstein Bilderdienst   125(B): Mary Evans Picture Library   160(A): Peter Newark's Western Americana   160(C): Mander and Mitchenson Theatre Collection   161(A): Ullstein Bilderdienst   161(B): © The Condé Nast Publications Ltd.   162/3: Bulloz/Bibliothèque Nationale   164(A): Mansell Collection   186(A): Courtesy of The Coca Cola Company   186(BL, BR): Mary Evans Picture Library   202(A,CR): Mary Evans Picture Library   202(CL): Michael Holford/Victoria and Albert Museum